INTERNATIONAL
MAIN COURSE
COOKBOOK

Books by Hyman Goldberg:

INTERNATIONAL MAIN COURSE COOKBOOK

THE BEGINNER'S COOKBOOK

OUR MAN IN THE KITCHEN COOKBOOK

HOW I BECAME A GIRL REPORTER

INTERNATIONAL Main Course COOKBOOK

by HYMAN GOLDBERG

CHARLES SCRIBNER'S SONS ❖ NEW YORK

This is for Naomi and Gabriel,
Et Urbi Et Orbi

TABLE OF CONTENTS

FOREWORD BY
Arthur Godfrey

My late and good friend Hyman Goldberg said that when he came to my studio as a guest to demonstrate on the "Mighty CBS Range" (which you can buy for about $3.95 in any appliance store) how to cook his recipes, the aromas that wafted through the studio and into the entire building, made me "moan with joy or at least scream with intense pleasure."

I'm not sure that Hyman was entirely accurate when he used the words "moan" and "scream" and "intense," but I know that I did make noises that indicated pleasure when I smelled his cooking and ate the food he fixed. I know, too, that a great number of you folks heard my happy cries, for many of you wrote to tell us so. People in Kansas, in California, and even as far away as Hawaii and Alaska swore they could smell the delicious aromas he created in our studio in New York City.

It was in January 1969 that Hyman committed what we in the business call "a radio first." While hundreds of people through the years have *talked* about cooking on the wireless, nobody ever actually cooked on radio before Hyman had the temerity to do it.

Word has come back to me that he went around saying that his anecdotes "make Arthur Godfrey howl with laughter." That I cannot deny. He was a witty man and his stories never failed to break me up. And not only me, but also Richard Hayes and Jerry Alters and the boys in my band, all of whom are very good eaters, but very reluctant laughers. As you turn these pages, you will see what I mean, for my friend Hyman was that rare bird, a witty writer who talked the way he wrote and wrote the way he talked.

I've been asked often by publishers to write a cookbook, but as I've said publicly many, many times, I'm strictly a meat and salad man and that's about the extent of my culinary repertoire. Anyway, why *should* I write a cookbook? Hyman Goldberg has done it for me and if I can follow his instructions, which are written with utmost clarity and in a style that makes it fun to read, certainly you can. If you do, I'm sure you will follow his motto, which is: "Cook and Laugh!"

ARTHUR GODFREY

PREFACE BY THE AUTHOR

Why an *International Main Course Cookbook*? Well, it used to be that most middle-class United Statesers started their everyday principal meal with an appetizer, followed by soup, then the main course, and ended with a dessert. But for a couple of generations now, most people have made do with just a main course, accompanied by a cooked vegetable, or a green salad, or both, ending with coffee and perhaps a dessert. And that's why I chose to have only main courses in this book.

About *International*: a majority of the dishes in this book are truly international, despite the names of the countries I have set down in parentheses after them, for they are known in many parts of the world with only slight variations. Put oregano in *gefilte fish*, and it becomes *pesceballo*, or Italian fish balls; add *pâte à choux* (pastry batter) to the ground and chopped fish and it becomes the French *quenelles*. Add paprika to a stew and it becomes Hungarian *gulyás*; add sour cream and it becomes Russian Stroganoff; add curry and it is Indian; add salt herring and it becomes Swedish *grytstekt*.

There are some dishes that are *so* international that it would be pointless to designate any country of origin.

As for the designations, "Brooklyn" and "A. Godfrey Studio," well, those places, as all the world knows, are independent principalities.

I once wrote a book which the publisher insisted on calling, *How I Became a Girl Reporter*, and also, for about six months wrote a newspaper food column under the by-line Prudence Penny.

I don't want people to misunderstand. That book was a kind of autobiography, published in 1950 when I'd been a reporter in New York City for various newspapers—nine of them, sadly, now defunct—for twenty-six years. I'd started as a police reporter, covering murders, riots, and criminal trials—including the kidnaping of the Lindbergh baby and the subsequent trial of Bruno Richard Hauptmann—and then wrote feature stories about girls—most of them actresses, but some in other professions—for a Sunday newspaper supplement. On that newspaper, the late, lamentable *New York Mirror*, because I wrote so many stories about girls, I was called "the girl reporter." That's why that publisher chose to inflict on my book that title, *How I Became a Girl Reporter*.

I wrote the food column as a side-job for the same newspaper under the by-line "Prudence Penny," because it was a Hearst paper, and on all papers under that ownership, all food writers wrote under that by-line because the management didn't want anyone building up a reputation under a real name. (Hearst had about twenty Prudence Pennys around the country, but I was the only male among them.)

So, folk, don't misunderstand: just COOK AND LAUGH!

HYMAN GOLDBERG
Stamford, Connecticut
JUNE, 1970

INTERNATIONAL MAIN COURSE COOKBOOK

SOUPS

PART ONE

I used this anecdote and recipe on the Arthur Godfrey Time CBS Radio Network program, which made Mr. Godfrey moan with pleasure.

I was reminded recently, when forced to visit briefly a terribly sordid spot in the "City" of New York where—in another incarnation—I served a long stretch under a succession of cruel masters in the vilest kind of durance, about something I'd thought foolishly that a benign Providence had helped me erase from my yin, or maybe it's yang, but you know; whichever. The thing I thought I'd forgotten is the word "cabbagehead" used pejoratively, meaning that whoever is so designated has a head, which, when peeled layer by layer, like a cabbage, see?, reveals nothing; nothing at all but more cabbage leaves. No kidding, any designee called "a cabbagehead" had, in that debased society, a legal right to throw at least one punch at the head of the calumnitorial designator.

What got me started on all this was a marvelous day spent in the company of my dearly beloved ma-in-law, a magnificent lady named Mrs. Malvina Katz, during the course of which one of the many courses she served up was a splendid concoction of her own daring design which I am pleased to present to you as:

MOTHER MALVINA'S FANTASTICAL
FRIGID HOT-WEATHER COMMIXION

3 quarts water (12 cups)
one firm young cabbage, approximately 3 pounds
"plenty" of salt
1 tablespoon butter
"about" 3 cups chopped onions (you got a mama, you know
    that's how mamas give recipes)
juice of "about" 2 lemons (approximately 6 tablespoons—and
    lime juice is okay, too)
3 tablespoons (approximately) brown sugar
3 large eggs
¼ teaspoon pepper (maybe more later)
one pint sour cream

If I told you to use a large pot to bring to boil the 3 quarts
of water you'd have a right to hate me for aspersing your intelligence. While the water is getting hotted up, cut the cabbage up
and then chop it. Not fine, but not coarse, either. Yes, students,
if there are any farfoilteh (means "spoliated" in Middle Litvak)
cabbage leaves on your head discard them. Put the chopped cabbage into a colander placed in your sink. Sprinkle the cabbage
with some of the "plenty" of salt as you go. Use salt freely and
unstintingly. In a large fry pan, hot up the tablespoon of butter,
and add the onions, stirring to coat them all, cover the pan and
cook over low heat until onion is soft, but not browned. Beat
the remaining ingredients—lemon juice, sugar, eggs, salt, and
pepper—into the sour cream.

Squeeze out of the cabbage as much liquid as you can. Easiest way is to put all the cabbage into a kitchen towel, ball it up,
and squeeze mightily. Put the chopped squeezed cabbage into
the boiling water. When the water returns to the boil, cover and
cook, simmering over low heat, for 30 minutes.

After 30 minutes of simmering, remove the pot of cabbage
from the heat. Beat 1 tablespoon of the cabbage soup at a time

into the egg mixture, in a large bowl, starting beating immediately and intensely. Keep doing this until you have at least 1 quart of the soup beaten into the egg mixture. (That would make 64 tablespoons, give or take a couple, but, of course, when you have about one-half of that much of the hot soup combined with the egg mixture you can use a ladle holding as many as 3 or 4 tablespoons, and do it faster. But remember: BEAT VIOLENTLY!

When it has cooled, taste it. It should have a faintly tart taste with the merest hint of sweetness. It should be pleasingly seasoned, with neither salt nor pepper making themselves apparent to you. Correct whatever seasoning needs correcting, and remember also that when food is cold the power of seasoning is considerably diminished.

This should be eaten icy cold. It is wonderfully cooling, in appearance as well as taste. Dark bread is perfect for this. With butter, possibly cheese. You can add infinite embellishments, like pitted black olives (not too salty); pieces of roasted red peppers, sweet or hot, or both; or pimiento pieces. These added ingredients make the soup extremely pleasing to the eye, which, of course, stimulates the appetite. Sometimes puree half the cooked cabbage in a blender and combine it with the unblended soup; makes it thicker, of course.

SERVES SIX.

A newspaper reporter was interviewing a pretty young chick who was the eldest daughter of a candidate for a high office in the state government. He had already elicited from her the fact that she traveled with her mother, going wherever her father was making speeches. "I think," said the reporter, a fatherly kind of type, "that is just wonderful, young lady," he said in a fatherly manner, "but tell me, isn't it true that wherever he goes in the state he makes the same speech? Doesn't that get kind of boring to you?" The pretty chick smiled prettily. "Oh, no," she said, "you see, my Papa does give the same speech all the time, but each time, he hollers in a different part of the speech."

What I want to holler about now is:

CHICK PEA SOUP WITH FRANKS OR ANY KIND OF WURST (Germany)

one 1-pound can chick peas (garbanzos)
one can or bottle of beer or ale (what I like best is stout, but it's
    stout-making)
2 cans chicken soup, each 13¾ ounces
one pound frankfurters, knackwurst, bratwurst, or other kind of
    wurst
2 cups chopped onions
1 rib celery, chopped with greenery
1 carrot, grated
2 tablespoons tomato paste or ketchup or chili sauce

Drain the chick peas. (They also come dried, but have to be soaked overnight and then cooked for a couple of hours.) In a large pot, combine the beer and the chicken soup. Skin the franks, or whatever, and bring beer-soup mixture to the boil. Cut the franks or whatever wurst you chose—hey, how about kielbasa, the Polish-type sausage?—into thin rounds and, over low heat, with no fat or anything added, fry them in a fry pan (where else?) until they are slightly browned on both sides. Pour off fat as it accumulates in pan, but save 2 tablespoons.

When the franks or whatever are cooked, put them into the pan of beer-soup. In the 2 tablespoons of fat you saved, fry the onion, celery, and grated carrot until the onion and celery are soft and turning golden. Add them to the mixture.

Stir into the soup the tomato paste or whatever. Taste for seasoning. What with the seasoned soup, the sausage, and the tomato paste, you may think this is a little too salty. If you think it is, add some boiling water to the soup. This will be even more filling if you add leftover cooked chicken, beef, or pork to it.

SERVES FOUR

The cop on the beat was astounded to see a great big shiny car that he knew was in the price range of about $6,000 parked in front of the dingy little shoe repair shop. He stuck his head into the store. "Say Joe," he said to the shoe man, "we're getting some real class around here, aren't we? Whose car is that out front?" The shoe man shrugged. "It's mine," he said. The cop was flabbergasted. "Yours?" he asked flabbergastedly. "How come you bought a car like that?" The shoe man shrugged again. "Well," he said, "you know I can't afford to have a telephone, so I have to go three blocks to that big auto agency which has the only public phone in the neighborhood, and it ain't nice, going into a store all the time, without buying anything." Go to your friendly neighborhood supermarket and buy the stuff with which to make:

A HAPPY BEEF SOUP
WITH WONDERFUL STUFF (Russia)

2 pounds, approximately, cabbage, shredded
1 teaspoon salt
3 to 4 pounds flanken, or short ribs
4 cups onions, sliced thin
one large green pepper, chopped
2 ribs celery, chopped with greenery
2 cans condensed beef broth (each 10½ ounces)
2 cans water
one can (10½ ounces) condensed tomato soup, or 4 tomatoes, peeled and mashed
4 tablespoons lemon, or lime juice, or wine vinegar
2 tablespoons sugar, brown, preferably
¼ teaspoon, or more, pepper
8 to 12 peeled new potatoes, or 4 to 6 large potatoes, quartered

Throw away coarse or discolored outer leaves of cabbage, shred the rest of the leaves into a colander, sprinkling with salt as you do. Let it stand in sink overnight. Next morning, squeeze out water—you'll find a surprising lot of liquid. Cut off as much fat as you can from the meat. In a large, heavy pot, over high heat, sear the meat, pouring off fat as it accumulates. When the meat is well-browned, add the onions, chopped pepper, and celery to the pot, putting the meat on top of the vegetables. Reduce the heat to medium, cover pot, and cook until pot steams. Reduce heat to low and cook for at least one hour, stirring meat and vegetables several times.

In a separate pot, combine the beef broth, water, and tomato soup. Stir, bring to the boil, lower heat to a simmer, add lemon juice and sugar and cook for 20 minutes. Taste the soup mixture. It should be sweetish and sourish, but neither flavor must overwhelm the other. Taste and correct flavor if necessary, adding pepper.

Add potatoes to the soup 30 minutes before serving. Add cabbage 15 minutes before serving. Remove pot with the meat from heat, add the gravy from the meat pot to the soup, stir and taste and correct seasoning—sour, sweet, salt and pepper—with no one flavor predominant. When the balance of flavors is as you like it, remove bones from the meat, add meat to the soup, cook for 15 minutes. Serve soup first, then meat, potatoes, and cabbage—or all together if you have large plates.

SERVES SIX TO EIGHT.

The lady in the fish market was looking over all the different kinds of fishes on display in the store, and she was muttering to herself while the fishmonger waited patiently for her to make a selection. Finally, she pointed to a great piece of fresh salmon. "How much is that salmon?" she asked. "That's $2 a pound," replied the fishmonger. "Two dollars a pound!" the lady yelped angrily, "that's absolutely crazy, that fish store on the next block sells fresh salmon for $1.50 a pound." The fishmonger shrugged. "So, why don't you buy it there, lady?" he asked. "Because today they happen to be fresh out of fresh salmon," the lady said. Again the fishmonger shrugged. "Lady, when I'm fresh out of fresh salmon I charge only $1.00 a pound."

Few people these days make their own soups, more's the pity, because there are so very many canned soups that are excellent, but even the soup producers try to encourage the use of fresh ingredients to their soups to give them a touch that is unmistakably homemade, and here we have one for you which uses a condensed soup to make:

MUSHROOM BARLEY BEEF SOUP (Israel)

one cup pearl barley (see note)
2 cans (10½ ounces) condensed beef broth
2 canfuls water
4 tablespoons (¼ cup) rendered chicken fat or peanut oil
1 cup chopped onions
½ pound (or more) fresh mushrooms, sliced (or two 4-ounce cans of mushroom pieces, drained and dried)
2 pounds chuck beef, plus soup bones

Bring the condensed soup and water to the boil, add the barley, reduce it to simmer, covered. NOTE: one cup of barley to the approximately 40 ounces of liquid in this recipe will make four plates of a wonderful rich, thick soup, but, if you don't want all that thickness, cut the barley down to ¾, ½, or even ¼ cupful.

In a large frying pan, hot up 2 tablespoons of the fat or oil, and in it fry the onions and mushrooms until the onions are browned. You can do this quickly if you use high heat and stir constantly, but watch it carefully, for onions will turn from browned to burned in a split second. Add the onions and mushrooms to the soup.

In the same large fry pan, hot up the remaining fat or oil and in it, over high heat, brown the meat all over, and pour off the fat. Add the meat and the soup bones, let the soup come back to the boil, reduce the heat to simmer, and cook covered for at least 1 hour. Throw away bones.

Serve the soup, with the barley and mushrooms, as a first course for dinner. Serve the meat with a cooked green vegetable, and any kind of gravy you like. What I prefer is a horseradish accompaniment with boiled meat. There are some perfectly acceptable commercial horseradishes in the stores. Combine some of the horseradish with some of the soup, and you can make the stuff as mild or as strong as you like. The red horseradish is made by the addition of beet juice and grated beets to the other ingredients which are vinegar, and water, and seasonings.

You know, of course, that soup, like stew, improves when eaten the day after or even two days after it is made. Even freezing seems to improve it. A food chemist told me that this is because the flavors of all the ingredients have more time to "marry" when allowed to stand refrigerated or frozen. This is not the case with human marriages.

SERVES FOUR.

The boy had been calling her for weeks to ask for a date and she'd always had some excuse. This time she said she'd go out with him. "I'll go out with you," she said, "but first I have to tell you this: I don't drink, and I don't let boys maul me around." After a short silence the boy said, "You've got me all wrong." The girl was delighted. "You mean you didn't expect to ply me with liquor and then maul me around?" she asked. "No, no, that's not it, what you're wrong about is that you think you're going out with me," the boy said, and disconnected.

There's absolutely no connection between that story and this recipe for:

HOT BORSCHT WITH MEAT

8 medium-sized beets, peeled
3 quarts water
2 cups chopped onions
2 cloves garlic, minced
1½ to 2 pounds bottom round
soup bones
4 cups shredded cabbage
1 teaspoon salt
¼ teaspoon pepper
¼ cup each (approximately), sugar—preferably brown—and
      lemon juice
2 eggs beaten

Grate coarsely 4 of the beets, cut the others into 1-inch slices. Bring the water to the boil, add the grated and cut-up beets, the onions, garlic, the meat, from which you should trim off as much fat as you can, and the soup bones.

When it comes back to the boil, lower the heat, cover the pot and let it simmer for 1½ hours. Most soup recipes say you should skim the top of the soup after it has boiled for 10 minutes or so. I say don't skim, because what you are skimming is stuff full of good taste and nourishment.

After 1½ hours of simmering, add the shredded cabbage and the salt and pepper, stir, and let it simmer with cover askew —pot partly uncovered, so much of the liquid can be cooked away, making what is left richer, for 30 minutes. Add the sugar and lemon juice and stir until sugar is dissolved. Cook for another 30 minutes, cover still askew. Taste the soup. It should be somewhat sweet, somewhat sour, with neither flavor overwhelming the other. Correct the seasoning, if necessary.

Beat into the beaten eggs 1 tablespoon of hot soup at a time. When you have beaten in 8 tablespoons, one at a time, reverse the process, beating the egg-soup mixture, a bit at a time, back into the soup. Throw the bones away. Cut the meat up. Serve the soup, with some grated and some sliced beets in each plate, and some of the meat, cut up into bite-size pieces, in each plate. There's a lot left over? Great! Gets better and better in the fridge.

SERVES SIX TO EIGHT.

This fellow came back from London with some woolen material which his British friends assured him was splendid stuff and a great bargain. He took it to a small tailor shop near his home and told the man he wanted it made into a suit. The tailor measured him, and then he measured the material. The tailor shook his head sadly.

"Mister, I'm sorry," he said morosely. "You haven't got enough material for a suit." The fellow was greatly disappointed, but he thought he'd try another shop, anyway. The second tailor measured him and the material and smiled happily. "Mister," he said joyously, "I'll make you the best suit you ever had!"

Sure enough, two weeks later, after a couple of fittings, the suit was ready, and it was a splendid set of threads. But the fellow was curious. How come, he asked the tailor, that this other tailor said there wasn't enough material for a suit? The tailor asked where the other tailor's store was located, and the fellow told him. "Hohoho!" laughed the jolly tailor. "I'll tell you why for him it wasn't enough! He has twin sons, but I have only one son!" Here is a dish that will serve a family with quintuplets, called:

NEW YORK FISH CHOWDER (formerly New England)

3 pounds mixed fish (cod, haddock, bass, any combination of
    firm-fleshed fish)
3 quarts cold water
½ teaspooon salt
6 peppercorns
1 bay leaf
⅛ teaspoon thyme
3 ribs celery
flour
¼ pound salt pork, cubed
2 onions, sliced
3 medium potatoes, cubed
¼ cup butter
1 quart milk

If you have an obliging fishmonger, ask him to skin and bone the fish and ask him for a couple of extra fish heads and bones, but don't despair if all you can get are fish steaks or fillets; we'll suggest an alternative method for making the fish stock. Wash the heads, bones, and skin, add all these scraps to the water along with the salt, peppercorns, bay leaf and thyme, bring it to boil and simmer, covered, over low heat, for 1 hour. Strain the stock and discard everything in it.

Now, if you can't get the fish scraps, all you need are a couple of pint bottles of clam juice and an equal amount of water; mix it together, and you've got a passable stock. If you've made the stock, fine; the clam juice is fine, too.

Chop the celery. Cut the fish into 3-inch pieces and dust with flour. Fry the pork until it is brown, and brown the onion slices. Put the pork into a pot, cover with the browned onion, add the chopped celery, potatoes and fish. Pour into the pot the stock or clam-juice water mixture. Add hot water to cover contents of pot, if necessary. Bring it to boil, and let it simmer 30 minutes. Add the butter, then the milk, bring it to boil and remove from heat and serve with crackers.

SERVES FOUR.

PASTA, RICE, CREPES, ETC.

PART TWO

Every once in a while I'm asked to speak at a meeting of ladies' organizations and invariably the organization is a charitable one whose president always explains carefully that they can't pay their invited speakers a fee because all the money they collect from dues, cake sales, bingo, and so forth are used for their charitable work. Not long ago, however, I was startled when the president of one of these organizations handed me a check after I'd spoken to the group, apologizing because it was so little money.

"We try," the lady said, "to use as much of the money we raise for our charitable work." This, of course, was quite embarrassing, and I said I couldn't take money that would otherwise go to charity. This pleased the lady immensely.

"Then you don't mind," she said, "if we put it into our special fund?"

Of course not, I said grandly, and asked what this special fund was.

"Well, some day," said the lady, "when we get enough money in this fund we're going to hire better speakers."

What could be better than:

SPAGHETTI ALLA CARBONARA

6 slices bacon, fried crisp
2 eggs, beaten
½ cup grated cheese (what I like is a mixture of Parmesan and
    Romano)
1 pound spaghetti
½ teaspoon salt
¼ teaspoon pepper

In a frying pan, cook the bacon over low heat, slowly, draining off the fat from time to time, until the bacon is quite crisp. Lean bacon is best for this. A good substitute for the bacon is boiled ham, sliced very thin, fried crisp, and cut up. And several times I've done this for groups of friends using fried, thin slices of corned beef, or tongue, and they loved it.

Beat into the beaten eggs the grated cheese, and add the bacon, crumbled, or the ham, corned beef, or tongue, chopped up.

I've said it before, and I'll keep saying it: DON'T pay attention to the cooking directions on spaghetti packages. They always tell you to overcook it. Listen to me and boil up a large pot of water, add a teaspoon of salt, and a teaspoon of olive oil to the water. The oil will help to prevent the spaghetti from sticking together.

When the water is boiling, add the spaghetti, all at once, stir with large spoon until all of the spaghetti is submerged in the water, and begin timing just as soon as the water returns to the boil. After 6 minutes of cooking in the boiling water, taste a small piece of the spaghetti, and, if it is cooked through and chewy, drain it immediately. If it is thick spaghetti, taste a small piece every minute after it has cooked for 6 minutes until it has reached the consistency you prefer.

Put half of the egg-cheese-bacon sauce mixture on a hot serving platter, add the spaghetti, pour rest of the sauce over it, sprinkle with a little salt and the pepper, and mix the spaghetti with two large spoons, getting it all coated with the sauce. Makes a fine easy, quick and economical main course.

SERVES FOUR.

In the year 1620, an English mathematician named Edmund Gunter devised a standard of measurement, still used by surveyors. He called it "a chain." The chain is precisely 66 feet long. It has 100 links, each link being 7.92 inches long. It was established by him that one mile would be 80 chains, thus, 66 multiplied by 80 gives us 5,280 feet. See? And an acre, he declared, would be 66 squared (66 multiplied by 66) multiplied by 10, thus giving us the figure 43,560 square feet.

What good this information will do you I haven't got the slightest idea, except that if you are a pretty lady, and a strange man were to come up to you in the street or someplace and say, politely, "I beg your pardon, Miss, but would you happen to know how many square feet there are in an acre?" you would not be so startled by this weird approach as to say, "No, I don't. How many?" You would be able to say, "Yes, wise guy, there are 43,560 square feet in an acre and you better beat it before I call a cop."

You have got to beat it if you're going to make:

CANNED SALMON OR TUNA FILLED CREPES (The Bronx)

4 eggs, beaten
1 cup flour
$\frac{1}{4}$ teaspoon salt
milk or water
$\frac{1}{2}$ stick (4 tablespoons) melted butter, oil or marge

Beat and stir the flour gradually into the beaten eggs. Add salt. Bit by bit, add milk or water, stirring all the while, and beating—with a fork or whisk—until you have a batter with the consistency of light cream. Get a small fry pan quite hot. Dip a paper napkin into the melted fat and rub the fat, leaving an almost imperceptible coating, all over the pan. Pour in just enough batter, tilting the pan fast as you pour, to cover the bottom of the pan lightly, quickly pouring excess batter back into the unused batter. Bubbles will form on top almost immediately, and in seconds the crepe will begin to draw away from the sides of the pan. Lift up the crepe slightly with a spatula, and when it is lightly browned, flip it over and brown other side lightly. Keep doing this until you've used up all the batter. Rub the pan with fat-soaked napkin after each third crepe is done. Don't bother to keep them warm.

FILLING

2 tablespoons butter (you'll have some left over from the melted crepe butter)

$\frac{1}{4}$ cup each, minced onion and mushrooms

2 tablespoons flour

1 pound (approximately) flaked and chopped canned salmon or tuna, drained, with skin and bones removed

salt and papper to taste

1 pint (or more) sour cream

In hot butter, fry onion and mushroom mixture until onion is golden. Sprinkle with flour and stir. Stir in chopped fish. Taste mixture and season to taste. Stir in sour cream and remove from heat. Lay the crepes out on a large oiled baking pan. Put some of the mixture on one-half of each crepe, fold them over. Leave some of the filling over to pour over each crepe. Bake in oven preheated to 350 degrees for 15 minutes to hot it all up.

This will feed a lot of people.

A man had the only lightweight aluminum ladder on the block and every single day of the week and twice a day or more on weekends one or another of his neighbors came to his house to borrow it. This irked him considerably. He decided to put a halt to it. "No," he said firmly to the next neighbor who wanted to borrow his ladder, "I can't let you have it, my wife is making pasta fazoola."

His neighbor looked puzzled. "So your wife is making pasta fazoola, so what's that got to do with your ladder, you don't need a ladder to make pasta fazoola?" The ladder-owner sneered. "That's how much you know, wise guy," he said sneeringly, "because when a guy don't want to lend out his ladder any more, pasta fazoola is as good a reason as any."

PASTA e FAGIOLI
or PASTA FAZOOLA (Mulberry Street, N.Y.)

1 pound dried kidney beans
one 1-pound can tomatoes (Italian-style, preferably, with a bay
    leaf in it)
1 clove garlic, minced
1 carrot, chopped (about ½ cupful)
1 onion, chopped (about 1 cup)
½ cup chopped celery
½ pound elbow marcaroni
¼ cup (4 tablespoons) olive oil
½ cup (or more) grated Parmesan cheese
salt and pepper

In water to cover, soak the beans for 24 hours or so. Next day, several hours before you want to serve it, drain the beans, cover with fresh water, add about 1 tablespoon of salt and bring the water to the boil, and simmer, covered, for 1 hour. (Once I used diluted condensed chicken broth instead of water and it was wonderful.) After 1 hour of simmering, add to the pot all of the ingredients except the macaroni, olive oil, cheese and salt and pepper, and simmer for another hour. (Makes 2 hours, right?)

Meanwhile, back at the range, bring to the boil, in another pot, of course, enough water, slightly salted, to cover the macaroni; add the macaroni; start timing when the water returns to the boil; stir from time to time; and taste a piece after 8 minutes. If you like your macaroni *al dente* (or cooked through but still chewy), 8 to 10 minutes should do it.

When the pasta is as you like it, drain it in a colander and add it to the simmering beans. Add the oil, stir the contents of the pot, add salt and pepper a little at a time, tasting to suit your taste, pour it all into a great big, deep dish, sprinkle with the grated cheese—have more grated cheese at the table—and serve to lots of people.

Crisp hunks of Italian bread. Butter. Wine? Beer? Milk? Sarsaparilla? Root beer? Should be a salad there, too.

You can, of course, swing with this dish adding let's say maybe some sliced franks, or sausages rendered of fat, hunks of lean beef, chicken meat, shrimp, anything that might strike your fancy.

SERVES FOUR.

The prisoner kept pestering the guards, telling them he wanted to be transferred to another jail. Finally one of the guards brought him to the warden's office. "What's wrong with this prison?" the warden asked angrily, "do you think you'd be treated better in any other jailhouse?" The prisoner shook his head. "No, no, Warden," he said, "you've got it all wrong. This isn't such a bad place, I've been in much worse jailhouses. I want to go to another jail because I don't think it's fair my being here with all these other guys." The warden looked at him wonderingly. "Why isn't it fair to you?" the warden asked wonderingly. "You keep getting me wrong, Warden," the prisoner said, "it's not fair to all these other guys being locked up with me because I've talked to all of them, and I seem to be the only guilty one in this jail." I pleaded guilty a long time ago to my love for plebeian dishes that self-professed "gourmets" scorn, as, for an instance:

CHILI CON CARNE (Brooklyn, via Texas)

1 pound dried kidney beans
2 tablespoons peanut oil
1 cup minced onion
1 pound ground chuck
one 1-pound can whole, peeled tomatoes
1 tablespoon (or more) chili powder
1 teaspoon (approximately) salt
2 (or more) large cloves garlic, pressed or mashed
possibly tomato juice

Put the kidney beans into a pot, add enough water to just cover the beans, cover the pot and let it soak overnight.

If you want to have the chili next day, you'd better start cooking the rest of the stuff at least 4 hours before you plan to eat it. Add 2 cups water to beans, start simmering. Get the oil hot in a large fry pan, and in it fry the onion until it is soft. Add the meat to the pan, and cook it over medium heat, stirring and breaking up the meat until it is well-browned. Transfer the onion-meat mixture to the pot with the beans, add the tomatoes and all the juice in the can, the chili, salt, and pressed garlic.

Cover the pot and simmer, stirring from time to time, for 3 to 4 hours. Taste it from time to time, and correct the seasoning, if you think it necessary. Always remember that when you judge the taste of food that has in it hot stuff like chili, or curry, or hot sauce, that it is the aftertaste that is important. So be judicious in your use of chili powder.

As with all foods, people's preferences vary. Some people like their chili pretty thick, others like it more liquid, almost like a soup. If you find that the chili is getting too thick, add tomato juice to suit your taste.

Going to let you in on my secret. There is, on the market, a can of condensed chili beef soup. What I do when I get a sudden, overwhelming yen for chili, is add ½ can of beer to this, bring it to the boil, and you know what? I add 1 tablespoon of curry to it, and it is a wonderful chili-curry-con-carne.

SERVES FOUR.

When I was a small kid, a cretinous teacher sent me to the principal's office to be punished after she had told me to stand up in class and tell everybody what I would ask for if a good fairy were to appear and say that if I asked for three wishes they would be granted. What got me into trouble was saying I didn't believe in guff like that, and if it was all right with her I would turn down the dubious offer of three wishes and take, instead, three:

CHICKEN LIVER POTATO KNISHES (Jewish)

4 tablespoons melted chicken fat, or oil, or marge or butter
1 cup minced onions
2 tablespoons minced garlic
4 cups mashed potatoes
2 eggs, beaten
1 teaspoon salt
$\frac{1}{4}$ teaspoon pepper
flour
12 chicken livers, fried and mashed

In a large fry pan, get 2 tablespoons of fat hot and in it fry the onions and garlic until the onions are golden brown. In a mixing bowl, combine half the fried onions and garlic with the mashed potatoes, and 1 of the beaten eggs. You beat the eggs both together? Well, why not? Use half of the beaten eggs for this and you'll have 1 beaten egg left, right? Add the salt and pepper, and just enough flour to make a rather stiff batter. Refrigerate it and it'll get stiffer.

Now, what we have left is half the fried onion-garlic mixture, 1 beaten egg, 2 tablespoons of fat, and 12 chicken livers. After you have washed and dried the chicken livers and separated them and removed any fat from them, get the remaining fat hot in the fry pan, and fry the livers until, when you prick one, no blood flows. Mash them with a fork. Add the remaining fried onion-garlic mixture to the livers, and stir to combine everything thoroughly.

Break off a hunk of the mashed potato dough, flatten it, and put some of the chicken liver mixture in the center and fold the dough over, enclosing it entirely. Do this with all the dough and all the liver. Oil a baking pan. Brush every knish with the remaining beaten egg, put them on the pan and bake in oven preheated to 350 degrees until the knishes are browned and crisp.

SERVES FOUR.

Two retired spinster teachers were spending a quiet evening at home. One was knitting and watching teevee and the other was reading a newspaper. The one who was reading suddenly threw the paper down on the floor. "What is it that has upset you, my dear?" the other asked. Her overwrought roomie was flushed with anger. "Did you see," she asked, "that story about the woman in Nevada who, at the age of 28, was widowed four times, and that she had each of her husbands cremated?" The other spinster sighed.

"Yes," she said, sighingly, "here we are, old spinster ladies with never even one, and there she is with husbands to burn."

It would be difficult for a girl to become a spinster if she knows how to make:

SPANISH BAKED EGGS AND RICE (Spanish Harlem)

1 tablespoon each, butter and olive oil,
1 cup onion, chopped
$\frac{1}{4}$ cup pimiento-stuffed olives, sliced in half
$\frac{1}{4}$ teaspoon pepper
one can condensed chicken broth plus:
one canful water
1 cup rice
(taste for saltiness after rice is cooked)
8 eggs
$\frac{1}{2}$ cup (or more) any kind of grated cheese you like

In a large frying pan, get the butter-oil mixture hot and in it cook the chopped onion, stirring, until it is soft.

Add the pimiento-stuffed olives to the pan and stir. Sprinkle with pepper. Add the soup and water and stir, and cover the pan. When the soup mixture comes to the boil, pour the rice into it, stir quickly, and cover the pan again and lower the heat so that the liquid just barely simmers. Cook, covered, until almost all of the liquid is absorbed by the rice.

Stir the mixture, fluffing up the rice, and taste it. The chicken soup, of course, has salt in it and your taste may not require any additional salt.

Rub oil or butter on the bottom and sides of a baking pan wide enough to allow you to pack the rice mixture into it to a depth of about one inch. Make certain that most of the cut-up pimiento-stuffed olives are on top of rice.

With a spoon, form eight hollows in the rice mixture. Break an egg into each hollow. Sprinkle the cheese over the egg whites, leaving the yolks standing free of cheese.

In oven preheated to 350 degrees bake the dish for about 15 minutes, give or take one or two, when everything will be hotted up splendidly and serve this delightful food to four people for a wonderful supper, so beautifully suited for Lent—or any time of year, indeed—which is so colorful, with the yellow egg yolks standing forth, the cheese slightly browned, the white rice studded with the red and green of the pimiento-stuffed olives. Enjoy! Enjoy!

SERVES FOUR.

He was the handsomest, richest, most amiable bachelor in town, and for years all the girls and their mothers in the set in which he moved had tried vainly to harness him. At a party, the mother of the prettiest, richest, most amiable girl in town cornered him. "How come," she asked, "you are so impossibly dead set against getting married?"

The bachelor smiled happily. "I have made a study of all the married people I know," he said happily, "and I have found the same terrible thing about each of the marriages."

The mother of the most amiable, prettiest and richest girl in town was indignant. "And what, pray," she asked, "is that one terrible thing in those marriages?" The bachelor smiled amiably.

"Well," he said, "sometimes it's the wife, other times it's the husband." One of the many wonderful things about mine is that we both love:

OUR MOTHERS' QUICHES (Odessa Gubernya, Russia)

one 8 or 9-inch unbaked pie shell
$\frac{1}{2}$ pound slab bacon, sliced thin, cut into pieces approximately 1 inch long
1 pound onions, chopped
$\frac{1}{2}$ pound mushrooms, or 1 four-ounce can pieces, or a jar of button mushrooms
$\frac{1}{4}$ cup parsley, minced
$\frac{1}{2}$ pound cheese, chopped (we prefer Swiss, you use what you like)
2 eggs
$2\frac{1}{2}$ cups (approximately) milk
$\frac{1}{8}$ teaspoon each pepper and cayenne pepper

This, according to the slavish followers of French cuisine, is a dish native to the Lorraine region of France, but if that's true how come both our mothers, who came from Odessa, made it and taught us both how it is done? Pfui.

If you are a kosher lady, you can substitute lox for the bacon, chunks of any smoked or salted fish, or meats like tongue, or corned beef, and, of course, you will use, instead of the bacon fat, butter, or oil depending on whether you use dairy or meat AND, OF COURSE, kosher ladies will use broth instead of milk if meat is used.

Fry the bacon, pouring off fat and saving it, until quite crisp. Fry the onions and sliced mushrooms in large fry pan until onions are quite brown, stirring very often over medium heat, using bacon fat sparingly—or butter or oil, as the case may be. Sprinkle with parsley and stir.

I like Swiss cheese because it lends a piquant, nutty flavor, but does not overpower everything else in the dish. Beat the eggs into the milk, add cheese. Taste a bit of the fried bacon. If it is very salty, use little, if any, salt.

Combine all the ingredients except the cayenne pepper. Pour it into the prepared pie shell—you did prepare one beforehand, didn't you?—sprinkle cayenne pepper over all and bake for 35 to 40 minutes in oven preheated to 350 degrees.

The top should be brown, and the quiche, when shaken forth and back, should quiver just a small quiver.

If there is filling left over after you've filled the pie shell, fill a smaller pie crust with it, or bake it as you would a custard. It is wonderful cold. You will notice, students, that I have not insulted your knowledge or intelligence by explaining that the French word "quiche" is pronounced as though it were spelled "keesh."

SERVES FOUR, MAYBE THREE, MAYBE TWO.

A lady out walking with her youngest son met a friend she hadn't seen since her marriage. "And Harry, here, is two years younger than his brother," she said. "What a handsome young man," the friend exclaimed. "Do you know that you have your mother's eyes and forehead?" The mother shrugged deprecatingly. "Everyone says that Harry has his father's chin," she said. "Yes, lady," said the small boy, "but you know what else? I've also got my brother's old pants and shoes." You say you have some leftover cooked beef handed down from yesterday's roast? Well that's fine. If you don't want the beef for sandwiches, how about using it for:

SPAGHETTI AND MEATBALLS
WITH A DIFFERENCE (Mexico)

1 tablespoon oil
½ cup minced onion
1½ to 2 cups cooked beef, ground or chopped fine
1 egg, beaten
¼ teaspoon salt
1 teaspoon chili or curry powder
1 can condensed cream of mushroom soup
½ can water
1 pound thin spaghetti (spaghettini, or vermicelli)

Get the oil hot in a small fry pan and in it cook the onion until it is soft.

In a mixing bowl, combine the cooked onion with the beef, egg, salt, and chili powder. (Curry powder is good, too.)

Form the mixture into small balls. In a saucepan, combine the soup with water—of course, you can use beer or wine instead of water—bring to the boil and drop the meatballs in. Reduce the heat, cover the pan and simmer slowly while you cook the spaghetti.

Bring to the boil 2 quarts of water, add a little salt and about 1 tablespoon of oil, and put the spaghetti into the boiling water. Stir the water-covered spaghetti with a kitchen spoon or fork, and the softened part of the pasta will allow all of it to fall below the surface of the water. When the water returns to the boil, start timing. If you have thin spaghetti, it will be cooked through, but still chewy, the state described by Italians as *al dente*, literally meaning, "for the teeth," in exactly 6 minutes.

Drain the spaghetti in a colander, put it into a large, heated bowl, and cover with the mushroom soup sauce and the meatballs. Toss it at the table, and have there hot, chopped, dried red pepper flakes for anyone who likes hot, and grated Parmesan cheese for those who want it.

SERVES FOUR.

Shloimey and Yente Talabender were attending a concert. Suddenly Yente nudged her husband. "Look," she whispered, "that rich millionaire, that big braggart, that big phoney, makes out he's a cultured man—Graf Patutsky—he's fast asleep." Shloimey looked at his wife with loathing. "So, for that," he said, "you wake me up?"

Wake me up anytime for:

CHINESE SPAGHETTI AND MEATBALLS (Peking)

½ pound very thin spaghetti (spaghettini or vermicelli)
4 tablespoons peanut oil
1 cup each, minced onion, sweet pepper, and packed down
    shredded lettuce
1 tablespoon garlic cloves, minced
1½ pounds ground beef (chuck, preferably)
½ cup salted peanuts, each one split
¼ teaspoon pepper
2 tablespoons cornstarch
2 tablespoons soy sauce
1 cup beef broth
½ cup water chestnuts, chopped

Bring to the boil 2 quarts salted water, add spaghetti, and when the water returns to the boil start timing. Taste a piece after 6 minutes. It should be cooked through, but still chewy. If you like it that way, drain the spaghetti, putting a colander in the sink and pouring water and spaghetti into it. Don't worry about keeping the spaghetti hot, because we're going to hot it up soon.

While the water for the spaghetti is coming to the boil, and while it is cooking, get 2 tablespoons of peanut oil hot in your largest frying pan, or in another pot. Add the minced onion, sweet pepper, lettuce, and garlic, stir to get it all coated, and cook over medium heat, stirring often, until onion is golden.

And while all this is going on, with wet hands, combine the ground beef with the peanuts and pepper, and form them into balls, whatever size you like.

Add the remaining oil to the pan with the frying vegetables, add meatballs and stir gently, browning the meatballs all over. Combine the cornstarch with the cold soy sauce and beef broth, stir until the cornstarch is dissolved, add it to the pan and cook over high heat stirring, until the sauce is thickened. Add the chopped water chestnuts and stir.

Taste the sauce. The soy sauce, you know, of course, is salty, and so is the beef broth, and there is pepper in the meatballs. But you may want more salt and maybe more pepper, too.

I didn't forget the spaghetti sitting there forlornly in the sink. If your fry pan is large enough, add the spaghetti to all the stuff in it, and cook, stirring, just to hot up the pasta. If your fry pan is too small, combine everything in the pot in which you cooked the spaghetti.

SERVES FOUR, MAYBE SIX.

A girl we know—her name is Nellie Myers—went to the movies with a girl friend not long ago, and she was terribly upset, she told us. Seems she and her friend came there in the middle of the feature, and they could find single seats only, in different rows. Nellie sat there for a while and then she thought of a solution.

She tapped the arm of the man sitting next to her, leaned over, and whispered, "Excuse me, but are you alone?" The fellow didn't move. But out of the corner of his mouth, he whispered hoarsely, "Knock it off, girlie, my wife is sitting with me."

Nellie was so mortified she got right up, walked out of the movie house, went home and broke her diet with:

FETTUCCINE NELLIE (Aunt Pattie's Lane)

1 pound thin spinach macaroni
2 tablespoons olive oil
¼ pound butter
1 cup Parmesan cheese, preferably freshly grated
1 cup heavy cream, scalded
salt and freshly ground black pepper

Cook the macaroni in boiling, salted water for 6 to 8 minutes, adding the olive oil so the macaroni won't stick together. The macaroni should be chewy, not mushy. Melt the butter, toss the grated cheese into the melted butter, and stir it well. Scald the cream. Heat it until it just begins to steam, but don't let it boil. Drain the macaroni well, put it into a heated bowl, cover it with the butter-cheese mixture, spill in the scalded cream, and toss it around wildly, so that all the macaroni is well coated. Add salt—maybe 1 teaspoon—and freshly ground black pepper—maybe ¼ to ½ teaspoon—and serve it with wine.

Look, if you like white wine, drink white wine; if you prefer red wine, then drink red wine. I think those precious people who set down cretinous rules about which wine to drink with what food are great big bores.

SERVES FOUR.

The girl had married and gone to live in San Diego, and this was her first visit back home in Massachusetts in two years. She was telling her mother all about her home out West, and her neighbors, and her social life, and, of course, all about her husband.

"And how does he treat you?" asked the mother. "Is he generous to you?"

The girl smiled ecstatically. "Oh Mother," she cried out happily, "he is so generous to me! He gives me everything I ask for!"

The mother smiled cynically. "That," she said, "shows what a fool you are; obviously you aren't asking for enough."

You can expect to be asked for more if you serve:

SMOKED SALMON-ONION-POTATO
KUGEL (PUDDING) (Russia)

4 tablespoons butter ($\frac{1}{2}$ stick)
1 large onion, sliced thin
5 potatoes, peeled and sliced thin
6 slices smoked salmon
2 eggs
1 cup milk
$\frac{1}{2}$ cup heavy cream
$\frac{1}{4}$ teaspoon (or more) pepper

Hot up the butter, fry the onion slices, separating the rings, until they are nicely browned. Remove the onion from pan and set aside. In the same pan, fry the slices of salmon gently, just enough to remove the pinkness, and remove from pan. Now butter a casserole generously and in it put successive layers of potatoes, smoked salmon, then onions. Finish up with a layer of potatoes. Beat together the eggs, cream, milk and pepper and pour this mixture over the potatoes. Bake it uncovered in oven preheated to 325 degrees until the top layer of potatoes is well browned.

If you can get freshly smoked salmon, ask the man to cut it from the belly, for this is the choicest part (and so, of course, the more expensive) but any supermarket or grocery or delicatessen will have canned smoked salmon which is pretty good, too. Of course, I omitted salt from the list of ingredients because smoked salmon is salty enough. This kind of smoked salmon is called "lox"; don't want you to be using Nova Scotia smoked salmon, which is far more expensive.

SERVES SIX FOR LUNCH, MAYBE FOUR FOR DINNER.

You know, of course, that no one can be a success in politics if he—or she—cannot remember both names and faces, and once I participated in a spectacular feat of this sort. About 25 years before this event, I had been introduced to James Aloysius

Farley, before he became postmaster general of the U.S. of A., and chairman of the Democratic Party's National Committee, after he successfully managed the election campaign of Pres. Franklin Delano Roosevelt. I was just one of the mob of about 26 newspaper reporters who had never been introduced to him, and he shook each of us by the hand, looked us straight in the eye—he had to bend down some to do that to me, for he was a great giant of a handsome man—and repeated each of our names.

Then, I didn't see him for 25 years, and again I was in a mob of newspaper reporters. This was an unruly one, with photographers jostling reporters, and reporters hollering various obscenities at the photographers, and suddenly I was pressed right up against Mr. Farley, and I emitted a loud outraged scream of pain.

"What's the matter?" asked Mr. Farley. "You stepped on my little foot," I said, sobbing quietly. "Gee," said Mr. Farley, his own eyes suddenly brimming with unshed tears, "I'm awfully sorry, Mr. Goldberg." *And that was almost exactly 25 years after I had been introduced to him!* Only successful politician I know who has a terrible memory for faces and names, uses a trick to get by. What he does when he can't remember someone's name—which is all the time—he asks, solicitously, "Tell me, how is the old complaint?"

Who's going to complain—nobody, I hope—if you serve them:

CHINESE ALMOST ANYTHING FRIED RICE

2 cups rice, cooked in 4 cups chicken soup (preferably done day
    before and refrigerated)
2 eggs, beaten
2 tablespoons soy sauce
5 tablespoons peanut oil
1 cup chopped scallions (green onions), with firm greenery
2 cloves garlic, minced
2 cups (or more) Almost Anything, cooked, like maybe chicken,
    beef, tongue, corned beef, ham, lamb, shrimp, maybe
    pastrami? Anything you got lying around the house.

Rice in Chinese restaurants is alway fluffy—each grain separate—because they cook it the night before it is to be used, and
refrigerate it and fluff it up and then steam it in a colander over
boiling water.

Beat the eggs with the soy sauce and let it stand while you
heat 2 tablespoons of the oil in a large pan and fry the scallions
(green onions) and garlic until the scallions become soft and
slightly browned. Add all but 1 tablespoon of the oil, pour in the
rice and stir quickly over low heat until all of the rice is coated
with oil. In a small frying pan heat the remaining tablespoon of
oil and pour in the egg-soy sauce mixture, and cook, stirring,
until the eggs show the first sign of setting, but are still quite
runny. Pour the eggs quickly into the rice, raise the heat, and stir
violently until the rice is thoroughly coated with egg. Add the
cooked, cut-up meat, or whatever, and cook, stirring, until the
meat or whatever is hot, and the rice nicely browned.

You know what I like with this kind of dish, whether it is
chicken, beef, shrimp, or whatever? I like chutney and salty
peanuts with it, that's what. And beer. Look, do you like beer?
Well, if you are drinking a beer you like—isn't that stupid? why
would you be drinking it if you didn't like it?—try it just slightly
chilled, not icy cold.

SERVES FOUR.

FOWL

PART THREE

The advertising copywriter had been working for the agency for several years, but he was not regarded there as anything but a dependable mediocrity, and so he went on working, getting no promotions, no increases in salary, no plaudits, no nothing. And then he got married. Everyone was astounded by the sudden change in his work. His superiors praised his work. He was given raise after raise. He kept getting moved into larger and more impressive offices. His secretaries became more and more beautiful. Finally, he was made a vice president. The agency threw an office party to celebrate his promotion, and for the first time people in the agency met his wife. She was very pretty.

Although people in the agency had asked the new vice president the secret of the remarkable change in the quality of his advertising copy, he had never responded except to put on a mysterious Mona Lisa-ish kind of smile. After he'd had his fourteenth martini, one of the other vice presidents in the agency asked him for his secret for perhaps the nineteenth time. "Have you met my wife?" the new vice president asked. The other man said he had. "She's very pretty, isn't she?" the new one said, and his colleague agreed. "Did you talk to her?" The old vice president said he had. "Well, now you know my secret," said the new vice president. "I show her every line of copy I write, and if it doesn't grab her, I change it, and when she digs it, that's the way it stays, because if she gets the message, then I know everyone in the agency will like it and understand it, because she's even more stupid than she is pretty."

Marvelous eating, and a pretty sight, too, is a:

STUFFED ROAST CHICKEN OR CAPON

one roaster, 3–4 pounds, or capon, 5 to 6 pounds
salt and pepper
½ pound chicken livers
1 large onion, sliced
one pound mushrooms, chopped

Wash and dry the bird inside and out, dry it thoroughly with paper towels, and remove all fat you can get at in cavities. Rub salt and pepper inside and out. Wash, dry, and separate livers, having removed all fat and membranes. Save giblets for a stew or soup. Melt chicken fat in a large fry pan and fry the livers until they are browned all over, which will take about 2 minutes. If blood flows when they are pricked with a fork, that's fine for this purpose. Remove from pan. You may need some oil to fry the onions and mushrooms lightly, but I doubt it because a capon comes equipped with a lot of fat. Combine the fried livers and onions and mushrooms. Spoon it into the capon's cavity, sew it up securely.

Preheat your oven to 350 degrees. I like to use a V-rack for large birds. Whatever you use, a pan without a V-rack, or a V-rack in a pan, rub it with melted fat or a little oil—great advantage of the V-rack is that you don't turn the bird during roasting, so you don't have to sew the cavities closed, or skewer them. Set the bird on it, breast side down, and roast for 30 minutes to the pound, basting occasionally with pan juices. The skin should be crisp and nicely browned, and if slightly pink juices run when you prick the thigh with a fork, that's fine, because then the bird will be done, but not overdone.

SERVES FOUR TO SIX.

The Englishman, visiting the U.S. for the first time, went to Shea Stadium to see a baseball game. The Mets and the visiting team had got one hit each, both of which were home runs with no one on base, and both runs were scored in the third inning. Because he had an appointment, the Englishman left in the tenth inning, by which point neither team had scored another run. He got a taxi with no trouble at all because he was the only man to leave the game. As they started towards Manhattan, the cabbie asked, over his shoulder, "What was the score when you left, Mac?" The Englishman was startled, because he couldn't understand how the cabbie could know that his first name was Mac, but as he had decided upon arrival in this country not to ask questions which would mark him as a foreigner, he replied, "It is a tie, 10,000,000 all."

Unless you've eaten in my house, chances are 10,000,000 to one you've never had:

ROASTED BOILED STUFFED CHICKEN

one chicken, 3 to $3\frac{1}{2}$ pounds
2 cans (each approximately 10 ounces) condensed chicken
    broth
$\frac{1}{2}$ can applejack, wine, or, alas, water (use the chicken broth
    can)
rendered chicken fat or oil
1 cup onion, chopped
$\frac{1}{4}$ pound fresh mushrooms, chopped, or 1 four-ounce can
    mushroom pieces, drained, dried
$\frac{1}{2}$ teaspoon thyme or basil
$\frac{1}{4}$ teaspoon pepper
$\frac{1}{2}$ pound elbow macaroni, cooked
$\frac{1}{2}$ cup broken nuts (any kind), unsalted
$\frac{1}{2}$ cup seedless raisins
$\frac{1}{2}$ cup cheese, grated
$\frac{1}{4}$ teaspoon paprika or turmeric

Remove giblet bag, dry and refrigerate the liver. Pick or cut off any fat in cavity of chicken and on giblets and melt it down in a frying pan, slowly. Wash the chicken and giblets. In a large pot, bring the broth and applejack or whatever to the boil, put the chicken in, add the giblets, cover the pot, reduce the heat and simmer slowly for 30 minutes, turning the chicken a couple of times.

While this is going on, fry the onions and mushrooms in the rendered fat. If you don't have about 2 tablespoons of melted fat, augment it with oil. Add the thyme, and pepper. While the chicken is cooking, boil the macaroni.

Take the chicken out of the pot. While it is cooling, cook the liquid in the pot over high heat until it is reduced to about 1 cup. Chop up the giblets, removing meat from the neck. Combine the onion-mushroom mixture with the macaroni, the giblets, and the nuts and raisins.

Add the cheese to the cup of broth, cook, stirring, until the cheese is melted and add it to the macaroni mixture, tossing to combine all the ingredients. Spoon the mixture into the chicken. You need not sew or skewer the cavity closed. Dry the skin thoroughly. Rub paprika or turmeric on skin of the chicken. Oil a V-rack, put the chicken on it, put rack on roasting pan and roast in oven preheated to 350 degrees until the skin is browned and crisp, which will take about 45 minutes.

What should you do with the liver you stashed away in the fridge? Don't tell anyone about it; fry it, lightly salted and peppered, and eat it all by yourself. You deserve a treat, you poor thing, you, slaving over a hot stove like that.

SERVES FOUR TO SIX.

A prominent English actor, a veteran of the stage, and movies, and TV, was seen by a friend, sitting in his club all by himself, morosely knocking down one drink of whiskey after another in quick succession. He sat down next to the actor. "Is there something wrong?" he asked solicitously. "Perhaps I can help you solve your problem?" The actor sobbed. "When the Queen's Honor List was published the other day," he said sobbingly, "my name was not on it, even after a lifetime of glorifying the English theater; there were businessmen who were made barons, and you know that even those unspeakable Beatles all have Orders of the British Empire, but I, after all these splendid years as a star, am still merely 'mister.'" His friend patted him solicitously and rose. "You know," he said, "that the Prime Minister is a very dear old friend. I will call him right now and see if we can't rectify this cruel injustice."

After a few minutes, the friend of the Prime Minister came back, beaming happily. "All is well, old friend," he said, "the Prime Minister gave me wonderful news for you. He said that he couldn't get you a title, but he offered something much better." "What," the actor sobbed, "could possibly be better than a title?" His friend patted his shoulder. "Just listen patiently for one moment," he said. "The Prime Minister told me that he gave you permission to say that you had been offered a dukedom, but that you turned it down."

Fit for a duke is this splendid:

BAKED PAPRIKA CHICKEN (Hungarian)

2½- to 3-pound chicken, cut up, or favorite parts
4 tablespoons melted chicken fat
¼ cup fine bread crumbs
¼ cup grated cheese, Parmesan or whatever you like
1 teaspoon salt
¼ teaspoon pepper
½ teaspoon tarragon, dried
2 tablespoons fresh parsley, minced, or 1 tablespoon dried
　　　parsley flakes
1 teaspoon paprika

Cut or pick off any pieces of fat on the chicken and melt it down. You won't get, most likely, 4 tablespoons from 1 chicken, and if you haven't got any stashed away in your fridge, shame on you, but augment what fat you've got with oil.

In a mixing bowl, combine the melted fat with all of the other ingredients except the paprika, and you will get a paste-like mixture. Dry the chicken parts thoroughly, and press the mixture all over each chicken part. Oil a baking dish large enough to hold all the chicken parts without piling one on top of the other. Put them into the dish, sprinkle with paprika.

Preheat your oven to 350 degrees, and bake the chicken for 1 hour, turning the chicken once. What should you serve with this? Whatever you like.

SERVES FOUR.

Two young fellows got on a bus at the beginning of the route. As it went on, more and more passengers boarded the bus, and then, finally, one of the young fellows closed his eyes, put his arm on the seat in front of him, and then put his head on his arm. His friend nudged him. "What's the matter?" he asked, "aren't you feeling well?"

The other fellow shook his head. "No, I feel fine," he said in a muffled voice, "it just gets me mad as all-get-out to see young fellows keep their seats on a bus when old ladies are standing."

An old Chinese lady I knew years ago taught me how to make a wonderful dish of:

FRIED CHICKEN WITH VEGETABLES (Chinese)

2½- to 3-pound chicken (or parts)
2 cups chicken broth
2 tablespoons peanut or vegetable oil
1 cup scallions, minced (green onions), with greenery
1 clove (or more) minced garlic
10-ounce package chopped spinach or broccoli, thawed and
    well drained
12 (or more) cherry tomatoes, peeled
½ cup water chestnuts, drained, dried, and cut into thin slices,
    horizontally
4-ounce can mushroom bits, dried and chopped fine
1 tablespoon (or more) soy sauce
¼ teaspoon pepper
2 tablespoons cornstarch
¼ cup wine or water

Cut the skin off the chicken, or parts, cut the meat off the bones in large pieces, and then cube them, removing and saving any fat you come across. Put the chicken skin and bones into a saucepan with the 2 cups of broth. Bring to the boil, and allow the broth to boil until it is reduced to 1 cup.

If you've been able to get enough fat off the chicken to make 2 tablespoons when it is melted down, in a large fry pan, forget about the oil. Otherwise, add enough oil to make 2 table-spoons.

While the broth is boiling, get the fat or oil hot, and in it fry the onions and garlic until the onion is soft. Add the cubed chicken meat, stir to get the meat all coated with fat, cover the pan, and cook for 15 minutes over medium heat, stirring from time to time.

At the end of 15 minutes, take cover off pan, increase the heat, and cook, stirring, until the chicken cubes are nicely browned. Add the thawed and drained spinach or broccoli to the pan, cook, stirring over high heat, for 2 minutes.

You can peel tomatoes easily if you pop them into boiling

water for 1 minute. By this time, the broth should have been reduced to 1 cup. Strain the broth, add it to the saucepan, and throw away the skin and bones.

Add the peeled tomatoes to the pan, then the thin-sliced water chestnuts, and mushroom bits. Stir in soy sauce and pepper, taste for seasoning, and add more of whatever you think it needs.

Dissolve the cornstarch in the wine or water, add to the pan, and cook, stirring constantly until it boils up and becomes thickened.

Serve on a bed of plain, boiled rice, or noodles. Wonderful.
SERVES FOUR.

The boy had been brought to the school and enrolled in the first grade by his mother, and then, at 3 p.m., she waited outside of the school with all the other mothers. When they came home, the boy handed his mother a piece of paper.

"What's this?" she asked. "I dunno," said the boy, "teach' said you should fill it out and that I should bring it back tomorrow morning." It was a questionnaire. It asked all kinds of impertinent questions like how many other children in family? how long living at that address? what does the male parent do for a living and what is his favorite recreation.

Next day the teacher read the filled-out questionnaire: "We have nine children and another on the way, and sometimes on a weekend my husband finds a little spare time to play a round of golf."

To keep your husband's strength up, give him:

CRISP-FRIED CHICKEN
WITH GARBANZO-TOMATO SAUCE (Italy)

two 2½-pound broiler-fryers, cut up, or your favorite parts
1 teaspoon salt
½ teaspoon pepper
1 teaspoon turmeric
6 tablespoons rendered fat
2 cups chopped onion
1 small green pepper, chopped
1 clove (or more) garlic, minced
1 can (10½ ounces) condensed cream of asparagus soup
one 1-pound can whole tomatoes, Italian style, well-mashed
one 1-pound can chick peas (garbanzos), drained
¼ cup parsley, minced
¼ cup pimiento-stuffed olives, halved

Take from the chicken or parts all the fat you can get at. You will not, of course get off enough fat to make 6 tablespoons —which is what we want—of fat after it is rendered. But you'll get some; augment what you get with olive oil, to make 6 tablespoons.

Rub into chicken parts the salt, pepper and turmeric. In 2 tablespoons of hot fat, fry the onion, green pepper, and garlic, until the onion is well-browned. Remove from pan, don't bother to keep it hot. Adding more fat to the pan as needed, fry the chicken parts on all sides until they are well-browned and cooked through.

Don't crowd the pan, but remove finished pieces to a platter placed over a pot of very hot water, and cover chicken with an inverted bowl to keep the parts hot. Add to the platter the fried onion-green pepper mixture.

In a saucepan, combine the condensed soup, the can of mashed tomatoes, and the drained chick peas. Cook covered for 10 minutes. Add the parsley and halved olives. Serve the sauce separately.

SERVES FOUR TO SIX.

I have a book that says when Captain Cook discovered Australia, some of his sailors brought a weird-looking animal back to the ship.

Captain Cook stared at it in astonishment and asked the sailors what the animal was called by the aborigines. When the sailors said they hadn't asked any aborigines the name of the animal, Captain Cook told them to go find an aborigine and ask him. They came back, it is said, and told the Captain that the aborigines called it "Kangaroo."

And this book says it wasn't until many years later that it was learned that when an aborigine says, "kangaroo," he means: "What did you say?"

What do you say we have some:

CHICKEN WITH CRACKLINGS
AND VEGETABLES (Chinese-Polynesian)

2 pounds chicken breasts
2 tablespoons each, soy sauce and lemon or lime juice
2 cloves garlic, pressed or minced fine
⅛ teaspoon cayenne pepper
2 tablespoons (or more) peanut oil
1 large or 2 small sweet peppers, cut into ½-inch pieces
6 scallions (green onions), chopped with some greenery
½ cup chicken broth
1 tablespoon cornstarch

Take the skin off each chicken breast and wash and dry it thoroughly. Cut the skin into pieces about ½ inch long, ½ inch wide. Put the pieces of chicken skin into a large, cold frying pan. Easiest way of cutting the skin is with a small sharp knife, on a wooden chopping board, or with very sharp kitchen shears. Set the heat as low as you can get it. In a short time, fat will start rendering from the skin. Scrape the pan with a stiff metal spatula to keep the skin from sticking to the pan. As fat collects in the pan, pour it off, saving it. The pieces of skin, when done, will be browned and crisp, and delicious. Keep turning the skin frequently to ensure browning all over. This will take about 45 minutes, over very low heat.

Meanwhile, cut the meat off the bones, throw the bones away, and cut the meat into cubes of about 1 inch. In a mixing bowl, combine the soy sauce, lemon juice, garlic and cayenne pepper, and add the cubed chicken meat, stirring in order to get the meat coated. Cover the bowl and let the chicken marinate for at least 1 hour, stirring occasionally. After 1 hour, get the oil, plus the fat rendered from the skin, hot in another large frying pan or saucepan. Pour in the chicken cubes and marinade, and cook over high heat, stirring, for 5 minutes. Add the peppers and scallions, cover the pan, and cook for an additional 15 minutes over very low heat, after stirring to get the peppers and onions coated.

In the broth, dissolve cornstarch, add it to the pan, and cook, stirring, until the sauce is thickened. Taste the sauce for seasoning.

By this time, the pieces of skin should be well browned and crisp. Add the cracklings to the chicken and vegetable mixture, stirring, and serve on a bed of rice or noodles.

SERVES FOUR.

The judge looked with loathing at the bum who had been brought into his courtroom, charged with vagrancy. "Have you ever been arrested before?" he asked. The bum laughed, "Yes, indeed, Your Majesty," the bum said laughingly, "I sure have."

The judge wanted to know what he had been charged with before this time. "All the time the same thing, Your Eminence," said the bum, "just like now, for bumming."

The judge frowned. "Have you ever held a steady job?" asked the judge. The bum shuddered. "Nonono! Never!" he said shudderingly.

"Well, have you EVER earned an honest dollar in your life?" the judge asked. The bum pondered this question. "Well, about it being honest, I couldn't say, but in the last eight years I was paid $2 every time I voted for you," the bum said.

Now I elect to give you:

FRUITY FRIED MARINATED CHICKEN (Polynesian-Hungarian)

one 3½- to 4-pound broiler-fryer, cut up, or parts
½ cup orange juice
2 tablespoons lemon juice (half a lemon, or bottled)
½ teaspoon tarragon
½ teaspoon salt
¼ teaspoon pepper
flour
1 tablespoon turmeric or paprika
4 tablespoons (¼ cup) melted chicken fat or oil
1 cup onion, minced
1 tablespoon fresh orange rind, grated or 1 teaspoon dried

If you buy a whole chicken and cut it up yourself, instead of buying a cut-up whole chicken or parts, it will be not only cheaper, but you'll also get a bag of giblets as well as more chicken fat, because in many stores, when the meat cutters cut up chickens, they snitch the fat, sometimes for the store, sometimes for themselves.

Dry the chicken parts, put them into a large bowl, glass or earthenware, anything but aluminum, and pour the orange and lemon juice over them. Cover it. In hot weather, this can be marinated outside the fridge for 1 hour, changing position of the parts in the bowl, and spooning the juice over all, or 3 or 4 hours in the fridge, or even overnight.

Take them out of bowl, save the juices. Dry the chicken parts by patting them with paper towels. Rub into them the tarragon, salt, and pepper. Sprinkle the parts lightly with flour. Rub with turmeric—a faintly sweetish, faintly hot spice which is one of the ingredients in curry powder.

Start frying the chicken with 2 tablespoons of melted fat, or oil in a large fry pan, adding fat as needed. Have a large pot of very hot water, covered by a large, heavy platter which you'll bring to the table, with an inverted bowl on the platter. When the chicken parts are all golden on both sides, add minced onion to the pan, and put them all back into the pan. Cover it and cook over low heat for 20 minutes, when the chicken will be cooked through. Now fry all the chicken parts on both sides in uncovered pan, over medium heat and make the skin brown and crisp, but don't crowd the pan. Put the finished pieces on the platter, under the bowl, to keep them hot.

Pour into the pan the remaining fruit juice, and put in the grated orange rind, and cook, scraping the pan with a flexible metal spatula to get up the goodies. Pour juice and all over the chicken and serve to four people. Everything can be done hours before, up to the point of final browning of the chicken parts which takes about 10 minutes.

SERVES FOUR.

Two New York newspapermen were having lunch and, of course, they were verbally tearing all their colleagues into small pieces about the size of a knish.

"What ever happened to old Adelbert Methfessel?" one of them asked. "I don't run into him anymore."

The other fellow laughed. "Didn't you hear?" he said. "He was taken off the Broadway beat, and he was sent out to Hollywood to do a column from there. The night his first column was printed, some actor he'd written about beat him up."

The other fellow clucked. "My, my," he said between clucks, "I guess he's coming up in the world, nobody in New York ever thought he was important enough to beat up."

An important part of the chicken repertoire of anyone who cooks should be:

POLLO FRA DIAVOLO
(BROTHER DEVIL'S CHICKEN) (Italy)

one 3- to 3½-pound chicken, cut up, or parts
chicken fat, or butter melted, or olive oil
½ teaspoon salt
½ teaspoon crushed hot red pepper flakes
garlic (let your conscience be your guide), minced fine
¼ teaspoon dried oregano
½ cup dry wine, red or white

If you get a whole chicken and cut it up yourself, or a whole chicken that has been cut up and packaged, chances are you'll find enough fat on it to suit the purposes of this recipe. If you don't have 4 tablespoons of fat when you melt it down in your frying pan, add some oil or butter. Rub a little melted fat on each of the parts, and remove from the pan all but 1 tablespoon of the melted fat.

Fry the chicken pieces, a few at a time, without crowding the pan. Use a spatula to pick the chicken up, so it won't stick to the pan too much. Sprinkle with a little salt and the red hot pepper flakes as you go, as well as garlic and the dried oregano. Get each part well and truly browned on each side, adding fat as needed.

When all the parts have been well browned, put them back into the fry pan and cover the pan, preferably with a colandar turned upside down. This will let the chicken cook through, but will allow the skin to get crisp. Cook it this way for about 20 minutes, basting the chicken from time to time with the pan juices.

If you haven't used a colandar, have a pot of very hot water on the range, cover it with a baking pan, put the chicken parts whose skin is crisp on the pan, cover the chicken with a heatproof bowl, fry the pieces whose skin is not crisp until they do get crisp.

When all the chicken parts have been finished, there will be a lot of good stuff stuck to the pan. Pour in the wine, scrape the pan with a spatula to get the goodies up, and pour the sauce over the chicken. Serve with plain boiled rice or noodles. Have the red hot pepper flakes at the table in case any daring soul wants more hotness.

SERVES FOUR.

The businessman was dictating a memorandum, in answer to an underling's memo suggesting a change in company policy, and his new secretary was taking it down in shorthand. "Furthermore, I think this whole idea of yours is just about the most stupid . . ." the executive said, and then his voice trailed off, and he looked thoughtfully up to the ceiling for inspiration.

"Well," he said, finally, "maybe the word 'stupid' is a little too strong, but I can't think of another that means just that, but won't hurt his feelings too much. I tell you what, in the second drawer of your desk you'll find a copy of Roget's Thesaurus, look up 'stupid' and read me the list of synonyms."

The girl got the Thesaurus and leafed through it for a while. Then, smiling brightly, she asked her boss, "How do you spell 'stupid'?"

One of the smartest things I ever did was give a boss I once had, some:

DEVILISH FRIED-STEWED CHICKEN (Italian)

1 can (approximately 10 ounces) chicken broth
1 can water, or, preferably, dry wine, red or white
2½ to 3 pounds chicken parts
4 tablespoons chicken fat melted
1 large onion, chopped
½ pounds mushroom stems and caps, sliced
hot red pepper flakes or Tabasco sauce
   2 tablespoons flour

In a pot, combine the condensed soup with the wine, or, alas, the water. Bring it to the boil, put the chicken parts in and cook for 20 minutes, covered, with heat reduced so the liquid simmers. At the end of 20 minutes, take the chicken parts out of the pot and set them aside. Take ¼ cup liquid from the pot and set it aside to cool.

Note: if you haven't got 4 tablespoons of rendered chicken fat, add enough oil or butter to make up for lack. Get 2 tablespoons of the fat hot in a large fry pan. In it fry the chopped onion and mushrooms until they are browned, cooking over high heat, and stirring all the while.

When the mushrooms and onion are browned, transfer them to the pot with the broth-wine mixture.

Dry the chicken parts with paper towels. Get the remaining fat hot in the same large fry pan in which you cooked the onion-mushrooms. Fry the chicken parts until the skin is crisp and well-browned.

Taste the broth, add some salt, and a little bit at a time, add hot red pepper flakes or Tabasco until the sauce is as hot as you like it. Remember, the only reliable way to judge the degree of hotness is to wait a couple of seconds, after tasting, to judge the aftertaste.

Stir the flour into the cool ¼ cup of broth-wine until it is dissolved, add it to the broth-wine in the pot, and cook, stirring constantly, over high heat until it is somewhat thickened.

Put the chicken parts on a platter, serve the sauce separately, or pour it over the chicken. Have some crisp bread to glop up the sauce. A green salad is good with this.

SERVES FOUR.

The bunch of kids were shooting dice in the street when a clergyman came by. He stopped to watch. Then an argument began because one of the kids wouldn't give another one a cigarette and the boy who'd been refused the butt used some pretty dreadful language.

"Now, now, children," said the minister, and the kids all shut up and listened. "This is terrible. It is Sunday, and you are gambling, and smoking and using foul language," said the minister. "Wouldn't you fellows all like to to go heaven?"

The boys, greatly abashed, hung their heads in shame. "Yes, sir," "Sure do want to," "Of course," were the words that made the minister beam.

"And how about you?" he said to the one boy who hadn't responded. "Do you mean to say that when you die you'd rather go to The Other Place?"

The recalcitrant boy laughed out loud. "Oh, when I die?" he said laughingly. "Sure I want to go to heaven when I die, I just thought you were getting a group together to go right now."

You know what we'd like to be doing right now, instead of sitting here maundering? What we'd like is to eat:

A FIFTH OF MAUND OF CHICKEN PRIME (India)

one 4-pound chicken, cut up, or favorite parts
maybe some butter, margarine, or oil, but preferably chicken
    fat
1 cup minced onion
1 tablespoon garlic, minced
salt and pepper
1 tablespoon flour
1 pint sour cream (They do so have sour cream in India.)
2 tablespoons tomato paste
1/4 cup bread crumbs, unseasoned

First, let us explain that word "maund." A "maund" is a vague kind of weight measurement used in India and thereabouts, meaning anything from about 20 to 160 pounds. (Maundy Thursday—the Thursday before Easter—has nothing to do with this.) So the maund of chicken we want is about 4 pounds.

Cut off or tear off the fat and skin. Cut the meat off the bones. Cut up the skin, and put the skin pieces and the fat into a dry pan and cook over low heat until the fat is melted, all but small brown, delicious pieces, and if you pour off the fat from time to time, the skin will get browned, and crisp and wonderfully delicious. Hold on to all of this. Save the bones for soup making.

In a large pan, fry the onion and garlic in the melted chicken fat until the onion is soft. Add the chicken meat and cook until the cut-up chicken meat is browned all over. Sprinkle meat with about ¼ teaspoon of salt and pepper—you can always add more later. Sprinkle flour also.

In a small bowl, combine the sour cream with the tomato paste, which will give it a lovely, pink blush. Stir in the bread crumbs, which will thicken it. Pour this mixture into the pan, stir, cover the pan, and cook for 30 minutes over very low heat, so low that it barely simmers.

Now, add the unmelted bits of fat—those wonderful brown morsels of goodness, and the crisp pieces of skin—to the mixture, away from heat. Taste for seasoning, add salt, pepper, or whatever, to suit your taste. Serve to a maund of people, who will moan with joy.

SERVES FOUR.

She (weeping): "When I married you, I thought you were extraordinarily kind, and generous, and brave."

He (sneering): "You were not alone, my honey. Everyone who knew you thought that I was extraordinarily kind, and generous, and brave because I married you."

Weep no more, my lady, and make some:

HONEYED CHICKEN (Persian)

2½ to 3 pounds cut-up chicken, or parts
½ teaspoon salt
¼ teaspoon pepper
foil?
oil, or melted chicken fat
1 cup chopped onion
½ cup water
½ cup orange juice
2 tablespoons honey
½ teaspoon dry mustard

Rub into the chicken parts the salt and pepper. If you have a nonstick baking pan, you won't need the foil. But if you use an aluminum pan you should always line it with foil when you use honey in cooking because it is absolute, unmitigated hell trying to get the encrustation off a pan in which something was baked with honey.

Smear a little oil or melted chicken fat on the pan or on the foil, put the chicken parts in the pan, skin side down, and bake them for 15 minutes in oven preheated to 375 degrees.

Meanwhile, back at the range, put the chopped onion into a pan with the water and orange juice, bring it to the boil, dissolve the honey in the pan, and stir in the dry mustard.

When the chicken has been baked for 15 minutes, remove the pan, turn the chicken parts, pour some of the mixture over them, reduce the temperature of the oven to 350 degrees, and bake for 30 minutes longer, basting the parts at least twice. The skin should be crisp and a deep golden brown, and the skin and meat deliciously sweet and hot.

What is good with this is buttered noodles seasoned only with salt and pepper, and just a tiny sprinkling of paprika. And a green salad. With equal parts of oil and lemon or lime juice.

SERVES FOUR.

If you've ever come into the slightest contact with a proper Bostonian you know how uppity they are.

Like the Boston lady who asked the young girl her son had brought home to meet her, "Where are you from, my dear?" And when the girl said, "I'm from Ioway," the Boston lady smiled superciliously. "In Boston," said the Boston lady, "we pronounce it 'Oh-hio.' "

And the Boston dame, who, after listening to a rather lengthy report on a new acquaintance's travels, said haughtily, "I have no need to travel, for I am a Bostonian and I'm already here."

What have we got here but a:

BAKED CHICKEN WITH ORANGE SAUCE (France)

one 4-pound broiler chicken, cut up (or favorite parts)
½ cup orange juice
¼ cup port
½ cup chopped onion
½ teaspoon salt
¼ teaspoon pepper
1 tablespoon grated orange rind
if you want a thick sauce (gravy), 2 tablespoons cornstarch

Remove all pieces of fat from the chicken and giblets and melt them down in a small fry pan over low heat.

Refrigerate or freeze the giblets for use later in soups or stews. Fry the liver, put it on a hunk of bread, season it with salt and pepper, top with some chopped onion, and eat it sneakily all by yourself, but don't feel guilty, because there isn't enough to go around, is there? Certainly not.

Dry the chicken parts thoroughly, put them into a bowl and pour the orange and wine over them, stir the parts around to get them all coated, cover the bowl and let it marinate for 1 hour, or for several if you like, in the fridge. Take the chicken out of the marinade—which save—and dry each part. Spread some of the melted fat in a roasting pan. Get the rest of the melted fat—you should have at least 2 tablespoons—hot in a small fry pan and brown the onion in it over low heat, stirring from time to time.

Rub salt and pepper into each chicken part. Put the chicken—*skin-side down*—on the roasting pan, and, in oven preheated to 350 degrees, bake it for 1 hour, basting at least once with pan juices, and lifting pieces up with a spatula, turning after 30 minutes.

In the last 10 minutes of baking the chicken, decide whether you want a thick gravy or a light sauce. If you want it thick, add the grated rind to the juice-wine mixture and dissolve the cornstarch in it. When the hour of baking is done, turn off the heat, leave oven door open and put the chicken parts on a large platter, and put it into the open oven. Put the baking pan over heat on top of the stove, pour in the juice-wine mixture and cook, scraping the pan with a metal spatula to get up the good stuff stuck to the pan. Stir until the gravy is thickened, and pour it over the chicken. Of course, if you want a thin sauce, don't dissolve the cornstarch in the marinade. Have a salad, won't you?

SERVES FOUR.

The kindergarten teacher was trying to make the small boy feel at home on his first day in school. "And what did you have for breakfast this morning, Shloimey?" she asked. Shloimey cast his eyes up to the ceiling and thought. "This morning," he said, "I et six flapjacks." The teacher smiled gently. "No, Shloimey," she said gently, "you mean 'ate.'" Shloimey shrugged. "No, teach," Shloimey said firmly, "I wanted two more, but my mama said no, she wouldn't give me two more because I already et six."

Four to six people can make an exotic feast with:

GINGERY BAKED CHICKEN (Japanese)

½ to ¾ teaspoon powdered ginger
½ teaspoon salt
¼ teaspoon pepper
2 eggs
¼ cup chicken broth
flour
one 2½- to 3-pound fryer, cut up, or favorite parts

Put into a mixing bowl the ginger, salt, pepper, and 2 eggs. Add the chicken broth and beat to combine the ingredients thoroughly.

Beat into the mixture, gradually, so that no lumps form, just enough flour to give it a paste-like quality just a little thicker than sour cream.

Dip the chicken pieces into the mixture, getting them coated quite heavily. Put the chicken into a baking dish large enough to hold the pieces of chicken side by side and bake in oven preheated to 350 degrees, uncovered, for about 45 minutes, when the chicken should be crisp on the outside, and cooked through.

Pickled cucumbers or tomatoes, or both are good with this, and so is chutney. What I like, too, with this, is mashed potatoes jazzed up with browned sesame seeds and minced parsley.

The sesame seeds are available wherever herbs and spices are sold. One tablespoon of sesame seeds, browned slightly in 1 tablespoon of oil mixed into, and sprinkled over mashed potatoes, along with minced parsley makes the ordinary mashed potatoes into something new and wonderful.

SERVES FOUR TO SIX.

The manager of the store saw a lady customer walk in and, after exchanging only a very few words with a brand-new saleslady, stalk angrily out of the store, muttering. He quickly went over to the new young saleslady.

He: "What did that lady ask you?"

She: "She asked if she could try on one of the dresses in the window."

He: "And what did you say?"

She: "I told her of course she couldn't, because we didn't want the cops to come, and that she'd have to use one of the dressing rooms like everyone else."

There's room in the cooking repertoire of everyone for:

BAKED CHICKEN BREASTS WITH RICE
OR MASHED POTATOES (Portuguese)

4 chicken breasts, bones and skin removed BUT SAVE SKIN
½ teaspoon salt
¼ teaspoon pepper
4 tablespoons melted chicken fat, or oil, or butter
1 large onion, chopped
1? clove garlic, minced
¼ cup parsley, minced
4 cups potatoes, mashed, or 1 cup raw rice (when cooked
     makes 3 cups)
2 or 3 strips pimientos (or roasted sweet red pepper), chopped

Rub some of the salt and pepper into each chicken breast, and, as we said, hold on to the chicken skin. In a large fry pan, get 2 tablespoons of the fat, oil, or butter hot, and in it, over medium heat, fry the chicken breasts on both sides, until golden. Don't crowd the pan; the chicken is going to be baked pretty soon. Hot up the rest of the fat in same pan and in it fry the onion, garlic and parsley, scraping the pan with a metal spatula, to get up chicken goodies stuck to the pan.

Oil a baking dish or casserole, put into it a layer of mashed potatoes, or cooked rice into which you have mixed in the chopped pimientos or peppers, and over that put 1 or 2 of the chicken breasts—depending on width of baking dish—spoon on some of the fried onion-garlic-parsley mixture, and then cover that with some mashed potatoes or rice. Repeat this process until you have used all of the ingredients. The top layer should be mashed potato, or rice. Put over it all some, or all, of the skin you removed from the chicken breasts (should not put one piece of skin over another).

In oven preheated to 350 degrees, bake it until the chicken skin on top of the dish is browned and quite crisp, about 20 to 25 minutes. Have a mixed green salad with this.

SERVES FOUR, MAYBE SIX.

When the pretty young actress was ushered into the theatrical producer's office by his secretary, the man got up from behind his desk, shook hands with her and then he sat down in the middle of his couch.

"Come over here, my dear," he said, "and sit down next to me and tell me all about yourself, your experience, and all like that." The young actress looked at him dubiously.

"Where," she asked dubiously, "would you like me to sit, on your right? or your left?"

The producer smirked. "Makes no difference at all, honey," said the producer, "I'm ambidextrous."

You'll need two hands to make:

BAKED STUFFED CHICKEN BREASTS (Israel)

4 large chicken breasts (see note)
¼ teaspoon salt
¼ teaspoon pepper
½ pound chicken livers
rendered chicken fat, or margarine, or oil
½ cup onions, chopped
½ teaspoon dried thyme, oregano, whatever herb you prefer
½ cup mushrooms, chopped, or ½ of 4-ounce can of mushroom
    pieces, drained and dried
⅛ teaspoon salt
⅛ teaspoon pepper
2 eggs, beaten
bread crumbs

NOTE: In most markets you can get chicken breasts without bones but they cost more. You don't have to possess the skills of a brain surgeon to remove the bones; just takes a little patience and practice, and if you really enjoy cooking, and can spare the time, you'll soon master it. Some people think that a half chicken breast makes an adequate serving for one person. If that's what you think, then, of course, you'll cut down on the quantities of all of the following ingredients. Rub salt and pepper into the breasts—¼ teaspoon each for 2 halved breasts, a little more for 4 whole breasts, but not doubled in quantity. Wash the livers in cold water, separate them, removing fat and membranes. Dry them thoroughly on paper toweling. Dry the breasts, too.

In a large frying pan, hot up 2 tablespoons chicken fat, or whatever, and in it fry the chopped onions, stir in thyme or whatever, and the mushrooms. Fry until the onion begins to turn golden. Push the onion-mushroom mixture to the side of pan, add some more fat or whatever, and fry the chicken livers until they have turned gray on all sides, not more than 1 minute on each side. Remove the pan from heat, put the fry pan on a wet wash cloth on your working counter or tables so the pan will remain stationary, and cut up the livers, and combine them with the onion-mushroom. Stir in ⅛ teaspoon each of salt and pepper.

You can leave it to cool in the pan, or you can transfer the liver stuffing to cool quicker in a bowl. Loosen the skin on the chicken breasts, being careful not to tear it, and put equal portions of the stuffing between the skin and meat of the chicken. They used to make pretty strong toothpicks years ago, but the only ones we've seen for a long time are terribly fragile. So use skewers to keep the skin of the breasts closed over the stuffing. Dip the breasts into the beaten eggs, then into the bread crumbs.

Rub with melted fat or whatever a baking dish large enough to hold all the breasts flat, skin side down. In oven preheated to 350 degrees, bake the breasts uncovered, until the skin is quite browned and crisp, basting twice, turning once, which will take about 45 minutes. Bake potatoes at the same time. Have a salad.

SERVES FOUR.

His daddy was looking out of the kitchen window and saw the boy hit their neighbor's young son. His daddy hollered out of the window—it was open, we forgot to tell you—"You come right on in here, you!"

So the kid went into the house and as soon as he entered the kitchen his daddy gave him a severe clop on the head which made the kid yelp.

"You know why I gave you that clop on the noggin?" the daddy asked.

"No," said the lad, "why did you give me such an undaddy-like clop on the head?"

"Because," said his daddy, "you gave a clop on the head to that kid who is smaller than you, that's why."

"Oh," said his son, "I thought maybe it was because you are bigger than I."

What goes over big in my house is:

CHICKEN BREASTS WITH SWISS CHEESE SAUCE (Hungarian)

4 chicken breasts
1 can condensed chicken soup (about 10 ounces)
½ soup can dry wine or water
¼ cup fresh minced parsley, or 1 tablespoon dried flakes
2 tablespoons chicken fat, oil, or butter
2 tablespoons flour
¼ teaspoon pepper
½ cup chopped Swiss cheese
¼ teaspoon paprika

Put the chicken breasts into a pot, add the soup, wine (or water), and parsley. Bring to the boil and simmer for 30 minutes over very low heat, covered, occasionally changing the positions of the chicken breasts in the pot.

Take them out of the pot, remove the skin and throw it away, and cut the meat off the bones. If you let them cool a little, you can take the meat off the bones quite easily without a knife.

Put the chicken meat into a baking dish. In a fry pan, hot up the fat, sprinkle with flour, and cook, stirring until the flour is golden. Add the broth slowly, stirring all the while, until the sauce is smooth and thickened. Stir in the pepper and taste it to see if it needs salt. Spoon it over the chicken meat. Scatter the chopped Swiss cheese over the sauce, sprinkle with paprika, and bake in oven preheated to 400 degrees until the cheese is melted and bubbly.

SERVES FOUR.

The teacher in charge of the school yard during the lunch recess heard excited yells coming from a crowd of boys and rushed over, for his experience told him that a fight was going on. He pushed his way through the crowd and, sure enough, two boys were in the center, rolling on the ground and pummeling each other. The teacher separated the boys and held them both at arm's length. "Now what's this all about?" he asked. "Why were you two fighting?" One of the boys said sullenly, "I called him a liar, and he punched me, so I had to punch him back, didn't I?" The teacher asked the other boy if it was true that he had thrown the first punch. "Yes," the boy said, "but even if I am a liar, he shouldn't call me that because I'm a very sensitive child."

When I call friends to invite them to a late weekend breakfast they are always happy to get:

FRIED CHICKEN BREASTS AND HAM ON MUFFINS
WITH ONION SAUCE (South, U.S. of A.)

4 chicken breasts
3 cups water
½ teaspoon salt
¼ teaspoon pepper
4 slices (or 8) boiled ham
4 tablespoons melted chicken fat or butter
1 large onion, chopped
2 tablespoons flour
4 tablespoons parsley, minced fine
a dash or 2 of Tabasco
4 muffins, split and toasted

Bring the water to the boil in large pan, add salt and pepper and simmer the chicken breasts slowly, covered, for 35 minutes. Remove the chicken breasts. When breasts are cooled, remove and throw away the skin and bones. Boil broth until reduced to 1 cup.

Fry the sliced ham in large fry pan in the melted chicken fat or butter, remove the ham from the pan with spatula. In the same pan fry the chicken breasts until they are golden brown on both sides, and remove them from the fry pan.

Fry the chopped onion in the same pan, stirring until the onion is soft and just turning golden, sprinkle with the flour, and slowly add 1 cup of broth, stirring until it is slightly thickened, stir in the minced parsley, and Tabasco sauce. Put chicken and ham into sauce to reheat, put a slice of ham on each muffin half, on top of that put ½ of a chicken breast, and pour some onion sauce over all and serve.

SERVES FOUR.

Thomas Jefferson, that great and good man was, among other distinctions, author of the United States Constitution which said that "all men are created equal," but he admitted, privately, that occasionally *furniture* prevented this condition from continuing after men's birth. So, to remedy this sad situation, at dinners in Jefferson's home, people sat at a round table so that no one was at the head of the table and no one was at the foot.

Speaking of American history, Mr. David Schwartz, an indefatigable researcher and author of an "anecdotal U.S. history" says that a candidate for the Senate in a Southern state once told his constituency: "While yo' honest, God fearin', hard workin' folks down here are eatin' yo' home-raised ham and hominy grits and eggs, what do yo' think yo' Senator up yonder in Washington is eatin'? I'll tell yo'. He's eatin' fish eggs, that's what he is eatin'. IMPO'TED FOREIGN ROOSH-IAN FISH EGGS!"

Only the spice is imported in:

ROASTED ROCK CORNISH HENS ON BED OF LIVERS AND MASHED POTATOES (U.S.A.)

4 Rock Cornish hens, each about ¾ to 1 pound
rendered chicken fat, or oil, or butter
1 teaspoon salt
½ teaspoon each, pepper and turmeric
2 cups onions, minced
¼ cup parsley, minced
4 livers from hens, plus ½ pound chicken livers, cut up (see note)
½ teaspoon salt
¼ teaspoon pepper
4 cups potatoes, mashed

Wash the hens inside and out and dry them thoroughly. Save giblets in your freezer for soup or stews. Rub each hen with about 1 tablespoon melted chicken fat, oil, or butter. Rub some salt inside and outside of each hen. Rub skin of each hen with pepper and turmeric. (Turmeric gives the birds a wonderful golden color, and a delicate, exotic, faintly warm taste.) I don't truss my birds, threw mine away years ago. Roast breast side up in 350 degree oven for 45 minutes.

In a large frying pan, fry the onion and parsley until the onion is just turning golden. LIVER NOTE: The livers from the hens, plus the chicken livers, should have all fat removed, separated, and be washed and dried thoroughly. Sprinkle with salt and pepper. Cook the cut-up livers in pan with onions until there is just a little pinkness in the livers. (I like a little pinkness, for these delicate morsels are toughened when over-cooked.)

Combine the liver-onion mixture with the mashed potatoes. When the hens are finished, put the liver-potato mixture on a large hot platter. Arrange the roasted hens on and around the potatoes. I like roasted tomatoes with this. Cut 4 large tomatoes in half, core them, sprinkle each with 1 tablespoon bread crumbs, and drizzle a little fat, oil or butter over each. Put them into pan with the hens in the last 15 minutes of roasting. This dish will be pretty to look at as well as delightful to eat.

SERVES FOUR.

The man's wife had been treating him with scorn because she accused him of not having courage to stand up to his boss and ask him for a raise. "A man with the heavy responsibilities that your boss keeps piling on you," she kept saying, "and the ability to cope with such difficult problems should be getting a whole lot more money than you're getting, and if you don't ask your boss for more money, he won't have any respect for you."

This wore him down so much that he went to his boss. "Look here," he said to his boss, "do you have any respect for me?" His boss laughed at him. "Why should I have any respect for you? Isn't it enough that I pay you?" he asked laughingly. The man shook his head. "No Sir, Boss," he said, "my wife says that anybody who does work as difficult as mine, with my education and abilities, should be getting more money than you're paying me." His boss sneered.

"You just tell that stupid wife of yours," he said sneeringly, "that if some slob with less than your education and ability could do your work I'd fire you and hire him for less money."

Anyone with enough education to read this can easily make:

SPICY ROCK CORNISH HENS (OR CHICKEN) (India)

Four 1-pound Rock Cornish hens, split in two, or two 2-pound
    chickens, split
chicken fat, butter, or oil
$\frac{1}{2}$ teaspoon each: salt, pepper, turmeric, and powdered ginger
2 tablespoons lemon or lime juice
8 canned peach halves, save syrup
2 tablespoons honey

Remove giblet bags from hens or chickens. Cut off the wings. Wrap up gizzards, hearts, wings, and necks and store in the fridge or freezer, to use for soups, stews another time. Wash the livers, remove fat, and separate the livers, dry them, and put them in your fridge until later in the cooking. Split the hens or chickens into 2 halves. Remove fat and melt it down in a small fry pan. Wash and dry the parts.

Combine the salt, pepper, turmeric, and ginger with the lemon or lime juice. You will have a paste-like mixture. Rub equal portions into the skin of each part.

You will have some melted fat in the small fry pan, but not enough. If you have any stashed away in your fridge, add enough to the pan to make 4 tablespoons. Or augment the fat you've got with butter or oil. Spread about 1 tablespoon of melted fat on a roaster pan. Put the parts skin-side down on the pan. Drizzle about 2 tablespoons, in equal portions, over the parts.

Put the pan into oven preheated to 350 degrees, and roast for 35 minutes, turning once. Baste the parts at least 2 times, adding the remaining tablespoon of fat, with the pan juices. In last 10 minutes, put a peach half on each Cornish hen part and 2 on each chicken half, and pour over it some of the peach syrup into which you have mixed the honey. At the same time put the livers into the pan, turn them to get them coated with fat on both sides.

Serve 2 Rock Cornish parts, or one chicken half to each of 4 people, sharing livers equally. The livers will need some seasoning. Tell everyone to use salt and pepper to taste at the table. Have a pepper mill at the table.

SERVES FOUR.

It was at a session of the drama class in college and the students had been called upon, one by one, to go to the stage to do an improvisation, without speaking, and to do it so well that the rest of the students could recognize immediately what was being presented to them. The class had no trouble recognizing what each improvisation was about until it came around to Don Task's turn. He stood there on the platform, holding the lapels of his jacket firmly with both hands, swaying backwards and forwards and sideways. Silence reigned for several minutes until the teacher said, impatiently, "Well, Mr. Task, would you mind telling us what you represent?" Don Task smirked. "I'm playing the part of a man," he said smirkishly, "riding in a crowded subway car, jammed up against a young chick measuring 38–24–38."

Now is the time for all good men to get hold of some young chicks and:

BARBECUE CHICKEN (U.S.A.)

1 pound (approximately) of chicken *per serving* (preferably broiler-fryers or Cornish hens)
½ teaspoon salt per chicken
¼ teaspoon pepper per chicken
¼ cup melted chicken fat augmented with oil
¼ cup dry wine or wine vinegar
¼ teaspoon dried tarragon
¼ teaspoon oregano
¼ teaspoon turmeric

If you're using whole chicks or hens, split them in half, remove all pieces of fat. Melt fat down, combine with salt, pepper, spices, and wine. Rub split chicken with mixture. Build a high bed of coals on *only half* the fire-box and oil the grill and have it as close to the coals as you can get it. Put foil in the bottom of the other half of the fire-box to catch fat. You don't have to wait for ash to form on the coals. As soon as half of the grill is red-hot, turn that part over the foil container and put the halved chicks, skin-side down, doused with the baste, on it. As that part of the grill cools, turn the grill gradually, replacing chicken pieces with tongs, on the hot part of the grill. A total of 20–25 minutes on each side, basting often, will cook the chicks to perfection, crisp outside, juicy and meltingly wonderful inside. Hooha! Enjoy! Enjoy! No flare-ups!

Man on the commuter train was being bored almost to the point of screaming because sitting next to him, an utter stranger, a young fool who was sure to become an ever-older fool and who had been married only one week, was bragging about his bride's varied talents. When the fool said: "And you know, my little doll can talk for hours on almost any subject you could name," our man got up, pushed his way past to the aisle of the car, and hollered: "My wife, you simpering young fool, does better than your wife, because my wife can talk for weeks with no subject at all."

The subject of today's lecture, students, is:

STEWED ROCK CORNISH HENS (U.S.A.)

four 1-pound Rock Cornish hens
giblets from hens (save little livers for other use later)
4 tablespoons fat (chicken fat, preferably)
2 cups onions, chopped
1 cup carrot, cut into very thin rounds
1 tablespoon garlic cloves, minced
¼ cup fresh parsley, minced
1 teaspoon dried sage
two 10-oz. cans condensed chicken broth
one 10-oz. can dry wine.
maybe some salt, maybe some pepper
2 tablespoons flour

Rinse hens inside and out. Put them in large pot, along with rinsed giblets. In large fry pan hot up 2 tablespoons fat, fry onions, carrot, garlic and parsley until onions are slightly browned, stirring often. Spoon this over the hens in pot. Add broth, wine and water to the pot.

Bring the liquid to the boil, cook, covered, simmering over low heat, for 35 to 40 minutes.

Remove hens from pot. Pat them dry with paper towels, put hens on a roasting pan. Roast in oven preheated to 425 degrees for 15 minutes. This will make the skin crisp and delicious.

Meanwhile, back on the range, have liquid in pot cooking over high heat, to reduce quantity to about 2 cups. Stir often, to make certain vegetables in pot don't burn. Taste sauce, add seasoning if you like, but broth is seasoned, of course. Dissolve flour in ¼ cup water, add to sauce, boil, stirring, until sauce is thickened just a trifle. Serve 1 bird to a person, with the sauce on the side. A good thing to get you sauced with this is the same wine you used in cooking. Don't fall into the oven. Drive carefully. Be polite to pedestrians. Stay well.

SERVES FOUR.

Seems this couple suddenly became rich so they decided to do something sensational to establish their changed status. After long thought, they decided to buy a Rembrandt and a Rolls Royce.

One afternoon, the husband called his wife. "Well, dearie," he said, "this morning I did it; I bought a Rembrandt and a Rolls Royce and they said they would be delivered this afternoon. Did they arrive yet?" There was a long silence over the phone. Then the wife said: "Yes, darling, they did. But will you explain something to me? Which is which?"

You can show you know what's what if you make:

CHICKEN FRICASSEE (The Bronx)

one 4- to 5-pound fowl
giblets
4 tablespoons chicken fat, butter, margarine, or oil
3 tablespoons flour
5 cups chicken soup
1 cup onion, chopped
2 ribs celery, chopped, with leaves
1 carrot, chopped
1 bay leaf
$\frac{1}{2}$ teaspoon thyme
6 peppercorns tied up in cheesecloth
$\frac{1}{4}$ cup chopped parsley
$\frac{1}{4}$ pound fresh mushrooms or 4-ounce can stems and pieces
$\frac{1}{2}$ pound beef, chopped
1 egg, beaten
salt and pepper to taste
$\frac{1}{4}$ cup dry wine, red or white
2 tablespoons cornstarch

Cut up and chop the chicken into parts as small as you can manage. Remove all visible fat and hold on to it. (You should do this every time you cook chicken, for its fat is splendid for any kind of frying.) Wash and dry all the parts and giblets. In a large pan, melt the fat, butter, or hot up the oil. Put giblets and chicken parts—but not the liver—into pan, turn to coat all sides, sprinkle with half the flour, turn parts again and sprinkle with rest of flour, and fry until all parts are golden, but not browned. Add 4 cups of soup, cover and cook over low heat, simmering, for about 1 hour. Add the chopped onion, celery and carrot. Tie the bay leaf, thyme and peppercorns up in a piece of cheesecloth and add it to the pot.

Simmer for another 30 minutes, turn the parts, and add the cut-up mushrooms. Mix the beef with egg, salt and pepper, shape into small meat balls and add to the pan, along with the wine. Simmer for another 15 minutes and add the liver, cut up. Dissolve cornstarch in remaining cup of consommé and simmer for 15 minutes. Throw away cheesecloth bag. Remove chicken parts, giblets, mushrooms and meat balls to serving platter, spoon gravy and vegetables over it all, and serve with rice or mashed potatoes. There should be about 4 cups of gravy, and after 2 hours, the fowl should be deliciously tender.
SERVES FOUR TO SIX.

The main course the bride had cooked for dinner was a pudding, her first effort with this kind of dish. She watched anxiously as her husband took his first taste. He chewed and chewed and chewed reflectively. "How is it, darling?" she asked anxiously. "Tell me, dearest," he said, "you didn't buy this, or make it from a mix, or anything, did you?" She shook her head. "Oh, no, I made it all by myself, sugarheart." Her husband nodded. "That's what I thought," he said thoughtfully, "but tell me, honeybun, who helped you to lift it out of the oven?"

What the most ethereal bride will find as light as a summer cloud is:

CHICKEN PUDDING (Holland)

one 2½- to 3-pound chicken, cut up, or parts
1 teaspoon salt
¼ teaspoon pepper
flour
melted chicken fat, oil, butter, or margarine
½ cup onions, chopped
¼ cup parsley, chopped
1½ cups flour
1 teaspoon baking powder
4 eggs, separated, yolks beaten until lemony, whites beaten
    stiff
broth or milk
1 can (10½ ounces) condensed cream of mushroom soup
½ pound chicken livers

Take the skin off the chicken parts, cut the meat off the bones in chunks as large as you can manage. Save the bones and skin for soup, or cut the skin into ½-inch squares and, over very low heat, in a large frying pan, cook the pieces of skin, pouring off fat as it accumulates—save the fat for use in frying—until the pieces of skin are crisp and browned. They are delicious on bread, with chopped fried onion and rendered chicken fat, lightly salted and peppered, and make a wonderful hors d'oeuvre, and keep indefinitely in the fridge, tightly sealed.

Sprinkle chicken meat with ½ teaspoon salt and ¼ teaspoon pepper. (Leaves ½ teaspoon salt for use later.) Dust the chicken meat with flour.

Get 2 tablespoons of melted fat or whatever hot in a large fry pan and in it fry the onions and parsley until the onion is soft. Add the chicken meat to the pan, adding more fat, and fry, stirring often, until the meat is well browned.

Put the 1½ cups flour into a mixing bowl with the baking powder. Beat the egg yolks and stir them into the flour with a fork. Add just enough broth or milk to make a batter with consistency of sour cream. Fold into the batter the egg whites, beaten stiff. Oil a large baking dish and spoon the batter into it. Spoon into the batter the fried chicken-onion mixture.

Bake it in oven preheated to 350 degrees for about 45 to 50 minutes, when the batter should be puffed up and browned. Serve this with:

MUSHROOM CHICKEN LIVER GRAVY

Pour contents of the soup can into a small pan. In the fry pan you used to cook the chicken meat, get some melted fat, or whatever, hot, and in it fry the chicken livers until only a little pink shows when they are pricked with a fork. The livers should, of course, have been washed, dried, all fat and membranes removed, and separated, before frying. Cut them up. Put them into the soup and cook it until the soup bubbles.

SERVES FOUR, MAYBE SIX.

The Sunday school class was discussing the meaning of the prayer, and they had come to the part that goes, "And forgive us our trespasses, as we forgive those who trespass against us." The teacher asked for a volunteer to rise and explain just what those words mean. None of the children volunteered.

The teacher sighed and explained that in this case the word "trespass" meant "wrongdoing," so that when one asked for forgiveness of trespasses, one was asking to be forgiven for wrongdoing. "But," she added, "if you don't forgive those who trespass against you, which means, as I have just explained, forgiving those who do wrongs to you, you have no right to ask forgiveness for your own wrongdoing, now do you understand?"

The class said, in chorus, "Yes, teach, we understand."

So the teacher said, "Now, Asa Momser, tell the class, suppose you were playing out in the street and another boy came along and punched you and knocked you down, and then he kicked you for no reason at all, would you be able to forgive him his trespass, or wrongdoing against you?"

Little Asa stood up and pondered the question. "Well," he said, finally, "I might be able to if he was a lot bigger than me."

You will be forgiven anything, almost, if you serve:

CREAMED CHICKEN WITH A DIFFERENCE (Brooklyn)

one 3½- to 4-pound chicken, cut up, or favorite chicken parts
melted chicken fat
½ teaspoon salt
¼ teaspoon pepper
1 cup onion, chopped
1 cup celery with greenery, chopped
1 clove garlic, minced (this is approximately 1 tablespoon)
1 bay leaf, crumbled
1 can (approximately 10 ounces) chicken broth
1 can (same one) water
vermouth
2 eggs, beaten
1 cup light cream
8 chicken livers
giblets, chopped

Wash and dry the chicken parts and remove all pieces of fat and melt the fat down in a small fry pan. Rub salt and pepper into each piece. Put the chicken parts into a pot with the giblets but not the liver, add the onion, celery, garlic and bay leaf. Pour into the pot the can of chicken broth, bring it to the boil, cover, reduce the heat and simmer for 1 hour. From time to time, add equal parts of water and vermouth, to keep the liquid at a level of 2 cups all through the cooking. Beat the beaten eggs into the cream while this is going on. Fry the chicken livers in 2 tablespoons of the chicken fat, save the other fat in the fridge for use in cooking another time.

Cut the skin off the chicken parts and throw the skin away. Cut the meat off the bones in large chunks. Do you like to chomp on cooked chicken bones? I do. If you do, chomp. Trim fat and cartilage off the gizzard and slice it and the heart, and tear meat off the neck bone. Strain the broth. Combine the eggy milk slowly with the broth, beating rapidly. Put the broth-milk mixture into the pot, add the chicken meat and chopped giblets and cook, stirring, just long enough to get it all nice and hot. Serve this with 2 fried chicken livers in the center of each serving to four people. Looks nice garnished with parsley sprigs—which should be eaten—and cherry tomatoes.

SERVES FOUR.

The father had caught his young son telling an outrageous lie. "I'm going to have to punish you, so I'm going to spank you," he said. After spanking him and when the child had ceased sobbing, the father said, "Now I hope you've learned a lesson from this. When I was your age I didn't lie to my daddy." The boy's face brightened considerably. "How old do I have to be to get away with it, Daddy?"

You can get away with very little time at a hot stove by making:

CHICKENBURGERS (California)

4 tablespoons melted chicken fat, oil, or butter
1 medium onion, minced
1 clove (or more) garlic, pressed
4 tablespoons parsley
$\frac{1}{4}$ pound fresh mushrooms, minced, or one 4-ounce can
     mushroom pieces, drained, dried, and minced
2 cups or more cooked chicken meat, minced fine
$\frac{1}{4}$ cup cheese, grated
1 cup tomato sauce
breadcrumbs
salt and pepper to taste

In a large fry pan, heat 2 tablespoons of whatever fat you'll use and in it fry the onion, garlic, parsley and mushrooms until the onions and mushrooms are browned and most of the liquid has been cooked away. If you use canned mushrooms they should be drained and dried before you mince them.

Add the chicken meat, grated cheese, and tomato sauce; stir, and cook covered, over low heat, for 10 minutes. Cool it. Stir in just enough bread crumbs to form a stiff mixture that you can form into cakes.

None of the ingredients in this recipe is critical, so you can change the measurements and even the ingredients, of course, to suit your taste. Everything in the list of ingredients is cooked, so taste a bit and add salt and pepper to suit.

Flour your hands lightly when the mixture has cooled so you can handle it, form them into flat cakes or round ones, whichever you like, and fry them in the large frying pan in the remaining 2 tablespoons of fat, browning them on both sides.

These are good hot and equally good cold.

SERVES FOUR, MAYBE MORE.

The elderly gentleman came into the art gallery and told the owner that he greatly admired one of the paintings on display in the window and would like to see it up close. The art dealer took the painting out of the window, and the art lover examined it lovingly. "What are you asking for this painting?" the man said. The art dealer told him. After some polite haggling they agreed on a price and the man wrote out a check. But just before he handed the check over, he asked, "I don't recognize this artist's name. He's dead, isn't he?" The art dealer laughed. "Oh no," he said, "this man is quite young." The art lover tore up the check. As he walked out, he shouted angrily, "I detest modern art!"

Ordinarily, I detest turkey, for it is a mingy bird with no fat—and therefore no juice—which has to be served with a rich gravy after roasting in order to be made palatable. But it is a delight when roasted in the fashion I invented several years ago, which I call:

CHICKEN-FATTED TURKEY

one turkey
½ pound unrendered chicken fat (this is for an 8- to 10-pound
    bird; vary quantity of fat according to bird)
¼ teaspoon salt
¼ teaspoon pepper
1 teaspoon salt
½ teaspoon pepper
½ teaspoon turmeric

Rarely do you ever see a fresh-killed turkey—except in Chinese or kosher butcher shops—so the first step is to thaw your frozen bird. When the turkey has lost its frigidity, bare your arm—either one—up to the elbow, and loosen the skin—pull it away from the meat—at both cavities. Work your fingers cautiously between the skin and the body of the turkey, lifting up the loosened part with your other hand, and down the legs, also. Be careful not to tear the skin. Wash the chicken fat—you've already washed and dried the turkey, inside and out, haven't you? —and dry it on paper towels. Rub into the fat ¼ teaspoon each of salt and pepper.

Cut the fat up into small pieces. Take a handful of the seasoned pieces of fat, put your fist under the skin as far as you can, and withdraw it slowly, leaving bits of fat all over the bird. You should keep enough fat to make at least 2 tablespoons when melted; combine this with salt, pepper, and turmeric and smear over the skin of the bird. Stuff the turkey with your favorite stuffing, but I recommend most highly the stuffing I like best— one that I think I invented—which you'll find listed as a main course in the index under Chicken Liver-fried Rice-mushrooms and Everything Nice.

Here are recommended roasting times, in oven preheated to 325 degrees, for various sizes of turkeys: 6–8 pounds—3 to 3½ hours; 8–12 pounds—3½ to 4½ hours; 12 to 16 pounds—4½ to 5 hours; for turkeys over 16 pounds, up to 20 pounds, roast in 300-degree oven for 6½ hours.

If you don't follow my method of putting chicken fat under the turkey skin, rub melted fat, or butter, or oil over the skin, put it on a rack, breast side down, in a pan, and put a large, fat-soaked double length of cheesecloth over the bird, and keep pouring oil or melted fat over the cloth all through the roasting. Even a turkey roasted this way needs a rich, highly seasoned gravy. MINE DOES NOT!

Man was accused of assault in the first degree for having thrown his wife out of the window of their second-floor apartment. He was arraigned before the judge and asked, "How do you plead? Guilty or not guilty?" The man shrugged. "Well," he said, "I guess I plead guilty with an explanation." The judge was infuriated. "What do you mean," he roared, " 'guilty with an explanation'?" The man shrugged again. "Well, I did throw her out of the window from the second floor, but it was just a case of absent-mindedness."

When the judge stopped roaring about that, the man said: "You see, Your Honor, I actually forgot that just the day before we moved upstairs from the first floor."

Upstairs, downstairs, all around you, everyone will know you're cooking something really splendid when you make what the French and their slavish followers here call "Cassoulet" but which really is nothing more than a stew with fowl, maybe some meat, and sausages, and beans, which is really:

BRUNSWICK STEW (Southern U.S. of A.)

1 pound sausages (or frankfurters)
1 frozen turkey thigh (about 2 pounds), thawed
oil if you don't use sausages
1 pound onions, chopped
2 cloves (or more) garlic, minced
½ teaspoon thyme
¼ cup parsley, minced
¼ teaspoon pepper
2 cans condensed chicken or beef broth, approximately 10
    ounces each
1½ cans water
1 cup dry wine, red or white, makes no difference
one 1-pound can chick peas (garbanzos) with liquid

Put about ¼ inch of water into a large pot, bring it to the boil. Prick the sausages in several places with a fork, put them into the boiling water. Turn the heat low so it simmers. Pretty soon, the water will be boiled away, leaving fat in the pot with the sausages. Pour the fat off and save it. Keep pouring off the fat, and cook, stirring the sausages often, to brown them all over. Remove the sausages when they're done. Put 2 tablespoons of the sausage fat—or oil—into the pot and when it is hot, brown the turkey thigh all over. Take thigh out of pot. If you are using frankfurters, cut them into 1-inch slices, and we'll tell you when to put them into the pot.

Add some more fat—or oil—to the pot, hot it up, and add the onions, garlic, thyme, parsley, and pepper. Stir and scrape bottom of pot with a stiff metal spatula to get up the good brown stuff on the bottom. When the onions are browned add the broth, water and wine. Bring to the boil and put the turkey thigh into it. Simmer, covered, for at least 2 hours, maybe longer, because turkey thighs are pretty tough. At the end of 2 hours, take the thigh out of the pot and cut the meat away from the bones in large chunks. Put the turkey meat back into the pot. (Taste a small piece, and if it is tough simmer for a while longer. And taste the gravy for seasoning while you're at it.) Add water to the pot if it cooks away too much. Put the sausages or franks into the pot, add the chick peas and the liquid in the can and cook until everything is hot. Serve in a large deep platter, pouring the sauce over all.

SERVES SIX TO EIGHT.

Seems there was this elderly gent rummaging around in his attic and came across a pamphlet printed years ago by some kind of anti-automobile organization that farmers belonged to. (Horses in those days were always being spooked by horseless carriages and they were called "runaway horses.") The pamphlet advocated legislation that would force automobilists (that's what drivers of cars used to be called) to stop every once in a while, while driving at night, to fire off a rocket warning horse drivers of their approach. And the pamphlet further urged legislation about a horse that refused to pass a car that had been pulled off the road, and was not only motionless but also with the engine stopped. "In such a case," the pamphlet is alleged to have said (I doubt the veracity of this entire story), "the automobilist must disassemble his automobile and hide the parts in the shrubbery until the horse has passed the location."

The radio studio of A. Godfrey, Esq., was the location of the birth of:

TURKEY CACCIATORE

1 turkey thigh, 2 to 4 pounds
2 tablespoons rendered chicken fat, butter, oil, or margarine
½ pound or 1 pound onions, chopped
2 to 4 ribs of celery, strings scraped off with knife, and chopped
     with greenery
1 to 2 tablespoons minced garlic cloves
one 1-pound can tomatoes, preferably Italian-style, or 3 cups
     peeled chopped fresh tomatoes
one to two cans (about 10 ounces each) condensed chicken
     soup
½ canful each, water and red wine, to each can of soup
salt and pepper to taste

I get thighs frozen, and then thaw them in the fridge overnight, or several hours—watched carefully—out of fridge. In a large, heavy pot, with no fat, brown the onions, after stirring to get them coated with fat, along with the celery and garlic, until the onions and celery are soft, scraping the pot with a flexible metal spatula to get up the burned-on turkey skin and meat, which imparts a lovely taste to the dish. Put the turkey on top of the vegetables. Add the tomatoes. (To peel tomatoes easily, plunge them into boiling water for one minute, then into cold water, and with a small knife, the skin will come off as easily as removing a glove—easier—from your hand.) Add the condensed soup and water and wine and, let us say, ¼ teaspoon each of salt and pepper, and bring to the boil. Cover the pot and reduce the heat to simmer. Cook for at least 2 hours.

The amount of each ingredient is governed, of course, by the size of the turkey thigh. If you add chicken fat, let us say 2 additional tablespoons, the meat will be juicier and more flavorful. If a fork goes through the thickest part of the thigh, with not very much pressure, it is cooked to perfection. The longer you cook the thigh, the more tender it will be. But you must guard against overcooking, for the meat should be chewy, not mushy. Taste and correct seasoning of sauce, if necessary, before serving. A green salad is good, always. "Cacciatore" you know, means "hunters' style" but I never knew a hunter ate as well as this in the field.

SERVES FOUR TO SIX.

His father looked at the boy's report card. "You've done well in all of your subjects, son," he said, "but you have a very bad mark in history, and I don't understand that because you've told me that that's the subject you like best." The boy shrugged. "Well, it's not my fault," he said, "it's only because the history teacher doesn't like me." His father scoffed. "Oh, come on, now," he said scoffingly, "why should your history teacher dislike you?"

His son scowled. "I really don't know, Father," he said scowlingly, "except that it may be because one day in class he asked me: 'Who was the barbarian who captured Rome?' and I said, 'It was Hannibal, wasn't it?' and he said to me, 'Don't ask me, I'm asking you,' and I said, 'Well, if you don't know, teach, I don't know, either.'"

What I would like to teach you is the construction of a marvelously wonderful dish called:

KASHA VARNITCHKES AVEC BRAISED TURKEY THIGH (The Bronx)

1 turkey thigh, about 2 pounds
$\frac{1}{2}$ cup rendered chicken fat, vegetable shortening, or oil
1 pound onions, minced
2 large carrots, cut into thin rounds
2 ribs celery, chopped with greenery
2 cloves garlic, minced
2 cups chicken broth

Turkey thighs come fresh or frozen, and in various weights. If your thigh is frozen, you will of course thaw it. In a pot just large enough to let the thigh lie flat, hot up 1 tablespoon of fat and brown the thigh all over. Take thigh out of pot. Add 3 tablespoons of fat to the pot and in it fry half the minced onion, all of the carrots, celery, and garlic, using high heat and stirring constantly, until the onion is browned.

Put the turkey thigh back into the pot, add the broth and bring it to the boil. Cover and let it simmer slowly for at least 2 hours, turning the thigh several times, and spooning soup and vegetables over it.

While this is going on, make the:

KASHA VARNITCHKES

1 pound bowtie or elbow macaroni ("varnitchke" is the name
    for bowtie-shaped pasta)
1 cup kasha (buckwheat groats)
1 egg, beaten
¼ teaspoon each, salt and pepper
2 cups water
½ pound fresh mushrooms, sliced through stems and caps, (or
    one 4-ounce can, drained)

Bring to the boil 3 quarts salted water, add macaroni, start timing when water returns to the boil. After 10 minutes of boiling, taste a small piece. Some brands need more cooking than others. After first 10 minutes, taste every 2 minutes and when the macaroni is cooked through but still chewy, pour it into a colander. Dry the pot in which macaroni cooked.

Put the kasha into the dry pot and, over medium heat, stir it for 2 or 3 minutes. The box containing the kasha says "brown buckwheat groats" but it's better if you do your own browning.

Beat the egg, salt, and pepper into the water, and pour it over the kasha, adding 2 tablespoons of melted fat, or oil. Cover pot and cook over very low heat until all liquid is absorbed. Up there in the list of ingredients for the thigh, there was "½ cup rendered chicken fat," etc., so now what we have left are 2 tablespoons of fat, ½ pound minced onions, and the mushrooms, right? Sure.

Hot up the fat in a large fry pan and in it fry the onions and mushrooms until the onions are browned.

When the turkey thigh is tender—those birds are pretty tough—cut the meat off the bones into bite-size pieces.

In the large pot in which the macaroni cooked, and which is now holding the kasha, add the bowties or elbow macaroni, the turkey meat, everything that cooked with the turkey, including broth, and the fried onions and mushrooms. With a large kitchen spoon combine all the cooked ingredients thoroughly.

Taste for seasoning, and add salt and pepper if you think it needs some.

SERVES FOUR.

Actor: "Did you see my last TV show?"
TV critic: "I hope so."
And I hope you'll like:

DUCK STUFFED WITH STRAWBERRIES AND NOODLES AND OTHER GOOD STUFF (Brooklyn)

one duck, about 4 pounds
$\frac{1}{4}$ teaspoon each, salt, pepper, and turmeric
2 cups onion, chopped
$\frac{1}{2}$ pound sliced fresh mushrooms or one 4-ounce can button mushrooms or pieces, drained
$\frac{1}{2}$ pound noodles
$\frac{1}{4}$ teaspoon dried rosemary
$\frac{1}{2}$ cup (or more) sliced frozen whole, sweetened strawberries, or blueberries

If your duck is frozen, thaw it. Dry it, inside and out with paper towels. Rub into the skin half of the salt and pepper and all of the turmeric. Remove from cavities all the fat you can, cut it up and melt it down over very low heat in a large fry pan. In the melted fat fry the chopped onion and sliced mushrooms until the onion is golden and mushrooms soft and remove from heat.

In 6 cups of boiling water, cook the noodles until they are cooked through but not soggy; taste a piece after 8 minutes, and, of course you know that you start timing when the water returns to the boil after having put into it the noodles, and when the noodles are cooked drain them immediately in a colander. In the large frying pan, combine the noodles with the onion-mushroom mixture, sprinkle with rosemary but if you don't have any in the house remember to buy some the next time you're in the store. Add the berries and toss to distribute them throughout the mixture. Stuff the duck with the stuffing. Sew up the cavities, close with skewers, however you like. Put the bird on a rack, breast side up.

Roast in oven preheated to 350 degrees for 25 minutes to the pound, draining off fat from pan every 30 minutes, and save the fat—put it in a tightly closed container to keep in the fridge for use in cooking other dishes which need fat.

SERVES FOUR TO SIX.

The old lady bought a ticket for a plane trip to Denver. "How high does the pilot go to get there?" she asked the ticket clerk. "Your jet," said the ticket clerk, "will fly at an altitude of approximately 32,000 feet." The old lady gasped. "Goodness, gracious," she cursed, "that will never do, because I get dizzy and my ears hurt at high altitudes."

The ticket clerk was astonished, "But, Madame," the clerk said astonishedly, "why do you think they call Denver 'The Mile High City'?"

Now the old lady was astonished. "You mean to say Denver is a mile up in the sky? Then give me my money back, I thought Denver was on the ground."

In many places around the world peanuts are called ground-nuts and they make a fine addition to a:

STUFFED ROASTED DUCK (Africa)

one 5- to 6-pound duck
1 cup salted peanuts
3 large oranges (2 peeled, pulled into sections, pulp and seeds removed)
3 cups cooked and drained elbow macaroni, seasoned to taste
1/2 teaspoon salt
1/4 teaspoon each, pepper and turmeric

Rub inside of duck with 1/4 teaspoon each, salt and pepper. Combine the peanuts, the sections of the 2 oranges, pits and all pulp removed, and the elbow macaroni. Stuff the duck with this. Sew up the cavities or close them with skewers. Fry the liver and eat it yourself with some fried onion. Save the giblets for stew, or soup.

Rub salt, pepper and turmeric all over the skin. The turmeric—can be bought at any supermarket—is one of the many spice ingredients that go into the making of curry powder, and it imparts a slightly warm flavor and colors the skin a beautiful golden brown.

Put the duck, breast side up, on a rack—a V-rack is best—in a roasting pan. Cut the remaining orange in half, squeeze juice over duck. Hold on to the 2 orange halves. Roast it in oven preheated to 425 degrees at that temperature for 20 minutes. A lot of fat will have accumulated in the pan. Remove most of it.

Cut up the 2 squeezed orange halves, with remaining pulp, and put them into the pan. Reduce the heat to 350 degrees and roast, starting timing at this point, for 25 minutes to the pound, removing fat from pan, preferably with bulb baster, and baste with pan juices every 30 minutes.

The skin should be quite crisp—you'll hear a hollow sound if you tap it all over with a fork or knife, or whatever. If you find it browning too fast, cut the heat down to 325.

SERVES FOUR, WITH A COUPLE OF EXTRA HELPINGS.

The man sitting next to her at a dinner party asked if she had seen the latest Swedish movie, whose plot—somehow "plot" doesn't seem like the right word for this kind of movie, but it will have to serve—he had just outlined. "Yes," she said, "I saw it and I thought it was disgusting. What did you think of it?" He thought for a while. "I'm afraid," he said, "that I didn't like it as much as you did."

I don't think there is any food that I like more than:

ROAST GOOSE

one 8- to 10-pound goose
1 teaspoon salt
$\frac{1}{2}$ teaspoon pepper
10 cups (approximately) stuffing (see index for Chicken
     Liver-fried Rice, Mushrooms and Everything Nice)
rendered goose fat
orange juice
port or any other wine, sweet or dry, that you prefer

Your goose will undoubtedly be frozen. Start thawing it in the fridge two days before you plan to cook it. When it is thawed sufficiently, remove the bag of giblets, and all lumps of fat in the cavities. Wash the bird inside and out and dry it thoroughly with paper towels. Wash the fat, dry it, and cut it up into small pieces. Melt it down in a large frying pan over very low heat. Pour off and save the golden fat as it accumulates in the pan. DON'T throw away the bits that do not melt down; they are cracklings, or *grieben* in Jewish, and they are delicious.

Stuff the goose but don't pack the stuffing in too tight, or it will burst open during the roasting. What I like to do, instead of sewing or skewering the cavity closed is to put a large baking potato partway into the cavity, and put a few skewers through the loose skin into the potato. I cover the potato with foil, and remove the foil about 15 minutes before the goose is cooked. A beauty baked potato as a bonus!

I don't truss birds that are to be roasted in the oven; only purpose in trussing birds is when they are barbecued, for if they aren't, the wings and legs will be hopelessly over-charred and inedible. I use an oiled V-rack (in the case of a goose, I rub melted goose fat on the rack), put the rack into a deep broiler pan, and set the bird, on its side, on the rack, after rubbing salt and pepper all over the skin, and some melted goose fat, too.

Preheat your oven to 425 degrees. Remove fat from pan after 30 minutes, and reduce the heat to 400 degrees. Save the fat! It is even better than chicken fat for cooking other dishes! Remove fat—a bulb baster is the best utensil for this purpose every 30 minutes—and reduce the heat by 25 degrees until you reach 350 degrees. A goose of approximately 8 pounds should be finished in 2 hours. If your goose is closer to 10 pounds, after 2 hours reduce the heat to 325 degrees and roast for an additional 15 minutes. Best way to tell when your goose is cooked is by tapping it with a kitchen spoon. It is cooked when you hear a kind of hollow sound, and feel that the skin is paper-thin and it is a beautiful golden-brown all over.

Most people have never eaten roast goose, which I think is a shame; but men who have eaten this glorious bird say they don't like it because "it's too greasy." This, I think, is even more shameful, because it proves to me they've never eaten a properly roasted goose. From an 8-pound goose I render out, by cooking it in this fashion, about one quart of fat, leaving the bird sweet and juicy, but by no manner "greasy." Need a stuffing recipe?—see page 275.

SERVES SIX TO EIGHT.

FISH

PART FOUR

I have a book entitled "Best From the Farmer's Almanac" which is a treasure trove of old forgotten lore, wit, and information, some of which is quite useful. Under a heading called "A little of everything," I found these nuggets: "There is about one cent's worth of gold in 1,000 gallons of sea waters." And: "Eleven and twelve were once written, oneteen and twoteen." And: "There were only 10 students in attendance when West Point Academy opened in 1802."

Then I came to: "If you have to measure a short distance and have no ruler, use a dollar bill as a rough guide. The bill is just six and one-eighth inches long." I read this on one of the all-too-rare occasions when I had a dollar bill (I always have a ruler). And you know what? The Farmer's Almanac is *right!* But when I went one step further and discovered that if you put a one-dollar bill with George Washington's noble visage up, it is precisely six inches from the left-hand edge of the bill to the end of the engraving on the right! Oddly, if you turn the bill over with "In God we trust" up, it doesn't work because the white space on that side is wider. I know how to print dollar bills, but I can't tell you how to make them because my editor says that would be a violation of some law or other.

There's no law to bar me from telling you how to make:

SWEET AND SOUR FISHES (India)

16 little fishes (about 5 or 6 inches long), like smelts, or perch.
　　Use fewer fish if they are larger to any marked degree.
$\frac{1}{2}$ teaspoon salt
$\frac{1}{4}$ teaspoon pepper
flour
2 eggs, beaten with $\frac{1}{4}$ cup milk
butter, margarine, or oil
1 cup onion, chopped
1 rib celery, strings removed, and chopped with some of the top
1 can (approximately 10 ounces) condensed tomato soup
$\frac{1}{4}$ cup lemon, or lime juice, or vinegar
$\frac{1}{4}$ cup sugar, preferably brown
1 clove, crushed, or $\frac{1}{4}$ teaspoon powdered cloves

The fish should, of course, be gutted. Cut off heads and tails. If your fish are frozen it is a cinch to skin them. As soon as you see the first sign of thawing, cut an incision in skin just below the head all around the fish, hold head with a paper towel, grasp loosened skin with another towel, and gently pull the skin up.

Rub salt and pepper on fish. Dip into flour, then into beaten egg. In a large fry pan, heat butter or whatever, fry the fish over medium heat until browned on all sides adding butter or whatever as needed. When the fish have been fried remove them from pan, but don't bother to keep them warm.

In the same large fry pan, add 2 tablespoons of butter and in it fry the onion and celery, until they are soft. Add condensed soup to the pan, stir in the lemon juice or whatever, and the sugar, stirring until sugar is dissolved. Add the clove and stir. Taste the mixture. It should be sweet-and-sour, but neither flavor should overpower the other. Correct if necessary. Put fish back into the pan, spoon the sauce over them, and cook, simmering gently, for 5 minutes. This is marvelous hot or cold.

SERVES FOUR.

Fellow was telling a friend about the dream he'd had the night before. He spoke rhapsodically about the wonderful day it was, how the sun was shining brightly, with a breeze just cool enough to make it comfortable to be out in the middle of the lake wearing just swimming trunks, fish all around the boat leaping for joy and insects, while Elizabeth Taylor Burton, wearing the miniest kind of mini bikini there was, was smiling fondly at him as he made his first cast.

"And then," he said, "I said to her, Honey, wouldja please light me a cigarette and open me up a can of beer?" And then he stopped and smiled beatifically.

"Yeah yeah yeah," said his friend, "and then what happened?" "Wouldja believe it?" the dreamer asked rhetorically. "Just as I asked her that, I hooked into a six-pound bass."

STUFFED BAKED FISH (Creole)

any kind of whole fish you like, or catch, or buy, like a bass, bluefish, salmon, about 4 to 6 pounds
salt and pepper
2 to 3 cups of your favorite stuffing, or boughten seasoned bread stuffing (there's a particularly good cornbread seasoned stuffing in the markets), jazzed up with some cooked shrimp, which is great stuffing for fish
1 teaspoon dried dill weed or thyme
¼ cup minced parsley or 2 tablespoons dried parsley flakes
½ cup scallions, chopped (green onions) with firm greenery
¼ cup (4 tablespoons) rendered chicken fat, or butter, or 6 slices bacon
½ cup dry wine, red or white: or clam juice; or condensed, undiluted chicken broth or, alas, water

The fish is gutted and scales removed, of course, and I like the fins cut off, too. But I like to keep the head and tail on a fish because I think it looks pretty that way, but if you don't agree, you just go right ahead, friends, cut off the head and tail and I won't be angry or even hurt. Wash the fish inside and out in cold running water and dry it. Rub salt and pepper, ¼ teaspoon each, inside and outside the fish. Stuff the fish, not too fully. Don't bother to sew it up or close it with skewers because it isn't going to be moved during the baking.

Sprinkle the fish with the dill or thyme, or a combination of both, and with the parsley. Put the fish into a shallow roasting pan, scatter scallions over the fish, and dot with the rendered chicken fat. Now, listen: this is not a put-on—chicken fat is splendid with fish and many peoples, ours and the Chinese, have been using it that way for centuries. If you're not using the chicken fat or butter, the next best thing, put 3 of the bacon strips over the fish. Pour the wine or whatever over the fish.

In oven preheated to 350 degrees, bake it for one hour, basting it several times during the baking. If you used bacon, you'll have to put the remaining 3 slices over the fish in the last 20 minutes of the baking. Remove bacon when it is crisp and crumble it over the fish when you serve it. Depending on the size and thickness of the fish, it should be baked through in one hour to 75 minutes. Test it with a fork after one hour. If the fork goes through the fish, down to the bone with very little pressure, it will be done. To make certain, make a gash in the thickest part; when done, the flesh will not look shiny. Allow at least ¾ of a pound per serving. Boiled, parsleyed potatoes and a salad go beautifully with this.

SERVES SIX TO EIGHT.

Among the reasons why Charlie Chaplin was in such disfavor in the U.S. that his pictures were virtually banned here for a long time was because he remained a British citizen during all the years that he made his many millions of dollars in Hollywood. Many other English actors who remained in this country

did, however, become U.S. citizens. One of them was being berated by an actor who retained his British citizenship though he
hadn't been back to the mother country in 25 years.

"Name me one advantage," he said, "that you gained by
betraying the mother country and becoming an American citizen."

The new United Stateser smiled. "That's easy," he said,
"because for one thing, now it's *my* side that won the American
Revolution."

You can carry the day by cooking:

CHARCOAL (OR OVEN-BROILED) STUFFED FISH (Portuguese)

2 tablespoons olive oil

½ cup scallions, chopped or green onions, chopped

1 (or more) clove garlic, minced fine

3 or 4 boneless and skinless sardines packed in olive oil,
  mashed well

½ cup toast crumbs

½ teaspoon dried dill weed (2 tablespoons if fresh) or dried
  thyme

½ teaspoon salt

¼ teaspoon pepper

2 tablespoons butter, melted

one 3-pound whole fish

Get the oil hot in a large fry pan, cook the chopped scallions and however much garlic you like until they begin to
brown. Add the mashed sardines, with the oil from the can and
the toast crumbs, and continue to mash and stir, over low heat.
Stir the stuff in the pan until you have a mixture with a sort of
pasty consistency. Add the dill (or thyme), and ¼ teaspoon salt
and ⅛ teaspoon pepper. Keep it hot in pan on the grill.

Any kind of lean meat fish—striped bass, snapper, bluefish,
trout, or salmon—is fine for this. Ask your fishmonger to clean
and split the fish, but tell him to cut it only on the belly side,
just past the back bone, and to leave the head and tail on the

fish, and to separate the spinal bone from the meat, but to leave the bone inside the fish. If he acts irked and turns surly, curse him roundly, but in a ladylike manner, turn on your heel and find yourself another, less irky fishmonger.

Wash the fish in cold running water and dry it thoroughly with paper towels. Rub the skin with the remaining salt and pepper—¼ teaspoon salt, ⅛ teaspoon pepper. Brush skin with melted butter.

Best way to charcoal broil a fish on an outdoor barbecue grill is to use a basket-type grill, which, when closed on the fish, makes it easy to turn from side to side without danger of breaking the delicate creature. The grill should be well oiled and very hot when the fish is put into it. Too few people ever charcoal broil fish, and I think that's sad, because if you like fish, nothing is better than one grilled this way.

A split fish of about 3 pounds, held 3 inches from the bed of coals, will be done in 15 to 20 minutes, turning the fish every 3 or 4 minutes, and brushing it with melted butter before each turn. This can, of course, be done in the oven, turning the fish only once. I like to leave the spinal bone in because we think it adds something indefinable to the taste of the fish; like the head and tail left on because it looks prettier to me that way, and because I think it helps retain the natural juices of the fish. And having it split makes it easy to peek inside to see if it is fully cooked through.

After the fish is broiled to your satisfaction, remove it to a large, hot platter, open it up, remove the spinal bone, and spread the filling—remember that sardine mixture?—over one half, close the fish up again and cut it into 4 equal portions—not counting the head or tail. Should be served with lemon slices, garnished with cold, sliced tomatoes, thick slices of sweet Bermuda or Spanish onion, parsley, and, maybe, mixed cooked vegetables.

SERVES FOUR.

I heard about a fellow who loaned a friend $1,000 and then became worried because it was a lot of money, and he didn't have anything to prove that the friend owed him this great sum of money. He kept thinking, "Suppose, Heaven forfend, that something happens to him? Then what will I do?"

So he went to his lawyer and told him the story. The lawyer said he would think about it. The next day, the lawyer called him.

"I have the solution," said the lawyer. "Write your friend a letter and tell him that you are very sorry, but you have to have back the $2,000 you loaned him."

"But," said the man, "I didn't loan him $2,000, I only loaned him $1,000." The lawyer's sneer came over the phone very clearly.

"That's just it," said the lawyer, "he will write you an indignant letter saying you only loaned him $1,000, not $2,000. So you'll have it in writing that he owes you the money, see?"

And here it is written how to make:

FISH IN SOY SAUCE

one 2-pound fish (or two 1-pound fish, or four ½-pound fish, but they have to be whole fish, see?)
2 tablespoons oil
salt and pepper to taste (maybe ½ teaspoon salt, ¼ teaspoon pepper)
4 tablespoons soy sauce
2 scallions, chopped (green part, too)
3 tablespoons water
(and how about a couple of ounces of sherry, say?)

Put the oil in a pan big enough to hold the fish (or fishes) and add the salt and pepper. I don't have to tell you to have the fish cleaned and scaled, do I? I happen to think a cooked fish looks pretty with the head and tail on, but you do as you please; you want to cut off the head and tail, go ahead, cut off the head and tail. And these fish can be any kind of fish: a pike, maybe a sea bass, perhaps flounder, or a trout.

Okay. You got the oil in the pan, right? With the seasoning, right? So hot up the oil. Put in the fish and fry them on both sides, about 2 or 3 minutes per side. Now pour off about half the oil, pour the soy sauce over the fish, sprinkle them with the scallions, and add the water.

Reduce the heat and cover the pan and cook it for another 5 minutes, turn the fish, and cook for another 5 minutes. When the fish needs only 2 more minutes of cooking, add the sherry, if you are using it. Test the fish for doneness with a fork; if it flakes easily, your work is done.

SERVES FOUR.

Early in July, 1776, in Independence Square, Philadelphia, the Declaration of Independence was read to the colonials who had assembled in answer to the tolling of the Liberty Bell, and you know who read it? A man named Col. John Nixon, that's who did, and it was the first time it was ever read aloud in public. That bell, before the Declaration of Independence was read, was known merely as "The Bell."

And Independence Square was called, simply, "The Square." Every schoolkiddie knows that the Liberty Bell is in Independence Hall, which before our independence from Britain went by the name of "The Hall." All I know about Col. John Nixon is that he was the reader of the Declaration, and for all I know, that may have been the only thing he ever read in his whole life. In public, anyway.

Let us now get into the kitchen to go about making public some:

MIGHTY BEAUTIFUL WONDERFUL ICY-COLD BAKED MARINATED FISH (Created in Brooklyn for the delectation of A. Godfrey, Esq.)

1 pound fish fillets, any kind you like
1 teaspoon salt
1 egg
1 cup cracker meal
$1\frac{1}{2}$ cups minced onion
2 cloves garlic, pressed or minced (about 1 tablespoon)
1 tablespoon chicken fat or butter
1 can (about 10 ounces) condensed tomato soup plus 1 cup
     water
$\frac{1}{4}$ cup vinegar
1 teaspoon salt
2 tablespoons sugar
2 tablespoons mixed pickling spices tied into a cheesecloth bag

Pat the fillets dry with toweling. Cut each one in half. Oil a baking pan or dish large enough to hold all the fish pieces side by side. Rub salt into each piece. Dip each piece into beaten egg, then in cracker meal getting fish well coated all over. In oven preheated to 350 degrees bake the fish for 40 minutes, turning pieces once with a spatula. They'll be well-browned.

Make the sauce while the fish is baking. Fry the onion and garlic in hot chicken fat or butter, until the onion is browned. Pour into the pan the tomato soup and the water and stir. Add the vinegar, salt, sugar, and the cheesecloth bag of spices which should be smashed when in the bag with a heavy blunt instrument like a blackjack, a heavy food can or bottle of beer or booze. Bring it to the boil and stir, while it is boiling, for 5 minutes.

When the fish is finished, spoon some of the sauce into a crock or other refrigerator container, put fish into the sauce, add another layer of sauce, then more fish, then more sauce, until you've used up all the ingredients. The top should be covered with sauce. Let it cool. Refrigerate it for at least a day.

This can, of course, be eaten hot and it's delicious; but when it's eaten cold on a hot day nothing can make you happier.

SERVES FOUR.

Did you know that George Washington, not content merely with being father of his country, also fathered some of the most infamous puns ever visited upon a long-suffering world? Or so 'tis said. For an instance: General Washington was riding on his white horse one day when he sees a column of soldiers. Regarding his shoeless troops, Washington bursts out laughing. An aide—that's what they call a flunkey in the troops—says: "Why are you laughing, General Wash, sir?" So the General says, guffawing, "These are the times that try men's 'soles'! Harharhar!!"

But the aide, not only does he *not* laugh, but he gives the Gen. a peculiar look.

"Omigoodness," cursed the General (he was not yet the father of his country at that time), and he repeated the line, and when his lobbygow still looked puzzled, the Gen. screamed: "Sole, you young cretinous idiot! Sole, like in fillet!" And when the young oaf still looked puzzled, General Washington, he busted that second Lieutenant all the way down to an extremely private in the rear ranks.

Say, you know what? Let us all have some:

SOLE FOOD

1 pound flounder fillets, dried
½ teaspoon salt
½ teaspoon flour
¼ teaspoon pepper
¼ cup peanut oil
¼ cup milk or light cream
2 tablespoons parsley, minced
½ pint (1 cup) sour cream
1 teaspoon paprika

Rub salt into each fillet, dust with flour and pepper. Get oil hot in large fry pan. Fry fish over medium heat, but do not crowd pan, until both sides of each fillet are light brown and crisp. Make room in pan by putting finished fillets on a heavy platter set on top of a pot of very hot water, cover cooked fish with a large bowl.

When all fillets are fried, combine milk or light cream, parsley, and sour cream, pour into the same fry pan, cook over low heat, scraping with a flexible metal spatula. Sprinkle with paprika. Heat until some steam rises, but don't let it boil. Serve sauce in sauce or gravy boat.

SERVES FOUR.

After a great deal of shilly-shallying, hesitation and doubt, the fellow agreed to lend his neighbor his power lawnmower, in which he took great pride of ownership. (He was a rotten fellow and hated lending things to neighbors.) But the following day, his neighbor brought back the lawnmower and handed him a hedge clipper. "What's this?" he asked suspiciously. "I can't figure it out," the neighbor said. "I put the mower in my garage last night and this morning I found the hedge clipper on the floor next to it. The lawnmower must have spawned it in the night."

The avaricious fellow didn't believe this, of course, but he happily accepted the hedge clipper. Next day the neighbor asked for the loan of his 16-foot aluminum ladder. "Well," he said hesitatingly, "okay." The following day the neighbor returned the 16-foot ladder, and with it, handed over a 4-step kitchen ladder. "I left the 16-footer in the garage," he said, "and this morning there was this kitchen ladder. I guess the same thing happened." The avaricious fellow accepted it happily.

The next week the avaricious fellow enthusiastically agreed to lend his neighbor his great big Cadillac. (He had visions of a compact, you see?) But three days passed and the neighbor didn't return the vehicle.

"Hey, neighbor," he cried out when he next saw the man, "where's my Caddy?" The neighbor shook his head sadly. "It died," he said sadly. "DIED!" the fellow shrieked, "how can a car die?" His neighbor sneered. "Listen, fellow," he said, "if you can believe that a lawnmower can give birth to a hedge clipper, and a 16-foot ladder to a kitchen ladder, why can't you believe that a car can die?"

Believe me, what is good is:

POACHED FISH FILLETS (India)

2 pounds fish fillets (any lean fish, like bass, cod, haddock, halibut, etc.)
1 teaspoon salt
¼ teaspoon black pepper
¼ cup (½ stick) butter
3 cups milk
1 tablespoon lemon juice
1 teaspoon turmeric
chopped parsley

Wash and dry fish and rub with salt and pepper. In a pan large enough to hold the fillets side by side, melt the butter and put in the fish. Turn after 1 or 2 minutes, when the bottom should be slightly golden, cook the other side the same length of time and add the milk. Raise the heat and bring to a boil, sprinkle with lemon juice and turmeric. Reduce the heat and simmer for 8 to 10 minutes when the fish should be cooked through. (Test one of the fillets with a fork.) Remove the fish to a hot serving platter.

Now raise the heat and cook until the sauce in the pan is reduced by about one-third, pour over the fillets and serve, after sprinkling with parsley.

Turmeric lends a warm, sweet flavor and gives sauces a rich yellow color. You may like to vary this some time by adding a teaspoon of curry, when you add the turmeric, if you like it hot. SERVES SIX TO EIGHT.

They'd returned recently from their honeymoon and were having dinner in their new home when the husband said he had something to say that had been on his mind for some time. "You know," he said, with an air of great seriosity, "we agreed that if either of us had any criticism to make of the other, that we should always talk it over reasonably, like sensible, civilized people." "Of course," she said.

"Well then," said her husband, "you won't object if I point out to you some faults that you have, will you?" His wife shrugged. "Oh, darling," she said, "I wouldn't mind at all. But really, you don't have to bother. Before we were married I was engaged nine times, and it was my faults, all of which I know very well, that kept me from marrying nine younger, handsomer, more successful men than you."

No one who likes fish will ever fault you for making:

FISH FILLET MARGUERY (France)

4 fish fillets
1 cup clam juice
dry white wine
¼ cup light cream (optional?)
1 can (4 ounces) mushroom stems and pieces
2 tablespoons butter
½ pound shrimp, boiled
⅛ teaspoon cayenne pepper

The fillets of any firm-fleshed, lean fish are good for this dish: flounder, bluefish, cod, halibut, haddock, red snapper, striped bass, and sea bass are all fine. If you get the frozen fillets, you will, of course, thaw them first. Put the fillets into a casserole or baking dish large enough to hold them side by side, pour in the clam juice and just enough dry white wine to cover them. Bake them for about 15 minutes in oven preheated to 350 degrees. Drain and dry mushrooms and save liquid.

Hot up the butter in a small pan and fry the mushroom pieces and stems. Remove the baking dish and test one of the fillets with a fork; if it flakes easily, it is done. Distribute the boiled shrimp all over the fish (if they are large shrimp, cut them in half), do the same with the mushrooms and the butter in which they were sauteed, sprinkle with cayenne and then put it under the broiler just long enough so the surface is slightly glazed.

This is lovely with boiled, parsleyed potatoes, and if you are not fighting a losing battle with calories, adding ¼ cup of light cream to the clam juice and white wine will make a delicious sauce that is not too rich. I've told you before, but I'll tell you again—when something is cooked in wine or anything else that has alcohol, the alcohol is cooked out, but the inherent flavors of all the ingredients are enhanced and subtly changed. So don't be afraid that anyone will get glazed or sauced if you cook with wine or even booze.

SERVES FOUR.

"It isn't that I don't like your boy friend," the father said to his daughter. "He seems like a nice enough young fellow—the way young fellows go today—but what I don't like is that he hasn't got a job, and hasn't had one since he's been hanging around our house." The girl laughed delightedly. "Oh, Poppa!" she said delightedly, "if that's the only objection you have, then have no fear, because next week he's going to start making $50,000 a year!" Her father gasped. "What? You mean to say that this fellow, never had a job in his life, is going to make $50,000 a year?" The girl jumped up and down with joy. "Yes, Poppa," she said joyfully, "he read in the paper where the International Bankers' Protective Association is going to give a certain forger $100,000 a year to quit forging checks, and my sweetie is going to tell them he'll do that for half."

It was that great and good man, John Heywood (1497?–1580?), comedic writer-playwright-epigrammist-balladeer, who said: "Better is halfe a loafe than no bread"; and if you have any part of a loaf, how about making, to glop up the lovely glop, a:

SALMON (OR ANY OTHER FISH) LOAF (Western U.S.A.)

$\frac{1}{4}$ stick butter (or margarine or 2 tablespoons of oil)

1 cup onions, minced

$\frac{1}{4}$ cup parsley, minced

$\frac{1}{2}$ teaspoon dried dill weed (or thyme)

$\frac{1}{2}$ pound mushrooms, sliced through caps and stems, or 1 four-ounce can, drained and dried

$\frac{1}{4}$ stick butter (or whatever)

2 pounds salmon steak or two 1-pound cans, drained, flaked, skin and bones removed (see note)

one 8-ounce bottle clam juice or 1 cup chicken broth

2 eggs, beaten

1 cup unseasoned bread crumbs

1 teaspoon lemon or lime juice

$\frac{1}{4}$ cup grated cheese

$\frac{1}{4}$ teaspoon paprika

Hot up ¼ stick of butter (or whatever) in a large fry pan and in it fry the onion, parsley, dill (or thyme), and the mushrooms. Fry until the onions and mushrooms are soft and almost all the liquid in pan has been cooked away, but don't let anything get burned. You should have a paste-like mixture in the pan. Push it to the sides of the pan. Add to the pan the remaining 2 tablespoons of butter or whatever, and in it fry the salmon, flaking fish as it cooks, cover and cook 10 minutes. (NOTE: If you are using canned salmon, which is fine, it doesn't, of course, have to be cooked. Just drain it, throw away skin and bones and flake it.) Add it, to the mixture in the pan, along with the clam juice, the 2 beaten eggs, bread crumbs, and lemon or lime juice, and combine it all thoroughly. Of course, if it is awkward to do the combining in the pan because yours may be too small, do it in a mixing bowl because that's what mixing bowls are for, right?

Sprinkle with grated cheese, and then paprika and bake in oven preheated to 325 degrees, until cheese is melted and bubbling and everything is nicely hotted up.

SERVES FOUR, OR TWO IF THEY'RE REALLY HUNGRY.

"And how," the mother asked her young daughter when she came home from her first day at school, "did you like your first day in school?" The dear child hugged her mother happily. "Oh, Mother," she said happily, "school is wonderful, I just love it!" Her mother asked what it was she loved school for—the teacher, the lessons, or what? "Oh, not for any of those reasons," the little girl said, "it's just because I'm the prettiest little girl in the school!" Her mother was appalled. "Who told you that?" her mother asked appalledly. The dear child laughed. "Oh, nobody told me," she said, "but I saw all the other little girls."

I think every mother should teach every little girl, especially if she *isn't* pretty, to make:

FISH STEAKS ALLA SICILIANA (Italy)

2 tablespoons olive oil (or whatever)
1 cup onions, minced
2 cloves garlic, minced fine
4 fish steaks (see note)
$\frac{1}{4}$ cup parsley, minced
$\frac{1}{2}$ teaspoon dried dill weed or oregano
2 tablespoons lemon or lime juice, or vinegar
1-pound can tomatoes, well mashed
10-ounce package frozen peas, thawed and dried
$\frac{1}{2}$ cup grated cheese (any kind you like)
2 tablespoons butter

In a large fry pan, get 2 tablespoons of the oil, or whatever, hot. In it fry the onions and garlic until the onion is soft. Push the onions and garlic to side of pan, add some oil and when it is hot, fry the fish steaks over low heat, turning to brown them on both sides. Add oil as needed. Don't crowd the pan, but when you take the fish steaks out to make room for others, don't bother to keep them warm because they're going to be cooked some more. Oh, yes, the Fish Steak Note: Any fish steaks will do, salmon, swordfish, cod, halibut, any kind. I have quit using salmon steaks, which we are crazy about, because the price is just too preposterous. Also, of course, you can use fillets instead of steaks.

Before you turn the fish to brown underside, sprinkle with parsley, dill, and lemon juice.

When all the fish steaks have been browned on both sides, return them all to the pan, spoon over them the mashed tomatoes, cover, and cook for 10 to 15 minutes, depending on how thick the steaks are. If you use fillets, 5 minutes of cooking, after the fillets have been browned, will be enough. Add the thawed, dried peas to the pan, sprinkle with grated cheese, dot with butter and put it under the broiler just long enough to melt the cheese and brown it slightly. This will feed 4 people, maybe 6 if you have a soup first, or any other course. I like a large boiled, parsleyed potato with this. And a green salad.

SERVES FOUR, MAYBE SIX.

Young woman told the salesman in the toy shop that she was looking for something a 4-year-old boy would find interesting and which, at the same time, would be educational without the kid's knowing it. "Ah, yes, we have just the right thing right here," the salesman said. He reached up to a shelf, took down a box and emptied it on the counter.

The young woman looked at all the parts spread out on the counter. Then she looked at the box. "But there isn't even a picture here showing how the toy should look when it's assembled," she said.

The salesman laughed craftily. "You are absolutely correct, young lady," he said, "because the psychologists who work for this company designed this with the specific purpose of teaching a child at a very tender age just how life will be when he grows up. You see, it is absolutely impossible to assemble this stuff."

What is easy to assemble is:

COLD SALMON (OR SWORDFISH) STEAKS
WITH SOUR CREAM SALAD

2 pounds salmon steaks, cut into 4 equal portions (or you can
    use swordfish or other fish)
2 tablespoons butter
1 large onion, chopped
$\frac{1}{4}$ cup parsley
1 tablespoon dried dill weed or thyme
$\frac{1}{2}$ teaspoon salt
6 whole peppercorns
one 8-ounce bottle clam juice, or milk, or water
1 pint sour cream
1 large cucumber
6 pimiento stuffed olives
6 radishes
6 scallions

If the fish steaks have any skin, or bones, remove them. In
a large pan, hot up the butter and in it fry, over low heat, the
onion, parsley and the dill weed, until the onion is soft. Add the
salt, peppercorns, and clam juice.

Put the fish steaks into a large piece of cheesecloth, large
enough so the ends will hang out of the pan, but not so long that
there will be any danger of it catching fire. When the clam juice
comes to the boil, lower the fish steaks into the pan, reduce the
heat, and let it simmer for 20 minutes.

Remove the fish carefully. If you think you might want to
use the stock in which the fish cooked within a few days, it will
keep if sealed tight in a refrigerator container. Put the fish steaks
on a large platter for which you'll have to make room in your
fridge. Let them cool. Refrigerate the fish steaks for hours and
hours.

All the rest of the ingredients should be cold, also. Peel the cucumber and cut it into thin slices. Do the same with the olives and radishes. Chop the scallions. Mix the vegetables into the ice-cold sour cream. Serve this separately, with the cold fish. Dark bread and butter is good with this. So is beer, and wine, or sarsaparilla.

SERVES FOUR.

I know one fellow who has written so many cookbooks, about so many different specialties, that it seems the only thing left for him to do is the writing of "The Art of Cooking With Salt and Pepper"; "The Art of Cooking Without Pepper, But With Salt"; "The Art of Cooking With Pots and Pans," and so forth.

Every year at least three books are published on the subject of using leftovers in planning meals. Which brings me to the point about a lady who prided herself on never wasting any food. One night, when the family sat down to dinner, her husband immediately began eating. "Oh, dear," she said, "aren't you first going to ask a blessing?"

Her husband shook his head sadly. "No, dear," he said, "I will not; but if you can point out one single thing in this meal that hasn't been blessed once before I'll try and see if a small prayer will do it some good."

In summer, what is always good is something that can be cooked in the cool of the evening or morning and served cold for dinner that night or the next and, bless us all, such a dish is:

PICKLED SALMON STEAKS IN ASPIC

2 pounds salmon steaks
1 tablespoon butter
1 small onion, minced fine
$\frac{1}{4}$ cup parsley, minced fine
1 bottle (8 ounces) clam juice, or 1 cup chicken broth
1 tablespoon mixed pickling spices tied up in cheesecloth bag
maybe a little salt?
$\frac{1}{2}$ envelope (1–1$\frac{1}{2}$ teaspoons) unflavored gelatin
all kinds of garnishments, like lemon slices, red radishes,
        scallions (green onions), olives, anything.

Remove the skin and center bone from the salmon steaks, and divide them into 4 portions. In a saucepan, get the butter hot and in it fry the onion and parsley until the onion is soft. Add the clam juice or chicken broth—fish stock would be better, but how many people have fish stock on hand always?

Add the pickling spices tied up in cheesecloth, bring the liquid to the boil, let it boil rapidly, covered, for 5 minutes, add the pieces of salmon, and simmer the fish for 20 minutes.

Let the fish cool, covered, in the broth. Taste the broth, and if you think it needs salt, add some cautiously. When the broth and the fish pieces are cool, take out the bag of pickling spices and throw it away, unless you are sentimental about such things and want to preserve it, like a flower, in a book. Remove the salmon to a large platter and refrigerate it.

The broth is quite cool? right? Sprinkle the gelatin into the broth and when it has become soft, heat the broth, stirring, until the gelatin has been thoroughly dissolved. Cool it. Refrigerate the broth for about 30 minutes, when it should be slightly jelled.

Pour it over the fish pieces you've stashed away in your fridge, and refrigerate for hours and hours, or overnight.

Serve this pretty dish to 4 people, with some, or all of the garnishments we've suggested, or any of your own choice. Dark bread and butter is great with this. So is beer or any tipple you prefer.

Some of the worst bores I've ever known have been professional comedians because all they can do is tell jokes, all of which are written for them by professional gag writers, who steal them from each other.

These days, the only truly witty professional comedian I can think of is Buddy Hackett. To your father, or maybe your grandfather, the name of Joe Frisco, a vaudeville comedian, was a familiar one. He was champion.

One day at the race track Joe found himself completely broke, a condition that was organic with him. This time he was frantic because he'd been given a tip on a fixed race and didn't have a dime to put on the nag that was going to win. By accident, he ran into Bing Crosby, told him of his sad plight, and Crosby loaned him $100.

The horse did win, and it paid 20 to one. Joe Frisco went to the clubhouse restaurant, saw some friends sitting at a table, and he joined them, putting his winnings on the table in front of him.

Bing Crosby walked past the table, and Joe Frisco grabbed him by the sleeve and stopped him. He picked a $100 bill from the pile in front of him, and gave it to Crosby, saying, "Here, kid, sing us a song."

Let us sing a song in praise of:

FRIED FISH STEAKS IN CREAMY EGG BATTER (Russia)

4 fish steaks, any kind you like, approximately $\frac{1}{2}$ pound each
2 eggs, beaten with:
$\frac{1}{4}$ teaspoon salt and:
$\frac{1}{4}$ cup sour cream
bread crumbs
4 tablespoons butter ($\frac{1}{2}$ stick)
1 small onion, grated or minced fine
1 clove garlic, pressed or minced fine
$\frac{1}{4}$ cup parsley, minced
$\frac{1}{4}$ cup grated cheese (any kind you like, but not too sharp)

Remove any skin or bones on and in the fish steaks.

Beat into the eggs the salt and cream. Dip each steak into the mixture, then dip each one into bread crumbs, coating them heavily. Refrigerate for at least 30 minutes.

In a large fry pan, get 2 tablespoons of the butter hot, fry the onion, garlic and parsley until the onion starts to turn golden. Remove from pan for use later.

Add 1 tablespoon of butter to the pan, put in the fish steaks, cover the pan, and cook over low heat for 10 minutes, turning fish once.

Take the cover off pan, raise the heat, cook until steaks are well browned on the bottom, turn, with spatula and brown the other side.

Sprinkle the fish steaks with the grated cheese, dot with the remaining 1 tablespoon of butter and put a few grains of cayenne pepper on top of each steak. Put the pan in broiler just long enough to melt the cheese. Watch it carefully so it doesn't burn. Spoon onion mixture over all when you serve it to 4 people.

I like boiled, parsleyed potatoes with this. Do you?

Purely—if that is the proper word to use in conjunction with this essay—by accident, the preacher met one of his parishioners who had been conspicuous by his absence from the past few Sabbath services.

"What?" asked the preacher sententiously, "has made you so conspicuous by your absence at the past few Sabbath services?"

His whilom parishioner hung his head in shame. "My wife," he said, shamedly.

Of course the preacher wanted to know how the scoundrel's wife could have caused him to be absent when she—the scoundrel's wife—had attended the services faithfully.

"You remember, preacher," asked the scoundrel, "that sermon you preached where you said that for every woman there was a man and that also, on the other hand, for every man there was a woman?"

Of course the preacher remembered that sermon and he said so in no uncertain tones.

"Well," said the scoundrel, "my wife is mad at me because I found me that woman you talked about."

Other day I found myself making and then eating a fantastically good:

EGGY POACHED FISH

1½ to 2 pounds fish fillets or steaks
½ teaspoon each, salt and pepper
¼ cup fresh dill, minced, or 2 tablespoons dried dill weed or
    parsley
2 tablespoons chicken fat or butter, melted
1 large egg, beaten
½ cup milk or clam juice
2 tablespoons fine unseasoned bread crumbs
¼ teaspoon dry mustard

Dry the fish by patting with paper toweling. Rub salt, pepper, and half the dill (or parsley) into the fish. In a bowl, beat together 1 tablespoon of the melted chicken fat or butter, the whole egg, half of the milk (or clam juice), all the bread crumbs and all of the mustard.

Put the fish into the bowl to get the fillets or steaks coated all over. Put the coated fish on a piece of wax paper or foil, put it on a plate and put the plate of fish into the fridge, which will make the coating firm.

Put the remaining ingredients—dill, fat, and milk or clam juice—into a pot that is large enough to hold a colander comfortably with the bottom of the colander several inches over the bottom of the pot.

After an hour in the fridge, put the fish into the colander. Put the colander into the pot. Put the pot on the range. Cover the colander and part of the pot with foil, sealing the space between the two utensils as best you can. Cook over very low heat, starting your timing when you see the first whiff of steam, for 10 minutes for fish fillets, 15 minutes or longer for fish steaks, depending on thickness (thickness of fish steaks, of course). With pot holders to protect your hands, seal the utensils so that very little steam escapes.

With fish steaks that are more than ½-inch thick, turn them in colander after 7 or 8 minutes. Unnecessary to turn fillets. I've used salmon steaks, flounder, cod, and haddock fillets, and they were all splendid. When you serve the fish scrape up the stuff in pot and spoon it over the fish. If you give this to people who don't like fish, it will serve thousands, with or without loaves. ENJOY!

SERVES FOUR TO SIX.

As you undoubtedly know, politics in the earlier days of the U.S.A., really swung, and the things politicians used to say about their rivals were really scandalizing. One of the most famous splenetic political orators we've ever had was John Randolph (1773–1833), who was probably one of the most powerful and feared Congressmen our country ever had. The target for what was his most famous vituperation was Edward Livingston, a Congressman who was forced to resign his office when he became Mayor of New York City.

What John Randolph said about Edward Livingston was: "He is a man of splendid abilities, but utterly corrupt. He shines and stinks like rotten mackerel by moonlight." Wow! Holy mackerel! When you buy fish it should be by daylight, you should always sniff it if it isn't frozen, and if a fish has any odor but that of something clean, I think any judge would hold you guiltless if you took it and slapped your fishmonger in the mush with it.

My sermon for today is:

FISH-FILLED BAKED BREAD (Italy)

1 pound fish fillets (any kind you like)
flour
2 eggs, beaten
1 teaspoon, each, salt and oregano
French or Italian bread (should be 24 to 32 inches of bread)
4 teaspoons each, butter and oil
1 very large onion (preferably Bermuda or Spanish), sliced and
    rings separated
1 cup sour cream
$\frac{1}{4}$ teaspoon cayenne pepper

Dry the fish fillets. Dust them lightly with flour, dip each one into the beaten eggs into which you have beaten the teaspoon of salt and oregano.

Probably I should have listed the bread first, because what you do is cut the bread in half, horizontally, and remove as much dough as you can. Chop some of the dough as fine as you can, and dip the egg-coated fish fillets in the crumbs.

In a large fry pan, fry the breaded fillets in 2 tablespoons each, butter and oil, until they are browned on both sides, turning them carefully with a spatula. The bread should be cut into 4 sections, the length of each section of bread the same length as the fish fillets. Put 2 fried fish fillets into the bottom half of each length of bread, put onion rings on top of the fillets, spoon some of the sour cream and dust with the cayenne pepper.

Cover each section of fish-filled bread with its hollowed-out top half. Put the fish-filled bread on a baking pan which you've oiled lightly and brush the top of the bread with the remaining butter and oil mixture and any beaten egg that you have left over. Bake it in oven preheated to 350 degrees until the bread is well-browned and crisp.

Broiled tomatoes are wonderful with this. Cut 4 tomatoes in half, sprinkle with bread crumbs, put a dollop of butter on each tomato half, sprinkle lightly with salt and pepper, and broil with the fish-bread.

SERVES FOUR.

On the day before her scheduled wedding, the girl realized that she hadn't bought presents for her bridesmaids, which is, of course, the custom, so she rushed downtown to the best jewelry store in the city. By a rather far-fetched coincidence, she met in the store one of her best friends, who was to be one of the bridesmaids.

This girl friend had been married for about three months. When she saw the bride-elect, she rushed over, threw her arms around her friend, and weeping, said: "Oh, darling, I'm so glad I ran into you here, because as you grow older you'll always remember today as being one of the happiest days in your whole life."

The bride-elect was puzzled. "But darling, surely you know that I'm not getting married until tomorrow?" she said. The young married woman wailed.

"Of course I know that," she wailed, "that's why I say that you'll always remember today as one of your happiest days."

Any day can be made happier with:

FRIED FISH-FILLED PUFFS (France)

1 cup water
1 stick butter (¼ pound), cut into thin slices
⅛ teaspoon salt
1 cup all-purpose flour
4 medium-sized eggs
peanut or vegetable oil

Put the water into a saucepan, turn the heat up high, add the cut-up butter, and cook, stirring, until the butter is all melted and the water comes to the boil. As soon as the water boils, add the salt and the cup of flour, all at once. Reduce the heat to low and, with a large kitchen spoon, begin stirring and beating the mixture—this is going to take quite a bit of muscle —and you will find that the mixture gets stiffer and stiffer, and then suddenly, it will form a ball, leaving the bottom and sides of the pan clean. Break 1 egg into the pan, and stir, stir, stir. At first the mixture will become softened, but then it will get stiffer. Do this with each of the 4 eggs. To make puffs of a uniform size, it's best to use a lightly oiled egg cup or custard cup, or ice-cream scoop filled with the batter. Drop the batter on a baking sheet in mounds about 1-inch apart. Bake in oven preheated to 400 degrees for 15 minutes, then reduce the heat to 350 and bake for another 15 minutes.

While this is going on, make the:

FRIED FISH STUFFING

1 pound any kind fish fillets
2 eggs beaten into ¼ cup of milk
¼ teaspoon salt and pepper
bread crumbs
4 tablespoons butter
4 tablespoons oil
½ cup onion, minced
3 tablespoons flour
1 cup milk

When the puffs are puffed up, take the baking pan out of the oven, close oven door and turn off the heat. Hold each puff gently, but firmly with a pot-holder, jab a small knife all around each puff, and lift up the tops. Pinch out the moist centers of the tops and bottoms of the puffs. Put the puffs back into the oven and finish making the fried fish stuffing, thus: Dip the fish fillets into the egg-milk mixture into which the salt and pepper has been beaten. Coat the fillets with bread crumbs. In a large fry pan, hot up 1 teaspoon each of oil and butter and cook the onion until it is soft.

Remove the onion from the pan with a slotted spoon, put it into a bowl. Add an additional tablespoon each of butter and oil to the fry pan, and fry the fish fillets in it until both sides are browned, about 3 minutes on each side over medium heat. (The oil heightens the burning threshold of the butter.) Cut the fried fillet into pieces about 1-inch long and remove from the pan into the bowl with the fried onion. Add to the pan the rest of the butter and oil—2 tablespoons each, right?—and when it bubbles, sprinkle with the flour, and stir with a fork or whisk until the flour is golden—about 2 minutes—add the milk slowly, beating and stirring until the mixture is thickened.

Take the puffs out of oven, share out the little fried fish slices on bottom part of each puff, top with a little white sauce, put the top back on the puff, spoon sauce over each one.

SERVES FOUR.

In the interests of Accuracy and Fair Play, I would like to print a letter sent by the executive director of the Paris-Bourbon County (Kentucky) Chamber of Commerce commenting on an essay I once wrote. It reads (in part): "Thank you for mentioning Bourbon County in your article, however, Bourbon County is not a dry county." (I had said it was a dry county, having depended on a gink who until this instant had been a prominent unimpeachable source—I have now impeached this bloke—for the information.)

To show you how wet Bourbon County can be, let me recommend:

BAKED FISH WITH ANCHOVY-BOURBON-CLAM SAUCE (Kentucky)

2 pounds fish steaks cut into pieces $\frac{3}{4}$ inches thick
$\frac{1}{4}$ teaspoon pepper
1 stick butter ($\frac{1}{4}$ pound)
$\frac{1}{2}$ cup onion, chopped
1 small green pepper, chopped
$\frac{1}{4}$ cup pimiento, chopped, or roasted red pepper
2 anchovy strips, dried and mashed
1 teaspoon lemon juice
$\frac{1}{4}$ cup bourbon
1 cup clam juice, or milk, or water

Remove and throw away any skin or bones on the fish slices. Dry them thoroughly, sprinkle with pepper, put them side by side into a buttered baking dish. If you have a pretty one, with a cover, that can go from the oven to the table, that's beautiful. In a medium-sized fry pan melt 2 tablespoons of butter and in it cook the onion and pepper until they are soft. Add the chopped pimiento to the pan, away from heat and stir, and then spoon the vegetables on top of and around the fish. Melt the rest of the butter in the pan and stir in the mashed anchovies. Drizzle the fish steaks with some of the anchovy butter.

Cover the baking dish—foil is fine. Bake in oven preheated to 350 degrees for 20 minutes. Drizzle with remaining anchovy-butter at least twice. In the last 5 minutes of this baking period, combine the lemon juice, bourbon, and clam juice (or whatever). If you want your sauce to be thickened, dissolve 2 tablespoons cornstarch in the liquid while it is still cold, pour it into the fry pan. Bring to the boil, stirring until the sauce begins to thicken. Remove cover from baking dish, pour the sauce over and around the fish steaks and bake for the additional 5 minutes, when the fish should be thoroughly cooked.

SERVES SIX TO EIGHT.

The man was a notorious hypochondriac. At least once a month he came to his doctor, each time with a new complaint. The doctor examined him each time and told him he was in perfect health but the man kept coming back. This time he told the doctor that he had a constant itch. "All over the body?" the doctor asked. "No," said the man, "only right here," and he touched his abdomen. The doctor examined him. "I can't see anything wrong," said the doctor. "Of course you can't," the man said, "the itching is inside, what's in there, where I've got that itch?" The doctor said that was where the appendix is. "I guess we'll have to take out your appendix," said the doctor. The man blenched. "You're going to take out my appendix just because it itches?" he cried. "Of course," said the doctor, "how else are you going to be able to scratch it?" So the man quit coming to him.

People will keep coming to your house if you give them:

BAKED-FRIED STUFFED FISH FILLETS (Italy)

2 pounds fish fillets (any kind you like) dried with paper towel
$\frac{1}{4}$ teaspoon pepper
flour (very little)
1 stick ($\frac{1}{4}$ pound) butter, margarine, or $\frac{1}{2}$ cup oil
     (approximately)
1 cup onions, minced
$\frac{1}{4}$ cup parsley, minced
one 4-ounce can mushroom pieces drained and dried
2 (or more) anchovies, drained, dried and mashed, or 2
     tablespoons anchovy paste
two 3-ounce packages cream cheese, softened
$\frac{1}{4}$ cup fine dry bread crumbs
$\frac{1}{4}$ teaspoon paprika

Rub into the fish fillets—which should be approximately the same size—the pepper, and then dust lightly with flour, shaking off excess. In a large fry pan get 2 tablespoons of butter hot and in it fry the fillets over medium heat until just golden, lift gently with a spatula and fry other side the same way. Don't crowd the pan, and don't bother to keep the fish hot. Add butter as needed. In 2 tablespoons of butter fry the onions, and parsley, and mushrooms, until onions are golden. Combine the mashed anchovies and cream cheese, then add to this the fried onion mixture. Taste it; you may want another anchovy in the mixture. Smear a thick layer of butter in a baking dish. Put in a layer of fried fillets, spread the onion-cream cheese mixture on them. Cover with rest of the fried fish.

Hot up 1 tablespoon of butter in the fry pan, stir in the bread crumbs, and spread the buttered crumbs on top of the fish, dust with paprika and bake in oven preheated to 350 degrees until bread crumbs are browned, about 15 to 20 minutes.
SERVES FOUR TO SIX.

Lady in a state of great excitement called her friend on the phone. "Have you heard about our minister's son?" she asked excitedly.

The friend said, no, she hadn't heard anything lately about the minister's son. This made the excited lady even more excited. "Well, I could hardly believe it," she said, "but it's true. Instead of going to the Theological Seminary, he's going to a school for bartenders, can you imagine that?" Now came a moment of silence.

And then the friend said, not at all excited, "You know, my dear? that's not so bad if you think about it for a moment. As a bartender he'll do a whole lot better than his father in getting people to repent."

You'll have nothing to be sorry about if you make:

FISH AND RICE AND EVERYTHING NICE (Brazil)

1 cup rice
2 cups tomato juice
1 pound any kind of fish fillets you like
$\frac{1}{2}$ teaspoon salt
$\frac{1}{4}$ teaspoon pepper
1 egg
1 cup milk or clam juice
$\frac{1}{2}$ cup grated cheese (any kind, Parmesan, Romano, Swiss, any kind you like)
2 ripe bananas, cut in halves the long way
2 tablespoons butter
1 tablespoon brown sugar or honey

Pour the rice into the tomato juice after bringing the juice to the boil. Cover the pan and simmer it slowly until most of the tomato juice has been absorbed by the rice. The rice should be quite moist.

Butter a baking dish and put half of the rice into it. Rub each fish fillet with some salt and pepper, and arrange the fish over the rice. Cover the fish with the rest of the rice.

Beat the egg into the milk or clam juice and pour it over

all. Sprinkle with the cheese, put the sliced bananas on top, and dot the bananas with dollops of butter.

Cover the baking dish and bake in oven preheated to 350 degrees for 1 hour. In the last 15 minutes, uncover the dish and sprinkle with the brown sugar, or honey.

SERVES FOUR.

Man had an uncontrollable itch to gamble, especially on slow-moving horses, but he finally promised his wife that he had quit throwing away the food and mortgage money on worthless nags, though she suspected that he was a secret gambler now.

One evening, a friend dropped in to visit the couple, and, not knowing about his host's fraudulent reform, said jovially, "Well, Joe, how did you make out with Libby Jones yesterday?" The wife ran out of the room, sobbing, the man berated his stupid friend, and then went to mollify his wife.

When she came back into the room, the visitor—real dope, believe us—said, "Look, Mrs. Yifnif, Joe has really quit betting on the horses, believe me, and you misunderstood me entirely, because Libby Jones isn't a horse, she's an exotic dancer."

If you'd like to get with something less exotic and a good deal more simple, try:

FISH FILLETS WITH A NICE SAUCE (Brooklyn)

2 pounds fish fillets
1 egg, beaten
flour
1 stick butter
2 tablespoons parsley, minced
1 teaspoon lemon or lime juice
1 dash (⅛ teaspoon) Worcestershire
¼ teaspoon salt
1 envelope brown gravy mix plus 1 cup boiling water

Dip the fillets in the beaten egg, then into the flour. Fry the fillets in butter, adding some as needed, but do not crowd the pan, then put fish on hot platter over pot of very hot water, covered with a mixing bowl to keep them hot. Add parsley as you go. Combine lemon juice, Worcestershire sauce, salt, and envelope of brown gravy mix with boiling water, in a saucepan, where else? and pour over the fish.

A large, boiled, parsleyed potato is nice with this, and so is mashed. Because it is good, have a cooked green vegetable AND a mixed salad with this.

SERVES FOUR TO SIX.

If you haven't been plagued by the fact that it keeps taking longer and longer all the time for a letter to get to its destination through the U.S. mails, you are pretty unusual. Reminds me of an old timey story. (You have noticed, haven't you? that almost everything reminds me of an old timey story?) People all over the country who wrote letters to friends or relatives in this town kept complaining to the postmaster general that they never got answers to their mail, so a postal inspector was sent there to investigate. He found that a new postmaster had been appointed to take the place of the lately departed one. He found a limp mailbag lying on the floor. Inside were a bunch of letters. "Why haven't you put this bag of mail through?" he asked the postmaster. The postmaster was indignant. "Put this bag of mail through?" he asked indignantly. "Why, it isn't filled yet, that's why."

Why not fill your family with this delicious:

PUFFY BAKED FISH OMELET (Italy)

1 ½ pounds fish fillets (any kind of lean fish)
2 tablespoons butter
½ cup chopped green pepper
¼ teaspoon dill weed or seed
¼ teaspoon pepper
4 eggs, separated
2 or 3 anchovy strips, minced fine
¼ cup pimiento-stuffed olives, sliced thin

Dry the fish fillets. Heat 1 tablespoon butter in a small frying pan, fry the chopped green pepper, sprinkled with dill weed, stirring until it is all butter-coated, then cover and cook for 5 minutes, or until the pepper is soft, stirring a few times.

In a mixing bowl beat the green pepper-dill mixture into the egg yolks, with the pepper and minced anchovies.

Beat the egg whites in another bowl until they are quite stiff and then fold the egg whites gently into the yolk mixture.

Smear a baking dish with the remaining tablespoon of butter. Spoon the egg mixture into the baking dish and arrange the fish fillets in the dish, overlapping them. Sprinkle with the sliced olives.

Bake in oven preheated to 325 degrees for about 30 minutes, when the fish will be cooked through and encased in a lovely puffed-up, well-browned, greeny-red omelet.

Serve this with hot, crisp Italian or French bread and lots of butter. Or margarine?

SERVES FOUR.

The two friends met, after a long interval had elapsed since their last lunch together, and the talk finally got around to their respective families.

"How's your oldest boy? What's he doing these days?" asked one or the other.

The other shrugged and looked unhappy. "Well, he's just finished his first semester in college."

"Is that so?" asked the first. "Is it doing him any good?"

The other shrugged again. "It isn't doing him any good, but it's done a great deal for my wife. When she heard what his marks were, she stopped her obnoxious bragging about him."

A dish worth bragging about is:

STEAMED FISH WITH HORSERADISH SOUR-CREAM SAUCE

1½ pounds fish fillets or steaks
½ teaspoon salt
¼ teaspoon pepper
½ cup onion, minced
½ teaspoon dried dill weed, or parsley flakes (2 tablespoons if
    fresh)
1½ cups milk or clam juice
1 cup canned clams, minced
1 egg, beaten into 1 cup sour cream
horseradish
perhaps some beet juice

Rub the salt and pepper into the fish fillets or steaks. Arrange them in a colander. Into a pot in which the colander will fit with its bottom at least 2 inches from the bottom of the pot, put ½ of the minced onion and ½ of the dill or parsley. Add 1 cup of the milk or clam juice (with ½ of the clams). Put the colander into the pot. Pour the rest of the milk or clam juice over the fish, sprinkle over the fish in the colander all of the remaining onion, dill, and minced clams.

Cover the colander and the pot with foil, sealing the space between the two utensils as well as you can. Bring the liquid to the boil over high heat. You'll see some steam, no matter how well you think you sealed the opening between the pot and colander. With two potholders, tighten the foil over the space.

With fillets the thickness of flounder, which is as good a fish as any for this recipe, 10 minutes of steaming over low heat will cook them thoroughly. With fish steaks, of course, you will need a longer cooking time. After 15 minutes of steaming a fish steak, test one of the steaks with a fork. If it flakes easily, it is, of course, cooked through and ready to serve.

Let the fish remain in the colander, covered with foil, if necessary, while you make the sauce. Add to the egg-sour cream mixture as much horseradish—there are some excellent strong brands in the stores—as your taste tells you to. To make the sauce pretty, add a spoonful or two of beet juice. If you have inadvertently made the sauce too hot with horseradish, you can cut its strength with more beet juice, or some of the liquid in the pot.

Pour the pot liquid over the fish, and serve the horseradish sour-cream sauce separately. This is not just good, it is merely fantastically wonderful with cornbread, pumpernickel.

SERVES FOUR.

The ship piled up on some rocks, and two men from the crew managed, after clinging to some wreckage for a couple of days, to reach land. It seemed like a bleak, desolate shore where they were washed up. For several hours they wandered along the sandy beach, seeing no signs of habitation. They wandered, hungry and thirsty, for hours and hours.

Finally, one of them gave a triumphant shout, and, pointing into the distance, began a stumbling run. When his shipmate caught up with him, he was jumping up and down with joy.

"We've reached civilization! We're saved!" he hollered with joy. "Look at all these empty beer cans!"

I like to drink wine, rather than beer, with:

FRIED FISH FILLETS FLORENTINE (Italian)

one 10-ounce package frozen chopped spinach
6 tablespoons butter
1 cup onion, minced
$\frac{1}{2}$ teaspoon dried dill, or thyme
1 pound fish fillets (flounder, cod, halibut, etc.)
$\frac{1}{2}$ teaspoon salt
flour
2 eggs, beaten with 2 tablespoons milk
$\frac{1}{8}$ teaspoon cayenne pepper
$\frac{1}{2}$ pint light cream
$\frac{1}{2}$ cup grated cheese (any kind that's not too strong)
$\frac{1}{4}$ teaspoon paprika

Put the frozen cake of spinach into a pan large enough to hold it flat *and add no water, despite what the package instructions say!* Cook it, covered, for 5 minutes over low heat, turn the spinach and cook for an additional 5 minutes.

Uncover the pan, break the spinach up with a fork, and cook, stirring occasionally until almost all of the moisture has been cooked away. Cover the pan and remove from heat.

In a large fry pan, melt 1 tablespoon of butter and in it cook the onion and dill over medium heat, stirring until the onion is soft. Push the fried onion to the side of the pan. Melt 2 more tablespoons of butter in the pan.

Rub each fish fillet with salt, dust each one lightly with flour on both sides, then dip the fillets into the eggs which you have beaten with milk. Fry each fillet in the hot butter, over medium heat, not more than 2 minutes on each side, turning the fillets carefully with a spatula, or maybe 2 spatulas. Do not crowd the pan.

To keep the fish hot, set a large, heavy serving platter over a pot of hot water, put the fillets on the platter as they are fried, and cover the fish with an inverted bowl.

When you turn each fillet to brown the top side, sprinkle on it a little bit of the fried onion and dill. When all the moisture has been cooked out of the spinach, add 2 tablespoons of butter to the spinach, and ¼ teaspoon of salt, and stir in the cream and ¼ cup of the grated cheese. Cook over low heat, stirring.

Butter a baking dish or casserole lightly, spoon in the creamed spinach, put on top of the spinach the fish fillets—if there is any egg left over pour it on the fish—top with the remaining ¼ cup of grated cheese, dot with the remaining tablespoon of butter and sprinkle with the paprika.

Cook the dish in an oven preheated to 400 degrees until the cheese is melted and beginning to brown—about 10 minutes—and serve.

SERVES FOUR, MAYBE FIVE.

You know, of course, that there are now very few colleges that are exclusively women's colleges or men's colleges and how even their living quarters are not separate, and how the young men and women are allowed to have overnight—and longer—guests of whatever persuasion—not to mention sex—they choose? So here was this father and his college-student daughter having a discussion about this subject. The father took a strong negative position all through the heated debate.

"Now, look, Pater, let us be honest with each other. Are you seriously going to tell me that the only woman you ever went to bed with was Mater?"

"Of course I am not seriously going to tell you any such thing," the father said. "Aha," said the daughter triumphantly, "now we're getting someplace! And when was the last time?"

"The last time was," said her daddy, "48 years and 6 months ago, when my mother weaned me."

Seems to me I was weaned on a lovely fish dish my Momma called:

FISH WITH HORSERADISH SAUCE (The Bronx)

2 pounds fish fillets
½ teaspoon salt
flour
½ stick butter
1 cup onion, minced
¼ cup fresh parsley, minced
½ teaspoon dried dill weed or seed
horseradish
1 cup sour cream
⅛ teaspoon cayenne pepper

Dry the fish fillets thoroughly, rub salt into them, and sprinkle lightly with flour, shaking off excess. In a large fry pan, hot up 1 tablespoon of the butter and in it fry the onion and parsley, over high heat, stirring all the while, adding the dill, until the onion begins to turn golden. Add rest of the butter. Reduce heat.

Put the fillets into the pan, on top of the onion. Don't crowd the pan, but do two fillets at a time if necessary. When the fillets are slightly browned, turn them carefully with a spatula, brown the other side carefully. When all the fillets are slightly browned on each side, put them back into the pan, and now they can lie one atop the other, willy-nilly and also helter-skelter. Stir the horseradish into the sour cream, and quit adding horseradish when you are satisfied that the mixture is as strong as you like it. Oh, sure, of course, if you don't like horseradish, don't use any. And you know what just occurred to me? Suppose you don't like fish? Ah, well.

Pour the horseradishy sour cream over the fish in the pan, sprinkle with cayenne, cover the pan and cook for about 5 minutes over low heat, but don't let the sour cream boil.

SERVES SIX TO EIGHT.

Fellow on the Southern Railroad got into conversation with the man sitting next to him and soon learned that the man was an itinerant revival preacher. "Yes indeed," the revivalist hollered, "I been in Florida fighting the Devil, and then I went up to Atlanta giving that old Devil what for, and now I am on my way to the nation's capital, where I am going to do the same thing." The fellow approved heartily. "That's the stuff, Reverend," he shouted, "you just keep on chasing that old Devil right up North to those damnyankees!"

A nice Yankee lady in Maine, named Yenta Talabender gave us this lovely recipe for:

BAKED STUFFED FISH FILLETS (Maine)

1 pound potatoes, peeled and sliced thin
2 cups onions, minced
¼ cup parsley, minced
¼ teaspoon pepper
½ stick butter
2 pounds fish fillets
anchovies, chopped, with oil drained and saved
1 tablespoon capers, chopped
2 eggs
1 pint sour cream
½ cup cheese, grated
¼ teaspoon paprika

In a large fry pan, fry the potatoes, onions, and parsley, sprinkling with pepper, in the butter which should be frothing when you put those ingredients into the pan. Use a spatula to turn the potatoes and try not to break or mash them up. When the potatoes are slightly browned, remove the fry pan from heat.

Dry the fillets, put some chopped anchovy on each one, and roll the fillets up. Butter a baking dish or casserole, put in a layer of potatoes, onion, etc., sprinkle with the oil from the anchovy can, then put into the dish the fillets, rolled up, side by side. Beat the chopped capers, and eggs into the sour cream. Pour half of the cream mixture over the fish.

Top this with the remaining potato-onion mixture, combine the remaining egg-cream mixture with the grated cheese, pour this over all, and sprinkle with the paprika. Bake, covered, in oven preheated to 350 degrees for 35 minutes. Remove cover and bake for an additional 5 minutes. This dish is one of my favorites.

SERVES FOUR.

The phone in the hall rang and the lady of the house went out of the living room, where she'd been sitting with her husband, to answer it. She was gone quite a long while. When she came back to the living room she was pale. "What's the matter, honey?" her husband asked. "Who was that on the phone? Did you get bad news from somebody?" His wife sighed deeply and sat down. "Do you remember that Caribbean cruise we took last year?" Her husband said of course he remembered the cruise.

"Well, do you remember that couple that sat at our table?" He said of course he did. "Well, do you remember the woman saying that if we were ever around their home in Oshkosh we should come and stay with them for a week or so, and how you felt you had to say the same thing?" Now the husband paled. "Yes, dear," said his wife, "those idiots are on their way."

Maybe your guests are not too strong in their heads if they don't ask for the recipe when you give them:

BAKED FRIED FLOUNDER PIE (Maine)

8 fillets of flounder
½ teaspoon salt
¼ teaspoon pepper
2 eggs, beaten with:
2 tablespoons clam juice or milk
bread crumbs
1 stick butter or ½ cup oil
1 large onion, minced
½ pound mushrooms, sliced through stems and caps
¼ cup parsley
3 tablespoons flour
1 cup clam juice or milk
frozen pastry dough for 1 crust
paprika

Wash and dry the flounder—or other fish—fillets. Rub into each some salt and pepper. Dip each fillet into the eggs beaten with the clam juice or milk, and then into the bread crumbs. When all the fillets are breaded, refrigerate them for 1 hour, longer if you like. In a large frying pan, get 2 tablespoons of butter or oil quite hot. Over high heat, stirring all the while, fry the onion, and mushrooms, and parsley, until the onion begins to turn golden. Remove the onion-mushroom mixture to a bowl.

Add 2 tablespoons of butter to the pan and fry the fish fillets. Don't crowd the pan. Cook over medium heat, and when the bottoms of the fillets are browned turn them gently with a spatula. When they are browned on both sides put them on a large, heavy platter set over a pot of very hot water, and cover them with an inverted bowl to keep them hot. Add butter to the pan as needed.

When the fillets are all fried, put 3 tablespoons of butter into the pan, cook the flour, stirring, for 2 minutes over low heat, add clam juice or milk, slowly, stirring all the while, and cook until the sauce thickens. Put the fried fish into a buttered baking dish or casserole, stir the onion-mushroom-parsley mixture into the white sauce, taste it for seasoning, and pour it into the baking dish. Cover the dish with the pastry, make 2 or 3 gashes in the pastry to allow steam to escape, sprinkle with paprika and bake according to pastry instructions. A great pie.

SERVES FOUR.

When the first star appears in the heaven it marks the beginning of Passover, the eight-day Jewish holiday, a happy festival tinged with sorrow, marking the deliverance of the Biblical Hebrews from Egyptian bondage. During the period, only bread that is unleavened—matzos—may be eaten, and various other foods are also proscribed. It used to be—maybe it still is, for all we know—that every member of a family wore only new clothes for the holiday. Which brings to mind an ancient story about the desperately poor man who came to his rabbi several days before the holiday with a terrible problem. "Rabbi dear," he said, "I am in terrible trouble. Help me. I have no money for matzos, no money for sacramental wine, no money for meat, no money for new clothing for my wife, my children and myself." The rabbi comforted him. "I will help you with your troubles," he said, reaching for a piece of paper and a pen.

"How much do you need for matzos, sacramental wine, and meat?" he asked. The man said he needed 24 rubles for those items. The rabbi wrote down the figure. "How much for clothing for your children?" asked the rabbi. The man said he needed 75 rubles for that, and the rabbi wrote that down. "And a new suit for yourself?" the rabbi asked. He said he needed 50 rubles for that, and the rabbi wrote it down. "And a new dress for your wife?" the rabbi asked. Another 50 rubles, the man said. "Now let me think," said the rabbi. He thought, and then he looked up beamingly. "Your troubles are over," he said, beamingly. "Now you don't have to worry about matzos, meat, wine, clothing for your children, your wife and yourself.

"Now all you have to worry about is: where are you going to get 199 rubles?"

You don't have to be Jewish to worry, or to like:

EXTRAORDINARY BAKED GEFILTE FISH (AND TRADITIONAL GEFILTE FISH)

$2\frac{1}{2}$ pounds (approximately) white fish
$2\frac{1}{2}$ pounds (approximately) yellow pike
or $2\frac{1}{2}$ pounds (approximately) each of any two different
    varieties of fish
$\frac{1}{4}$ cup corn or peanut oil
2 pounds onions (yes, that's what I said, "2 pounds"), chopped
    one whole head, about 15 cloves, garlic (now, now, don't
    get scared, I'll talk to you about this later), pressed or
    mashed
1 tablespoon salt
$\frac{3}{4}$ teaspoon pepper
$\frac{1}{2}$ teaspoon paprika
3 eggs
$\frac{1}{4}$ cup (approximately) water
$\frac{1}{4}$ cup matzo meal, or cracker meal
2 carrots, 1 grated, other cut into thin rounds (one cupful each)
$\frac{1}{2}$ cup (additional) oil
4 bay leaves
8 cloves

Gefilte fish, traditionally, are boiled fish balls, and you have undoubtedly seen jars of them in the supermarkets and groceries. But these commercial ones are mere shadows, pallid imitations of the real thing, because for the general public they cannot be seasoned well enough. All commercial gefilte fish have one thing in common—they contain no garlic. Gefilte fish without garlic is like an egg without salt. Of course, garlic may not be used by Jewish people during the Passover season, and this, probably, is why they never use the wonderful stuff in the store-boughten fish balls. (Every national cuisine has a traditional fishball recipe. The French call theirs "quenelles"; the Italians call theirs "pesceballo" and the Chinese name for fish balls is "Jan-Yu-Bang.") What do you say we go into the kitchen and cook some?

Don't want to scare you, but it is best to begin working on this recipe two days before you plan to serve the gefilte fish. They must be filleted, all skin and bones and head and tail removed—and, of course, gutted—but all of the scraps, except for the guts, must be saved for making fish broth.

If you have a grinder, hand-operated or electrical, that is fine. And if you have a blender, as well, that will save you a lot of labor and time. But, of course, gefilte fish can be made without these gadgets. Put the heads, tails, bones, and skin of the fish, thoroughly washed, into a pot. Add 3 quarts of water, 1 teaspoon salt, ½ teaspoon pepper, 2 cups of onions, chopped—these ingredients are apart from the ones listed in the recipe above—and one large carrot chopped. Bring to the boil and then simmer, covered for several hours.

In a large fry pan, hot up the ¼ cup of oil and in it fry the onions, and mashed garlic uncovered, over low heat, stirring often. The onions must be well-browned, and a lot of the liquid cooked out of them. When the onions are quite brown—but not burned—remove from heat, and then refrigerate it—tightly covered, of course—overnight. Strain the fish broth, throwing away all the solids. Refrigerate the broth—you should have about 1 quart—overnight. If you have a grinder, grind the fish meat twice through the finest blade. If you don't have a grinder, but do have a blender, cut the fish meat into very small pieces and blend small quantities at a time at high speed, turning the motor on and off quickly. If you don't have a grinder or a blender, you will have to chop the fish in a wooden bowl with a chopper—they come with one or two blades—along with the fried onions and garlic.

If the 15 cloves of garlic frightened you, let me reassure you; when the fish is baked, it will taste delicious, but you will *not* detect any garlic in the finished product.

Add the salt, pepper, and paprika, and chop, blending all the ingredients thoroughly. Add 1 egg and chop until all traces of the egg are no longer visible. Add and chop, add last egg and chop, chop, chop. Add the matzo or cracker meal and the remaining water and chop, chop, chop. Add the grated carrot and chop until all traces of the carrot are no longer visible.

Now put the ½ cup of oil into a large baking or roasting pan, put it into your oven, and set the heat at 350 degrees. After 5 minutes, take the pan out of oven. Wet hands and form the fish mixture into flat cakes, about 1 inch thick. Put the cakes, after forming them, into the oil in the pan, wetting your hands from time to time. Put a thin round of carrot, pressing it down, on top of each fish cake. Put 1 bay leaf and 2 cloves in each of the corners of the pan. Bake the fish until the cakes are a deep golden brown, basting them with some of the broth you stashed away in your fridge, and the oil in the pan, every 10 minutes. They will be finished baking in about 45 minutes. From time to time lift up one of the cakes with a spatula to see that the bottoms of the fish cakes are not burned. If the bottom seems to be browning too much, reduce the heat to 325 degrees, but the bottoms will have to be darker than the sides or tops of the gefilte fish, in order to be cooked through. Now, you know what you have? A *magnificent* gefilte fish, that's what you've got.

If you want traditional, boiled gefilte fish, form the fish mixture with all of the aforementioned ingredients, into balls about the size of a pingpong ball. (If you want the fish Passover-style, omit the garlic.) Bring the fish broth to the boil, drop the fishballs into the broth and when the broth returns to the boil reduce the heat to barely simmer the broth, and cook the gefilte fish, covered, for 1 hour. They will swell up considerably in the broth.

Done either way, this is good hot or cold. You should have horseradish with gefilte fish, and dark bread (except, of course, if you observe the Passover).

SERVES FOUR TO SIX.

This kid—name of Zebediah—stumbled over the word "revitalize" in English class, and the teacher asked him: "Zeb, do you know the meaning of that word, 'revitalize'?" Zebediah shook his head. "No, teach," he said. The teacher thought for a moment. "Now," she said, "let us see if we can figure out the meaning, all by ourselves. Your father works hard to make a living, doesn't he?" Zebediah nodded. "He sure does, teach," said Zeb. "All right, then, after working hard all day, what does he do after he finishes working?" Zebediah yelped astonishedly. "Hey, teach," Zebediah yelped astonishedly, "you know what? My Mom keeps asking him that all the time."

Once I made a cheap but wonderful fish dish and now all the time my loved ones keep asking for:

SALMON (OR TUNA) AND SARDINE LOAF (The Bronx)

1 8-ounce can salmon or tuna
1 can boneless and skinless sardines (they're almost always
     about 3½ ounces)
1 tablespoon lemon juice
¼ cup onion, minced
1 tablespoon oil from sardine can
¼ cup parsley, minced
2 cups mashed potatoes (instant is fine)
¼ teaspoon pepper
4 eggs, separated
½ cup grated cheese
parsley sprigs, lemon slices, red radishes, cherry tomatoes,
     cucumber slices, corn, pumpernickel, or rye bread and
     how about beer, not too cold?

The salmon—or tuna—must be mashed up well with the sardines and the lemon juice, until it has a pasty consistency. Fry the onion in a small pan in the oil from the sardine can and add it to the mixture, along with the parsley. Combine this with the mashed potatoes, pepper, and the egg yolks, getting everything combined thoroughly. Beat the egg whites until they are stiff, and fold gently into the mixture.

Butter a baking dish and spoon the mixture into it gently. Sprinkle the cheese—any kind you like—on top, and bake in over preheated to 350 degrees until the cheese is melted, say about 30 minutes? This is good cold or hot.

SERVES FOUR.

The salesman had checked into the motel late the night before and had gone right to bed. In the morning, while he shaved, he turned on the TV set and was furious when he found that it didn't work. On his way to the office to make a complaint, he noticed as he left his room, that over the doorway was a sign reading, "Honeymoon Lodge." Then he saw four other rooms which had the same sign over their doorways.

Angrily, he told the man at the desk about the out-of-order TV set. The man seemed unconcerned. "Listen, Mister," the man said, "you got no cause to complain, that was the last empty room you got last night and you would have had to drive another 20 miles to the next motel." So the salesman shrugged. "Okay, okay," he said, "but how come my room and four others I saw got signs saying, 'Honeymoon Lodge,' over their doorways?"

The man laughed. "Generally we give those rooms only to young couples, and you know what? None of them has ever complained that their TV sets weren't working."

A working lady can do all the preparatory work the night before and then, about half an hour after she comes home the next day, serve up a beautiful:

SALMON (OR TUNA) POTATO SOUR CREAM PIE (U.S.A.)

6 large non-baking potatoes
½ stick butter
2 cups onions, chopped
¼ cup parsley, minced
1 pound canned salmon or tuna, drained (skin and bones removed)
2 anchovy strips, dried and mashed, or 1 tablespoon anchovy paste
1 teaspoon flour
½ pint sour cream
¼ cup (or more) grated Swiss or other cheese
¼ teaspoon cayenne pepper

Boil the potatoes until a fork goes all the way through with very little pressure. Let them cool.

In a frying pan hot up 2 tablespoons (half) of the butter and fry the onions and parsley, stirring almost constantly, until the onions are golden. In a mixing bowl, combine the fried onion-parsley with salmon and anchovy, mashing with a fork.

Wipe the frying pan dry with a paper towel, and in it brown the teaspoon of flour. Stir the flour into the sour cream (which will prevent the cream from curdling when it is baked), and add this to the salmon mixture.

If you're going to serve this the next evening, cover the bowl securely and refrigerate, along with the boiled potatoes. If you're going to serve it the same evening do this:

Peel the potatoes and cut them into thin slices. You have 2 tablespoons of butter left, right? Use ½ tablespoon to smear on a pie plate. Put a layer of potatoes into the plate. Spread the salmon-sour cream mixture over the potatoes. Cover with the rest of the potato slices. Combine the remaining 1½ tablespoons of butter with the grated cheese, dot the potatoes with this. Sprinkle the cayenne pepper over all. Bake, uncovered, in oven preheated to 350 degrees until the potatoes and the cheese are browned, or golden, however you prefer, which will take 20 to 30 minutes. Serve with a green salad.

SERVES FOUR.

Long time since I heard this story, and since at least one, maybe two generations have come along since the protagonist was at his height, maybe it should first be noted that John Barrymore—not to mention his brother, Lionel, and sister, Ethel, and several of their ancestors—was world-famous. Take my word for it, okay? John Barrymore, who, in addition to his artistry, was possessed of the most handsome, unforgettable appearance of anyone all through his long career, was shopping in a haberdashery in Beverly Hills, Calif. When he had made his purchases, the clerk asked: "Is this a charge, sir? Or will you pay?" Mr. Barrymore glared. "Charge it," he said coldly. "And the name, sir?" said the clerk. "Barrymore," said the great actor, angrily. "Which Barrymore, sir?" said the clerk. Mr. Barrymore roared, furiously, as he stalked out of the store, "Ethel, of course."

If you have a stalk of celery in your fridge make:

BAKED SALMON LOAF (U.S.A.)

1-pound can of salmon (sure, you can use tuna)
½ cup ketchup, catsup, or tomato sauce
2 tablespoons oil (I like olive oil for this, but any other is okay)
1 medium onion, minced
1 rib celery, minced
1 slice bread (white, rye, any kind) crust removed, shredded
      and chopped fine
¼ teaspoon each, salt and pepper
one can (10½ ounces) condensed cream of celery soup

Empty the can of salmon, along with its liquid, into a mixing bowl. Throw away the skin and bones, and flake the salmon. Add the ketchup or whatever. Get the oil hot in a frying pan and in it quickly fry the minced onion and celery over high heat, stirring constantly, until the onion and celery are soft.

Add the fried onion-celery to the bowl, add the chopped bread and the salt and pepper. Combine all the ingredients thoroughly, with a fork or your hands, and pack the mixture down into an oiled loaf pan or casserole.

In your oven, preheated to 350 degrees, bake it for 30 minutes. At the end of the 30 minutes, spoon the condensed soup over it and bake for an additional 15 minutes.

If you want to do most of the work on this dish—there really isn't very much, is there?—beforehand, you can do everything up to the step of adding the condensed soup, refrigerate it overnight, or for a couple of days, and then, when you want to serve it, preheat your oven to 400 degrees, spoon the soup over the salmon loaf, and bake it at that heat for 30 minutes to get it all nice and hot.

Or you can serve it cold, omitting the condensed soup, with a salad of green vegetables.

SERVES FOUR.

The man had told the attorney all the facts behind the lawsuit a rival had brought against him, and then he asked the lawyer what he thought his chances were for being acquitted and avoiding a jail sentence. "Well," said the lawyer, "it is a tricky case, and I'll tell you frankly that a jury would most likely find you guilty, but, of course, we can appeal on legal grounds, and it will be a long hard fight through the courts. Can you afford that?" The man nodded. "I've got a half-million dollars," he said grimly, "to fight against going to jail." The lawyer smiled. "I'm happy to hear that," he said, "because it's been my experience that no man goes to jail with that kind of money." And you know what? That lawyer was absolutely right. Because when the man went to jail he was completely tapped out. (Means penniless.)

Even if you are far from being tapped out you can enjoy this cheap and easy:

BAKED FISH-POTATO CASSEROLE (N.Y.)

2 tablespoons oil or butter
1 sweet pepper (green or red), chopped
1 cup onion, chopped
1 pound potatoes, mashed, or 2 envelopes 5-servings instant
    potato granules, prepared according to package
    directions
1 pound canned salmon or tuna
tomato, or chili sauce, or ketchup
grated cheese

In a fry pan get the oil or butter hot and in it cook the chopped sweet pepper and onion until they are soft. Combine the mixture thoroughly with the mashed potatoes, and the drained, flaked salmon or tuna, removing any skin or bones.

Pack the mixture into a buttered baking dish. Cover with sauce, sprinkle the sauce with grated cheese—as much of any kind you like—and bake in a 350 degree oven until the sauce is bubbling, which will take about 30 minutes. If you drink champagne with this, everyone will know that you are not tapped out, but will think that you like the simple things in life and they will admire you.

SERVES FOUR.

The man came into the barroom looking unhappy, and he had three martinis in less than five minutes, and after each one he looked more and more dejected. When he ordered his fourth martini, the kindly, philosophical bartender began making it for him and said, "Look friend, don't you think you should take it a little easier on the sauce? Maybe you could tell me your trouble. That generally helps, I find, if a feller tells a stranger his story."

The drinking fellow looked even sadder. "It's my wife. For

twenty-six years she and I were the happiest people in the world, and then it had to happen." He paused. The bartender leaned over the bar. "Tell me, friend, what spoiled this twenty-six years of happiness?" he said. The drinking man sighed. "Then we met."

You'll want something cooling to drink along with:

HOT CURRIED FISH BALLS (India)

1 pound cooked fish (canned salmon or tuna, drained, flaked,
    bones and skin removed are fine)
2 eggs, beaten separately
$\frac{1}{4}$ cup onion, minced fine
$\frac{1}{4}$ cup parsley, minced
flour
bread crumbs
$\frac{1}{2}$ stick butter
$\frac{1}{4}$ cup oil
1 tablespoon (or more) curry
1 cup light cream or half-and-half
$\frac{1}{4}$ teaspoon salt

Flake and chop the fish fine, in a mixing bowl. Add one of the beaten eggs, the grated or minced onion, and the parsley. Combine all this thoroughly with your hands, moistened, adding just enough flour to form a mixture that is firm enough to hold together. Form the mixture into small balls about the size of a pingpong ball, and dip them, one at a time, into the remaining beaten egg, then roll them in the bread crumbs which should be spread out on a piece of waxed paper.

Put the breaded fish balls into the refrigerator for at least one hour. Put into a large frying pan the butter, and the $\frac{1}{4}$ cup of oil and heat it to the point where it just barely begins to smoke, lift the pan away from heat and lower the heat. Put the fish balls into the hot fat, a few at a time, trying to keep the temperature of the fat at the same level, just below the smoking point, and fry them, turning them gently with a slotted spoon or spatula until they are a deep golden brown color all over. Remove them, when they are done, but don't bother to keep them hot.

There should be 3 or 4 tablespoons of fat in the frying pan. Stirring all the time, add 1 tablespoon of flour and 1 tablespoon of curry to the fat. When the mixture is smooth, slowly add the light cream or half-cream-half milk, stirring or beating with a fork or whisk. When it begins to thicken, add the salt, stir, and taste the sauce. Wait a couple of seconds to get the aftertaste and if you think it needs more curry, or salt, now is the time to add it to the sauce. When the sauce is seasoned to your satisfaction, return the fried fish balls to the pan, stir the sauce and fish balls gently just long enough so the fish balls are hot. Parsleyed boiled potatoes are great with this.

SERVES FOUR.

Man had attended an office party the night before and now he was feeling terrible. Among other discomforts his right eye hurt. He looked in the mirror and saw he had a black eye. He felt just as awful as he looked. Maybe even more so. He didn't feel like eating breakfast but he went downstairs anyway. His wife didn't look at him or answer him when he bade her a hesitant good morning. Then a long silence ensued. The husband broke it. "I guess you've got a right to be sore at me this morning," he said sheepishly, "what with coming home so late and everything, and with a black eye to boot." His wife snorted. "I wondered," she said snortingly, "if you would remember how late you came home, and apparently you do, but what you don't seem to remember is that when you did finally get here, you didn't have a black eye."

And since I'm on the subject, why not have some:

BLACK-EYED PEAS AND SMOKED SALMON CREPES

2 eggs, beaten
$\frac{1}{2}$ cup flour
$\frac{1}{4}$ teaspoon pepper
milk or water
$\frac{1}{2}$ stick butter
1 cup onion, minced
$\frac{1}{4}$ pound lox (smoked salmon)
$\frac{1}{2}$ pound cream cheese, softened
1 can (10$\frac{1}{2}$ ounces) cream of mushroom soup
1 cup canned black-eyed peas, drained

Who ever heard of such a combination—black-eyed peas and lox? Nobody. Not until I thought of it, after that short essay up there, and you know what? Makes a fine combination, that's what.

Beat together the beaten eggs and flour, adding the pepper. Add to this mixture just enough milk or water to make a loose batter, about the consistency of light cream. In a fry pan—8 to 10 inches—melt half the butter and in it fry the minced onions over medium heat, until they are soft. Keep stirring the onion. Taste a piece of the lox. If it is very salty—varies greatly from time to time—soak it in milk for a couple of minutes, then dry it on paper towels. Chop up the lox and add it to the fry pan, with the onion, and stir until the lox loses its redness. Put the cream cheese into a bowl and combine it thoroughly with the onion-lox mixture.

Wipe the fry pan with a paper towel. There should be no trace of the onion or lox in the pan. But there should be a thin, almost imperceptible film of butter in it, so melt the remaining butter in the fry pan, pour the butter into a saucer, and blot the pan gently with a dry paper towel to pick up excess butter. Get the pan very hot. Quickly pour just enough batter into it to coat the bottom of the pan, pouring back any excess batter. Bubbles will form immediately on the top of the crepe, and when the sides draw away from the pan, turn the crepe with a spatula and brown the other side lightly. Continue until you have used all the batter. You should have at least 10 crepes. Rub the bottom of pan with butter-soaked paper towel after each 2 crepes, and keep the pan at the same temperature—just below smoking.

Put some of the onion-lox-cream cheese mixture at edge of each crepe, roll them up and tuck in ends. Butter or oil a baking dish and put the crepes into it. Combine the soup with black-eyed peas, spoon the mixture over crepes and bake in 350 degree oven for 20 to 25 minutes.

SERVES FOUR.

Fellow told me a story about the traveling salesman who was summoned to the auditor's office. The auditor handed his expense account to the salesman. "Is that your expense account?" the auditor asked. "Of course it's my expense account, it's got my name on it, hasn't it?" asked the salesman.

"Then maybe you can explain to me how you manage to spend $24 a day for food?" said the auditor. "That's easy, I skip breakfast," said the salesman.

Any day in the summer or winter, too, what is great is homemade:

LOX IN ASPIC (Hawaiian-Jewish)

2 pounds frozen salmon steak
lemon or lime juice
½ teaspoon salt
6 peppercorns
1 package (1 tablespoon) unflavored gelatine
two 8-ounce bottles clam juice or 2 cups condensed chicken
    broth

Don't buy "fresh" salmon. Buy the frozen, just as good, and only half the price. As soon as it begins to thaw, cut off the skin, throw it away. With a real sharp knife you'll be able to make paper-thin slices of the slowly thawing fish. Put the sliced fish in a large bowl. Add the juice of 2 large lemons or limes—about 8 tablespoons—or the same amount of bottled lemon or lime juice. Add salt and peppercorns. Stir to get all the fish slices coated with the juice and seasonings. Refrigerate overnight, stirring often.

Next day, soften the package of gelatine in the cold clam juice or chicken broth, then heat it in a pan until the gelatine is dissolved. Cool it, bubbeleh, cool it. Remove fish slices from the juice. Taste a piece. Cooked by George! Who *is* George? Anyway? It was "cooked" by the lemon or lime, not by George. Arrange the fish slices on a pretty platter. Put the platter in your fridge. Put the clam juice or broth in the fridge, also. Peek at it from time to time. As soon as it begins to jell, spread some over the fish, refrigerate, spread some more over the fish, leaving half of the jellied clam juice or broth to be cut up and scattered over the plate. Garnish with cherry tomatoes, scallions (green onions), red radishes, cucumbers or pickles, gherkins, whatever you like. Have dark bread and butter! Beer! Or sarsaparilla.

SERVES FOUR.

It was the coldest day of the winter. The young woman drove into the garage and blew her horn until one of the six men hard at work came over to her.

"What can I do for you? lady?" he asked. "I want you to install an air conditioner in my car," she said. "An air conditioner?" the man asked incredulously. "Yes, an air conditioner," she said.

The man shrugged. "Well, okay, but we're kind of rushed now with a whole lot of frozen radiators, can you come back next week?" he asked. "No, I've got to have it today," she said. "On the coldest day of the year, you're in a hurry to get an air conditioner?" he asked.

"Yes," she said, "last summer my rich uncle gave me money to buy an air conditioner for my car, but I spent it in riotous living and now he's coming to town tomorrow to visit me."

When your rich uncle comes to visit you give him some:

SMOKED SALMON CHEESY MASHED POTATOES (Jewish)

1 pound potatoes, peeled and cut in quarters
2 eggs, separated
$\frac{1}{4}$ cup hot milk
6 tablespoons butter
$\frac{1}{4}$ pound smoked salmon, or lox, chopped
$\frac{1}{2}$ cup grated Swiss cheese (or any other you like)
most likely no salt
$\frac{1}{8}$ teaspoon cayenne pepper

Boil the peeled and quartered potatoes in salted water to cover. With medium-sized potatoes quartered, it shouldn't take more than about 12 to 15 minutes to have the poatoes finished. Remove the potatoes with a slotted spoon to a dry pan and toss them over medium heat to dry them. Cook the 2 egg yolks in the potato water, simmering, for 3 minutes. Put the potatoes into a mixing bowl, add the yolks, and mash them together, adding hot milk and 2 tablespoons of butter. Beat and toss until the potatoes are quite fluffy. Add ¼ cup of the grated cheese, and the chopped lox and blend it thoroughly throughout the mixture. Beat the egg whites stiff and fold them in.

Lox is a much saltier version of smoked salmon than the so-called Nova Scotia salmon. If you use lox you won't need salt, but you may want to add some if you use the milder version.

Butter a baking dish and spoon the mixture into it, mounding it high. Sprinkle with the remaining cheese, dot with the remaining butter and dust the surface with the cayenne pepper. In oven preheated to 400 degrees, bake until the cheese is melted and is slightly browned, which should take about 10 minutes.

You can substitute almost anything for the lox, like chopped, smoked whitefish, chopped shrimp, chopped cooked ham or chicken, or any other meat. This is a marvelous dish in which to use leftovers, including cooked vegetables of any kind.

SERVES FOUR.

SHELLFISH

PART FIVE

Movie actress was applying for a passport and she was being asked questions about her life. "Are you," the passport clerk asked, "married?" The lady shrugged. "From time," she said, "to time."

A great party-time dish, delicious and festive, is:

SHRIMP THERMIDOR (France)

1½ to 2 pounds shrimp
2 tablespoons butter
2 tablespoons flour
one 8-ounce bottle of clam juice
¼ cup grated Parmesan cheese
¼ teaspooon each, pepper and dry mustard
1 cup heavy cream
2 tablespoons olive oil
1 clove (or more) garlic, pressed
taste for salt
¼ teaspoon paprika

Fresh, frozen, with, or without shells, all shrimp, I think, are best cooked in this fashion: Bring to the boil enough salted water, with a bay leaf in it and a little pepper, to cover the shrimp with about 2 inches of water over. Put the shrimp into the boiling water, cover the pot.

As soon as the water returns to the boil, drain it, holding the cover slightly askew with pot holders, and when all the water has been poured off, put the cover back on the pot and let the shrimp sit in the steam-filled pot.

In a saucepan, melt the butter over low heat, add the flour, and stir rapidly with a fork or whisk for about 2 minutes. Add the clam juice slowly, stirring all the while, until the mixture is smooth and somewhat thickened. Add the grated Parmesan cheese, and pepper, and mustard, and stir until cheese is dissolved. Add the cream, stir, cover the pot and remove from heat.

If your shrimp have been cooked with the shells, remove the shells and the narrow black vein, if any, along the top of the shrimp. Get the oil hot in a large fry pan, cook the pressed garlic for 1 minute, add the shrimp and stir them to get all the shrimp coated with the garlicky oil. This should take only 1 minute of cooking in the frying pan.

Put the saucepan containing the clam juice-cheese-cream mixture over medium heat, put in the shrimp, and cook, stirring for just enough time to get everything hotted up nicely. Sprinkle with paprika.

Since clam juice, which is salty, has been used for the sauce, taste the sauce for seasoning, and add salt if you think it is necessary.

I like Shrimp Thermidor served on a bed of plain cooked rice, with some minced parsley distributed throughout the rice. Some like it served on toast cut into triangles, some like it on toasted muffins. An accompaniment I like with this is chutney. Dill pickles are nice, too, especially the half-sour kind. And a mixed green salad.

SERVES FOUR TO SIX.

"Ladies and Gents of the Graduating Class," said the distinguished businessman to his commencement audience, just so there would be no misunderstanding about whom he was addressing himself to, "I have only two things to tell you as you Go Forth Into the World, and then I will sit down. First, I want to impress on your flabby, immature little minds that there is no such thing as a free drink on the house in any saloon, and the second thing is that you will never be hungry if you buy cheap and sell dear." And you know what? He really did sit right down.

Now, sit you down, friends and let us all have some:

SHRIMP CORN BAKE (Creole)

½ cup scallions (green onions) with firm greenery, chopped
½ stick butter or 4 tablespoons peanut oil
1 to 1½ pounds shrimp, thawed if frozen, shelled and veins removed if fresh, dried
one 8-ounce can creamed corn
½ teaspoon salt
¼ teaspoon pepper
1 cup chili sauce or catsup or ketchup
1 small green pepper, chopped

Fry the chopped scallions in 1 tablespoon of butter or oil until soft. Add the rest of the butter or oil and in it, over fairly high heat, fry the shrimp, stirring all the while, for about 2 minutes. Add the corn, salt, pepper, chili sauce and chopped pepper, combine thoroughly and bake in oven preheated to 350 degrees for 30 minutes. Taste and correct seasoning as necessary.

That was short and sweet, wasn't it?

If you don't like creamed corn, use whole kernel corn. There's hardly a time, these days, when fresh corn, from Florida, Texas, or wherever, is not available all year long. That's true, of course, with most vegetables, and fruit, too, except when there's a calamitous state of weather somewhere.

SERVES FOUR.

Man went to the dentist with a bad toothache. He sat down in the chair, and the dentist poked around and inspected the guilty tooth carefully. "I'm afraid," he said, "that there's nothing can be done to save it, it'll have to come out."

The man nodded. "I was afraid of that. Tell me, how long will it take you to extract it?" The dentist put his hand on the man's shoulder cheeringly, comfortingly.

"Not more than two minutes, and you won't feel a thing, old man," the dentist said.

"And how much will you charge me for it?" the aching man said.

"Ten dollars," said the dentist.

"Ten dollars?" the acher exclaimed. "Ten dollars for just two minutes' work?"

The dentist shrugged. "Well," he said, "if you like, I can pull it a whole lot slower."

What doesn't take too much time:

SHRIMP WITH SPAGHETTI AND STUFF (Italy)

1 tablespoon butter
1 cup chopped onion
one 1-pound can peeled tomatoes, well mashed
½ teaspoon salt
¼ teaspoon pepper
1 pound thin spaghetti (spaghettini or vermicelli)
1 pound shrimp, fresh or frozen
1 cup grated cheese (Parmesan, Romano, American, cheddar, whatever you like)

Put up 2 large pots of water to boil. In a large fry pan, get the butter hot and in it fry the onion, stirring over medium heat, until it is soft and starting to turn golden. Add the tomatoes, salt and pepper, stir, and cook over low heat. Taste for seasoning.

Put some salt into both pots of boiling water, and in one of them, 1 tablespoon of olive oil. Put the spaghetti into the pot with the oil, and put the shrimp, fresh—these should be shelled and deveined before cooking—or frozen, thawed into the other pot.

When the pot with the spaghetti returns to the boil, start timing. Within 6 minutes, if it is thin spaghetti, it will be *al dente*, or chewy; drain it immediately into a colander.

As soon as the pot with the shrimp returns to the boil, drain the water from the pot. Combine the shrimp with the sauce and in a large, deep platter, pour the sauce over the spaghetti, toss with large fork and spoon, sprinkle with cheese.

SERVES FOUR.

The boy and the girl had met at a party of a mutual friend, and both had come to it single. When it became rather late he asked if he could take her home, a very long subway ride, necessitating changing from one line to another, and then a bus which ran two blocks from her home, for she lived in the Bronx, the nothernmost borough of New York City, and the party was in Brooklyn.

"Are you sure," she asked, prettily batting her long eyelashes at the smitten young man, "that you want to take me all the way home?"

The boy nodded. "Sure, I'm sure," he said manfully, and all the way to her home—2½ hours time—they held hands and looked fondly at each other, and told each other all about themselves. When they came to her home, he kissed her gently, and whispered: "Will you meet me tomorrow evening at the information desk of the Waldorf Astoria, in Manhattan, which is roughly half way between your home and mine?"

The girl gasped. "The Waldorf Astoria? That's a pretty fancy place, isn't it?" The boy nodded. "Yes," he said, "it is a pretty fancy place, and furthermore it's on the same block as the hot dog stand I want to take you to."

I would like to take all you nice folk to my home to have some lovely:

BROILED GIGANTIC BUTTERFLY SHRIMP (Gulf Coast, U.S.A.)

24 (or more) huge shrimp
1 stick melted butter
2 cloves garlic, pressed or mashed about 1 tablespoon, or more
¼ cup minced parsley
¼ teaspoon dried oregano
¼ teaspoon each, salt and pepper
¼ cup fine bread crumbs

Cut a slit down the underside and then break off the shells. Remove the black vein if there is one. Put the stick of butter on a pan, put it into the broiler section of your oven about 3 inches from the source of heat. When the butter is melted, add all the other ingredients, stir them around in the broiler pan. Put the shrimp on the pan, turning them to get them coated all over. Broil for about 3 minutes, when they will be browned, turn the shrimp, spoon sauce in pan over all, broil for another 2 minutes on the second side. Bite into one of the shrimp. It should be cooked through.

SERVES FOUR.

It was in Dallas, Tex., where a blue-jeaned, 10-gallon-hatted young fellow named Wilfred Santa Anna drove his hot-rod across the busy intersection, beating the light by two seconds, narrowly missing a baby carriage being wheeled by a clearly enceinte lady, and scraping the fender of a taxicab—all within clear view of the cop, who blew his whistle and hailed Wilfred over to the curb.

As he walked toward Wilfred, who was grinning a shy, boyish, nervous grin, the cop pulled out a handkerchief. "You see this handkerchief?" he asked Wilfred. Wilfred nodded. "Yessir, Officer, I purely do surely see that there handkerchief," he said boyishly and nervously. The cop dropped the handkerchief to the pavement. "Okay, cowboy," said the law man, "now you make a U-turn, and on your way back let's see you pick it up in your teeth."

A toothsome dish is:

A CASSEROLE OF POACHED EGGS, SHRIMP AND CELERY SOUP (A. Godfrey's Studio)

1 pound shrimp, cooked (see Note)
2 cans condensed cream of celery soup
1 canful milk
¼ cup scallions (green onions) minced with greenery
1 cup cheese cubes (cheddar, American, what you like)
⅛ teaspoon cayenne
4 eggs
½ teaspoon paprika

Note: Makes no difference whether they are fresh or frozen shrimp, cook them the same way. Peel shells from fresh shrimp, cut out black veins; bring to the boil enough water to cover the shrimp, toss them in, and cover the pot. If you have frozen shrimp, put them in frozen. When the water returns to the boil, drain the water out immediately, holding the pot cover slightly askew, just enough to drain out the water, using two pot holders to protect your fingers. Cover the pot securely so the shrimp, all free from water, can sit in their own steam.

Pour the soup into a large flame-proof casserole or baking dish, or fry pan, stir in the milk, and cook over low heat, adding the scallions and cheese cubes. Stir in the cayenne. Taste the soup, and add salt if you think it is necessary—the soup is seasoned, you know—and perhaps another soupçon of cayenne. (A soupçon is ½ pinch.) If you've used a fry pan because you have no flame-proof casserole, pour everything into a casserole. Put the cooked shrimp into the casserole, break the 4 eggs, one at a time, into a saucer, and slide them into the soup. Sprinkle with paprika. Put the casserole in your broiler, about 2 inches from the source of the heat, until the whites of the eggs are cooked and the yolks still slightly quivery when you shake the casserole.

You can jazz this dish up in countless ways; add ¼ cup of sherry or applejack with the soup; you can use quartered, hard-boiled eggs instead of poaching them; minced clams are fine in it with the shrimp.

SERVES FOUR.

The tramp came across a roadside pub in England called "St. George and the Dragon," and he went around back to the kitchen and knocked on the door. A massive woman opened it and said, "What do you want?" The tramp took his shabby hat off his shabby head and said, "I wonder, Madam, if you could spare a bite to eat for a hungry man?"

The woman glared at him. "I should say not!" she hollered. "We sell food here, we don't give it away to no-good, lazy tramps!" and she slammed the door in his face.

A few minutes later she heard a timid knock on the door, opened it, and saw the same tramp. "What is it now?" she asked belligerently. "I wonder," said the tramp meekly, "if I might have a word, if he's not too busy, with George."

By George! If you like shrimp and clams, you are going to be crazy about, or, at least, not dislike:

GALLIMAUFRY OF SHRIMP AND CLAMS (Old English)

6 strips of bacon
1 cup of corn kernels cut off cobs (or whole canned)
¼ cup parsley, minced
1 cup onions, chopped
minced garlic cloves (at least 1 tablespoon)
1 cup sweet green or red pepper, chopped
1 cup potatoes, sliced very thin
10-ounce package (or 1 pound) frozen shrimp, thawed,
    drained, and dried (or fresh ones, shelled and deveined)
1 can (about 10 ounces) minced clams, or 1 dozen or more
    fresh ones, chopped
juice of ½ lemon (about 2 tablespoons)
2 tablespoons cornstarch
⅛ teaspoon (or more) cayenne pepper
maybe some salt

In a large, cold fry pan, arrange the bacon strips side by side. Cook over low heat. As fat is rendered, pour it off and save it. When the bacon strips are quite crisp remove them from pan and hold on to them. You will have at least ¼ cup of bacon fat. Put 2 tablespoons back into the fry pan, get it good and hot and add the corn kernels, parsley, onions, garlic, sweet pepper, and the potatoes, sliced very, very thin. Stir to coat everything with the fat, cover the pan, and cook for 10 minutes over very low heat, stirring occasionally. The onions, pepper, and potatoes will be soft and the onions and potatoes will be turning golden. That's just what we want.

Add 2 more tablespoons of bacon fat to the fry pan. (If you don't have that much, augment it with oil or butter.) Add the shrimp and the clams, saving the clam liquid for later, stir over high heat for about 5 minutes, when the shrimp and the clams will be cooked, and the onions and potatoes will be browned. Add lemon juice and stir.

Dissolve the cornstarch in the clam juice and add it to the pan, stirring and cooking until thickened. Add the cayenne pepper and taste.

If you would like it more peppery, add some more cayenne, you brave one, you, and add salt if you think it needs some.

What should you serve with this? Well, what I like with it is beer, or ale, chilled, about 40 to 45 degrees, but *not* icy cold. You want something icy cold, have sarsaparilla, but not beer, because icy cold destroys the flavor of beer. At the Biltmore, in New York, they have my favorite imported beer on tap, but it comes out icy cold. So, when I had a stein of it there once, I asked the bartender to give me a bowl of hot water in which to warm it up some, and he was delighted to oblige because he was an old-timey bartender and he agreed that it was sinful to have a good beer icy-cold. Earned me some stares, but *ish kabbible* (means: "I should worry!"). What does gallimaufry mean? It is a good English word, means "mishmash."

SERVES FOUR.

"Hey! Pa!" said the small boy, looking up from his book. "It says here that English is our mother tongue." His father nodded. "Why do they call it 'mother tongue'?" asked the small boy. "Haven't you noticed, son?" said his father, "who uses it most around this house?"

In my house, what we use often is this recipe for:

KIND OF A SHRIMP SOUFFLÉ (Swedish)

4 tablespoons peanut oil
1½ to 2 pounds shrimp, thawed and dried if frozen, cleaned and dried if "fresh"
1 cup onion, minced
2 tablespoons garlic cloves, minced (at least)
1 teaspoon dried dill weed
¼ cup fresh parsley, minced (or 1 tablespoon of dried flakes)
½ teaspoon salt
¼ teaspoon pepper
4 large eggs, separated, yolks beaten lemony, whites beaten stiff
½ cup any cheese you like, grated
2 cups mashed potatoes
about 1 tablespoon butter

Get 2 tablespoons of oil hot in a very hot large fry pan and in it fry the shrimp, over medium heat, shaking the pan, and turning shrimp with fork. Add some minced onion and garlic as you do, adding oil also as you go, and sprinkling with dill weed, parsley, salt and pepper. In about 8 to 10 minutes, depending on their size, the shrimp will be cooked through. Even though some shrimp in their raw state come pink when "fresh" or frozen, a lot of recipe-putters-down persist in saying "cook shrimp until they are pink." Don't overcook them, or they'll shrivel and get tough. Test-bite one after 8 minutes.

In a large bowl, beat the egg yolks and grated cheese—Swiss is good, and so are almost all other cheeses, including a smaller bit of strong ones like Roquefort or blue—into the mashed potatoes. (Once I used 2 tablespoons of Liederkranz in addition to Swiss, but I was the only one in our house who liked it, which was great, because then I had it all to myself.)

Combine the shrimp mixture with this mixture and then, gently, fold in the stiff egg whites with an over-and-under motion, either with your hands, or with a large kitchen spoon. (Hands are best.)

Oil a baking dish and spoon the mixture into it. Dot the top with butter and bake in oven preheated to 350 degrees for 20 to 25 minutes. In this time the mixture will have risen somewhat, and the top will be browned. All the work on this dish can be done beforehand, up to the point of baking. Isn't that nice?

SERVES FOUR TO SIX.

The four ladies were sitting at a sun-shaded table by the swimming pool at the Nitgedeiget Country Club, a plush, swank, exclusive establishment where membership was limited to rich tycoon types whose only problem was how to avoid paying more than $11 a year to the Internal Revenue. One of the elegant ladies asked a question. "What bugs me," she said elegantly, "is, how can I get my husband, Abednego, to tell me something about his affairs?"

The other ladies laughed raucously. Abednego's wife blushed furiously. "I mean his financial affairs!" she shouted furiously but quietly, "not the kind your husbands have."

The other ladies sneered. "Just tell him," one of them said sneeringly, "that you're embarrassed, because all your friends' wives are riding around in next year's model of yachts—85 feet and longer—and that you still have to pig it in last year's model. *Then* you'll hear about how tough the money situation is and all like that!"

How's about us all having something that's not good, just wonderful, like:

CHINESE STIR-FRY SHRIMP

¼ cup peanut or corn oil
½ cup scallions (green onions) with some firm greenery, minced
4-ounce can mushroom pieces, drained and dried
1½ pounds shrimp
¼ teaspoon pepper
2 tablespoons cornstarch
1 tablespoon soy sauce
8-ounce bottle clam juice
8 to 10 water chestnuts, sliced thin

Get a large fry pan hot and heat oil until you see a very faint whiff of steam. Lift pan from heat, immediately put in the minced scallions and mushroom pieces. Put pan back over high heat, stir vegetables rapidly and constantly for about 2 minutes, and the scallions will be cooked, but still crisp. Of course, if you can get fresh mushrooms and can afford them—fantastically expensive in hot weather—that's better. If shrimp are "fresh," wash, devein, and dry them: if frozen, thaw and dry them. Take vegetables out of pan with slotted spoon, keep in bowl. Add shrimp, sprinkle with pepper, cook over high heat, stirring constantly, for 5 minutes, when they will be cooked through—real large ones take longer, of course—but crisp. Taste one. DELIGHTFUL!

Remove shrimp to bowl. Dissolve cornstarch in soy sauce and cold clam juice. Bring to boil stirring over high heat, until it thickens. Put back into pan the cooked vegetables, shrimp, and sliced water chestnuts. Cook only until all ingredients are hotted up. Taste sauce. To increase saltiness use more soy sauce. On a bed of plain, boiled rice, this is great. On noodles, it's only wonderful.

SERVES FOUR.

The young husband nudged his young wife, who had been sleeping soundly. "What's the matter?" she asked sleepily. "Why are you nudging me awake from my sound sleep?" Her husband groaned. "Because," he said groaningly, "it's time to get up."

She looked out the window and saw that it was pitch dark. "Are you crazy or something?" she asked sweetly. "Can't you see that it's still pitch dark outside?"

Her husband groaned again. "Yes, I know it's pitch dark outside, but it's got to be time to get up and get ready to go to work because Baby just stopped crying," he said unhappily.

Happy is the man who comes home from work to have for dinner:

FRIED SHRIMP CAKES (Creole)

1½ to 2 pounds shrimp, cooked
½ teaspoon salt
¼ teaspoon pepper
¼ cup scallions with firm greenery, minced
2 eggs, beaten
flour
bread crumbs
2 tablespoons each, oil and butter
2 tablespoons garlic, minced
¼ cup parsley, minced or 2 tablespoons dried flakes

Cook the shrimp by putting them into a pot with enough water to cover them. Bring the water to the boil before putting the shrimp in, cover, and just as soon as the water returns to the boil, drain the shrimp. Mince the shrimp as fine as possible. Add salt and pepper and minced scallions and 1 beaten egg. Add enough flour to make a mixture that will hold together. Moisten your hands and form the mixture into eight cakes of equal size—you want to call them "patties," you go right ahead, folk, but don't expect me to call them that—and dip each one first into the remaining beaten egg, and then in bread crumbs.

In a large fry pan, get the butter and oil hot. Put the minced garlic and parsley into the hot fat and fry the shrimp cakes, pressing garlic and parsley into each one with a spatula as they fry. When they are well-browned on each side, remove them, drain on paper towels, and serve 2 shrimp cakes to each of four people.

You want to try something nice with this? Mix 4 tablespoons of strong horseradish into 8 tablespoons of mayonnaise and you have a wonderful sauce. You want to chop up some gherkins or sour pickles into the sauce? Sure, that's great, too. If I don't have French-fried potatoes with this I get unhappy.

SERVES FOUR.

Fellow had just inherited a house from his father-in-law, so he went to the bank and borrowed $20,000, putting up the house as collateral. With that money he went out and bought a foreign sports car, paying for it all the money he had obtained from the bank. Then he went back to the bank and tried to borrow another $20,000, explaining that he wanted to buy a boat, and offered his expensive sports car as collateral for that loan.

The banker looked at him in astonishment. "With two loans like that, on your salary," he said dubiously, "how are you going to buy gas for the car and the boat?"

The fellow became angry. "Listen," he cried out indignantly, "a fellow who owns a house, a car and a boat ought to be able to get credit for gas!"

Your credit as a cook will rise with:

CHOPPED MUSHROOMY SHRIMP ON TOAST (U.S.A.)

1 pound shrimp, fresh or frozen
1 bay leaf
6 peppercorns
one 10½-ounce can condensed cream of mushroom soup
½ soup can milk
1 tablespoon chives (or dill or onion), minced
salt (maybe)
4 slices toast

If you get fresh shrimp, fine; remove the shells and the black veins. Frozen shrimp come that way—you don't have to thaw them either. Bring to the boil enough water to cover shrimp. Tie the bay leaf and peppercorns into a little cheesecloth bag and put this and the shrimp into the boiling water and cook them until the water returns to boil. Throw the bag away and drain the shrimp well. Combine the soup with the milk, add the chives (or dill or onion), simmer it, taste it, and if you think it needs salt, why, add some. The soup, you know, is pretty well seasoned.

Chop up the cooked shrimp into pieces that are not too small, add them to the soup mixture, stir it around for a couple of minutes over low heat, put a piece of toast into each of 4 soup plates, and distribute the mushroomy shrimp over the toast. This is good, too, on plain boiled rice.

SERVES FOUR.

Fellow out hunting got lost in the words, and for four days and four nights he stumbled around, trying to find his way back to camp. At last, he gave up all hope and sat down, leaning against a tree. Suddenly he heard thrashing in the underbrush and a man carrying a rifle came into sight. Our fellow jumped up, ran over to the man with the gun, threw his arms around his neck and broke into loud sobs. "You don't know how happy you've made me. For four days and four nights I've been lost, just wandering around in circles," he said. The other fellow shoved him away. "Listen, stupid," he said, "don't be so excited, I've been lost for more than a week."

A dish that will create excitement is:

SHRIMP IN CLAM-TOMATO SAUCE

2 tablespoons butter or oil
1 cup onions, minced
1 tablespoon (or more) garlic, minced
$\frac{1}{2}$ cup sweet green or red pepper, minced
$\frac{1}{4}$ cup parsley, minced
1 large bay leaf, crumbled fine, or $\frac{1}{4}$ teaspoon powdered
$\frac{1}{2}$ teaspoon dried dill weed
8-ounce bottle clam juice
1 can (about 10 ounces) red clam sauce
$1\frac{1}{2}$ to 2 pounds shrimp (thawed if frozen)
salt and pepper to taste

In a saucepan melt the butter or get the oil hot, and in it cook the minced onions, garlic, sweet pepper, parsley, bay leaf, and dill until the onion is soft.

Pour in the clam juice and clam sauce, stir, and bring to the boil. You should be able to get the red clam sauce in any supermarket, but if, by any chance they don't have it in stock, use 1 can of minced clams, drained, plus 1 can (about 10 ounces) of tomato sauce.

Bring to the boil, add the shrimp, stir, and cook covered until the liquid comes to the boil. Let it boil for 1 minute, stirring. The shrimp should be cooked through, but quite firm and chewy. Generally I put the shrimp into boiling water to cover and drain it just as soon as the water returns to the boil, and then let the shrimp sit in the pot, covered, in which they were cooked, while I make the sauce that we will use with the shrimp. The steam in the pot, when the shrimps are cooked in water, cooks the shrimps a little more. But this is going to be served right away, so let the shrimp remain in the boiling sauce for one extra minute. Just before serving this on a bed of rice or noodles, taste the sauce to see if you think it should have salt or pepper— both of which are in the clam sauce and juice—to suit your taste.

One of the nice things about this festive dish is that all the work, up to the point when the shrimps are added to the sauce, can be done beforehand.

SERVES FOUR TO SIX.

The man came home from work and in the living room he found the young fellow who had been dating his daughter for almost a year. The young fellow looked worried, angry, and miserable. "Why?" asked the man, "are you looking so worried, angry, and miserable?"

The young fellow shook his head sadly. "Because your daughter got me to agree that we'd get married on the Fourth of July, and now she's upstairs calling all her friends to tell them about it." The girl's father snorted derisively. "Well," the girl's father said derisively, "you've got no one to blame but yourself, hanging around here like you did."

Everyone will hang around the kitchen impatiently waiting for:

FRIED SHRIMP AND FISH BALLS (China)

½ cup minced scallions (green onions), with greenery that's firm
clove garlic, approximately 1 tablespoon, pressed
4 water chestnuts, minced
1 pound raw shrimp, minced fine, and 1 pound raw fish fillets
     minced fine
2 eggs, beaten
¼ cup flour
¼ teaspoon ginger
1 tablespoon soy sauce
½ teaspoon pepper
fine bread crumbs
peanut oil for frying

When I say "minced" here, that's what I mean, minced real fine. If you have a grinder, put all those minced ingredients through the grinder twice. Most people, however, don't have a grinder and that's a shame, because you can get a hand-powered one in almost any hardware or houseware store or department for just a few dollars. You can also use a blender to grind all this up fine, but we know that thousands, maybe millions, of blenders have been used perhaps once or twice and then stashed away never again to be used because they are so pesky to use and clean, on account of the bottoms, where the blades are, are so narrow.

Anyway, mince or mash everything as fine as you can. Combine everything, except the bread crumbs and the peanut oil, in a mixing bowl. Wet your hands and form the mixture into balls of whatever size you prefer. Put enough oil into a pot to cover the balls, with about ¼ inch over. Heat the oil to just below the smoking point, roll the balls in bread crumbs, and fry them, not all at once, until they pop to the surface, and then for an additional 2 or 3 minutes, turning them gently with a long-handled slotted spoon. Take them out with slotted spoon and keep hot on a large platter set over extremely hot water, and cover the shrimpfish balls with an inverted bowl as you fry the rest of them. Plain boiled rice, chutney, and salted peanuts are wonderful with these marvelous concoctions.

SERVES FOUR.

Young fellow was looking very glum. "Why are you looking so glum?" his friend asked. "Last night," the young fellow said, "I had a date to take my girl out, and when I rang the bell, her father opened the door, and no sooner did I get inside when he began asking me how much I made a week, and what were my chances for advancement." His friend shrugged. "Well, what's wrong with that? You told me you wanted to marry her, didn't you?" his friend asked. "Yes, that's right," the young fellow said, "but what's wrong is that my girl heard her father ask me those questions, and she hollered from her room, 'No, Daddy, that's not the one I want.'"

What I want to talk about here is a seafood dish called:

FRUITS OF THE SEA (France)

1 pound shrimp, fresh or frozen
$\frac{1}{2}$ pound crabmeat, flaked
8-ounce can minced clams
4 tablespoons each, oil and butter
$\frac{1}{4}$ cup minced onion
$\frac{1}{2}$ teaspoon dried dill weed or seed
2 tablespoons flour
8-ounce bottle clam juice or milk or light cream
salt and pepper
$\frac{1}{2}$ teaspoon paprika
4 slices toast, each cut into 2 triangles

If your shrimp are fresh, shell them and remove the black vein. If they are frozen, thaw and dry them thoroughly. Chop up the shrimp, but don't mince them too fine. Frozen crabmeat, which I think is fantastically good, is also fantastically expensive —about $4.50 a pound last time I looked—so get the canned variety which is excellent and a whole lot cheaper. Save the liquid in the crabmeat can, and combine it with the clam juice from the can of minced clams.

In a large, deep frying pan, get 2 tablespoons each of oil and butter hot, and, over fairly high heat, cook the chopped shrimp, stirring constantly, for about 5 minutes, when the shrimp will be cooked through, but still crisp. About halfway in the cooking of the shrimp, add the minced onion and dill weed to the pan. When the shrimp have cooked for 5 minutes, add the remaining oil and butter, sprinkle with flour, and stir for 2 minutes. The liquid from the crabmeat and from the clams will not come to a cupful, so add either clam juice, or milk or light cream to make a cupful of liquid. Stir the combined liquid into the pan and keep stirring until it begins to thicken. Add the flaked crabmeat and minced clams. Taste the sauce and add salt and pepper to suit your taste. Add the paprika. Cook for just 2 minutes, to get everything hot.

Put 2 toast triangles on each of 4 plates, spoon the seafood and sauce over the toast, and serve.

SERVES FOUR.

Boyfriend was waiting in the front room with the father of his girlfriend. The father wasn't too crazy about the boyfriend. Indeed, it would be more accurate to say that he despised his daughter's boyfriend, a sentiment that the boyfriend returned in spades.

Finally the girlfriend came downstairs. She was greeted by a resounding silence. She pirouetted coquettishly. "How do you like my new dress?" she asked her boyfriend and her father. The boyfriend blushed.

"Well, I find it kind of puzzling," said her papa. "What do you mean 'puzzling,' papa?" she asked.

"It's puzzling," said her papa, "because I can't figure out whether you're trying to get out of that dress, or trying to get into it."

I'd like to talk you into making:

SCALLOPS A LA PEKING HOUSE
(China, via Second Avenue, NYC)

4 tablespoons peanut or soybean oil
2 scallions (green onions) minced with some of the firm greenery
1½ pounds scallops, sea or bay
1 cup clam juice or 1 chicken bouillon cube dissolved in 1 cup
    boiling water
½ teaspoon salt
¼ teaspoon pepper or a couple of dashes of Tabasco
½ teaspoon powdered ginger
⅓ cup water chestnuts, sliced in half horizontally
1 tablespoon cornstarch
¼ cup dry white wine

In a large fry pan, get the peanut or soy bean oil hot until it just begins to smoke, then lift it quickly from the heat when you see the first faint whiff of smoke. Drop into the pan the minced scallions, return pan to heat and cook, stirring constantly until the scallions are soft and just beginning to change color.

There is, as you know, quite a difference between sea scallops and bay scallops. The latter are smaller, and they are more delicate than the large bay scallops. Both come fresh or frozen. If frozen, they should be thawed before cooking in this manner. And if they are sea scallops, they should be cut in half, horizontally.

Cook the scallops, stirring, for 1 minute. Add the clam juice or chicken broth, stir, and add salt and pepper—or Tabasco—and taste. Correct the seasoning, if necessary, and stir in the powdered ginger.

Add the sliced water chestnuts (you can get these, in cans, in every supermarket) and stir. Dissolve the cornstarch in the wine, add it to the pan, and cook over high heat, stirring, until the liquid comes to the boil and becomes somewhat thickened. Serve this on a bed of boiled rice.

I call this recipe Scallops a la Peking House, because I learned how to cook it in this manner at the famous Chinese restaurant by that name on Second Avenue in Manhattan.

SERVES FOUR.

Everyone at the wedding reception agreed that they were a wonderful couple, and everyone seemed to be having a wonderful time, drinking champagne and eating all sorts of goodies, except one young fellow who stood out from the crowd because he looked so depressed. The brand-new husband, a good-natured young slob, walked over to the fellow, whom he didn't know.

"What's the matter, fellow?" he said. "Aren't you enjoying yourself?"

The fellow gave him a look of hatred. "No," he said.

"Well, cheer up, cheer up," said the happy bridegroom. "I know how to cheer you up. Have you kissed the bride?" The fellow looked at him venomously. "No," he snarled, "not lately."

How long is it since you made:

MUSHROOM-BAKED SCALLOPS (New England)

½ cup butter (1 stick)
½ pound mushrooms
2 tablespoons flour
1 cup milk
1 small onion, minced
¼ teaspoon dry mustard
salt and pepper
1½ pounds scallops (bay or sea), cooked
½ cup cheese, grated (Parmesan, Romano, Swiss, any kind of
        cheese you like)

Slice mushrooms and fry them in the butter. Remove the mushrooms from pan when they are soft. Add flour to pan, stirring, and then slowly add the milk, stirring until the sauce is thickened. Add all the other ingredients except the cheese, and stir over low heat for about 2 minutes. Pour it all into a casserole or baking dish and top with the grated cheese. Preheat your oven to 350 degrees and bake for about 15 minutes until the cheese is browned. Serve this on toast, with a green salad. If you are using small bay scallops, leave them whole; if they are sea scallops, which are larger, cut them in half. (Scallops, you know, are mollusks, with a pretty, wavy shell, and they come frozen—as well as fresh, of course—and if your supermarket doesn't carry them, tell the man you want them, see? He can get them if you are insistent enough.)

By the way, I've been using frozen and canned steamer clams which come from Chesapeake Bay, and they are just great. They don't need scrubbing, and they are freer of sand than any steamers I've ever eaten. If you like steamer clams one-tenth as much as we do, talk to the man in the supermarket about these and maybe you can get him to carry them, also.

SERVES FIVE OR SIX.

A man coerced his 14-year-old son to go to the birthday party of a daughter—the same age—of another friend, by threatening to cut off not only his allowance, but also to cut him out of his will. When the lad came home, sulky, of course, his poppa—in our set any kid that called his father "daddy" was considered to be a weirdo—asked him how the party was. "Lousy," said the boy.

"How were the refreshments?" asked poppa. "Lousy," said the boy. "Did you play any games?" the poppa asked. "Nah," said the boy, "the girls did, but not us." "Was there any dancing?" the poppa asked. "Yeah," said the boy. "Did you dance?" the poppa asked. The son looked at his poppa as though his old man was demented. "Nah," said the boy. "What else happened?" the poppa asked.

"Well, the birthday girl sang songs," the boy replied. "What kind of songs?" asked the poppa. "Were they classical?" The boy said, "Nah." So the poppa said, "Well, then they must have been popular songs." The boy shrugged. "Well," he said, "they were popular, but not any more, not after she sang them."

One of the many things that are popular in our house is:

CLAM PIE (Italian)

9 or 10-inch pie crust, unbaked
1 can (about 10 ounces) white or red clam sauce
4 eggs, beaten viciously
1 8-ounce bottle of clam juice
½ cup grated cheese
½ teaspoon salt
¼ teaspoon hot red pepper flakes

Bake the crust for 10 minutes in oven preheated to 350 degrees. Combine ingredients.

Pour the mixture into the pie shell.

Bake until the crust is browned and the filling is thickened but still quivers some when the pie is shaken.

SERVES FOUR.

It was the fourth day of a heat spell during which the temperature remained in the 90's, and people who had to be abroad in the streets kept passing out from the heat all over town. One of these was a lady who fainted right outside a bar. She was brought inside and several kindly people took turns in trying to revive her.

They bathed her brow with cold water, but it didn't help. One of the waitresses loosened her clothing, and that didn't do any good, either. They tried to give her a drink of cold water, but that didn't work. One of the bartenders said he knew the lady. "I'd bring her to right away with a drink of brandy," he said, "but I can't give her brandy because she's the head of the Temperance Society."

Just then the lady opened her eyes and sat up. "No," she said weakly, "I'm not the head of the Temperance Society; I'm president of the Society for the Suppression of Vice."

The bartender shrugged. "Well," he said, "I knew there was something I couldn't give you."

Here's something you can give your family:

POACHED OYSTERS IN LEMON SAUCE (French)

24 oysters
2 tablespoons butter
2 tablespoons flour
1 cup oyster liquid (if necessary, augment with clam juice)
$\frac{1}{4}$ cup heavy cream
salt and pepper
2 tablespoons lemon juice
1 egg yolk
$\frac{1}{4}$ cup dry white wine
paprika

If you can't get fresh oysters—which your fishmonger will open for you, saving the liquid—your supermarket has them shucked, in the fish section, or in cans. Melt the butter and blend in the flour, stirring. Add the oyster liquid to the pan, stir over low heat until it is slightly thickened, then add the oysters and poach them just until the edges begin to curl. Remove oysters from the pan and keep them warm.

Add the cream and then season with salt and pepper according to taste, and stir in the lemon juice, and remove the pan from heat. Beat the egg yolk into the wine and add it to the sauce slowly, stirring rapidly.

Serve this dish on toast, putting oysters on the toast, dousing with sauce, and then sprinkle each serving with a little paprika.

Now how am I going to tell you how many people this will serve? If you are as mad about oysters as I am, a dozen isn't too much, not at all too much. If there are going to be other courses in the meal, maybe 2 or 3 oysters will satisfy most people. But if the other courses are light, maybe 6 oysters per person will be enough. Look, for all I know, maybe you don't even like oysters.

SERVES FOUR AS A MAIN COURSE.

Scene: a car on a country road. Characters: a boy and a girl.
She: "Why don't you use two hands?"
He: "Be patient, honey, wait'll I find a place to park."
In springtime you can find:

SOFT-SHELLED CRABS (U.S.A.)

8 soft-shelled crabs
2 eggs
4 tablespoons clam juice (or milk)
½ teaspoon salt
⅛ (at least) teaspoon pepper
⅛ (at least) teaspoon cayenne
flour
bread crumbs
½ stick butter
¼ cup oil (preferably olive)
minced garlic (let taste or your conscience be your guide)
4 slices white toast, cut into 8 triangles
parsley (minced), olives, gherkins, red radishes, cherry tomatoes
tartar sauce

If you happen to have a crabby fishmonger, it's easy to prepare the crabs yourself. Stab the crabs between the eyes with a
sharp knife. Lift up the soft points of the shell and remove the
spongy gills, turn the crab on its back, and cut off the pointy,
hard piece at the end of the shell.

Beat together the eggs and clam juice (or milk) with the
salt, pepper, and cayenne. Dry the crabs on paper toweling. Dust
each one with flour. Dip them into the egg mixture, then coat
them with bread crumbs. If there is any of the egg mixture remaining, repeat this process until you've used it all up, and
coated crabs well with bread crumbs. Put them on a large platter, cover with wax paper, and refrigerate for at least one hour.

In a large pan, hot up the butter and oil. Press some of the minced garlic into each crab, fry them, without crowding the pan, until they are well browned all over. Keep finished crabs hot by putting them on a large platter set over a pot of very hot water, cover finished crabs with a large bowl, or with foil.

Put 2 triangles of toast on each of 4 hot dinner plates, put a fried crab on each piece of toast, pour butter sauce over all, garnish with parsley, gherkins, etc., and serve with tartar sauce. You can make your own tartar sauce by combining mayonnaise with horseradish and minced sweet pickles or gherkins. Fried soft-shelled crabs are wonderful, cold or hot. And you know, of course, that all of the crab is edible, shell and all. Joy to the world.

SERVES FOUR.

Spinster Lady: "Oh, how I dream of the joys, and contentment of married life!"

Married Lady: "That's a strange coincidence, dearie, because I have the same dreams as you!"

Have you ever dreamt of making:

MARYLAND CRAB CAKES

1 pound crabmeat, drained and flaked
2 eggs, beaten separately
$\frac{1}{4}$ teaspoon salt
dash of pepper
1 tablespoon Worcestershire sauce
1 teaspoon dry mustard
$\frac{1}{4}$ cup onion, minced
4 tablespoons butter
1 tablespoon parsley, chopped
bread crumbs
lemon wedges, parsley sprigs

Mix together the flaked crabmeat, 1 beaten egg, salt, pepper, Worcestershire, mustard, onion and 1 tablespoon of the butter, melted. Sprinkle with the chopped parsley, and form it into a ball and refrigerate it for an hour or two. Form the mixture into flat cakes, dip into remaining egg, coat them with bread crumbs and brown them well on both sides in the remaining 3 tablespoons of butter.

Serve, garnished with lemon wedges and parsley sprigs. Make the cakes small if you want them to be appetizers, large if they're to be the main course. But in either case, make them pretty flat and fry them thoroughly, over low heat.

I've had cakes like this made with half crabmeat, half minced clams and they are great. You can use canned minced clams, but be sure to drain and dry them thoroughly.

SERVES FOUR OR FIVE AS MAIN DISH.

The man noticed that his wife seemed terribly preoccupied about something, but he decided that it might be wiser not to appear to notice it. Finally, she broke the silence. "Tell me, Max," she said, "when did you last wear that lightweight blue suit I sent out to be cleaned and pressed?" The husband pondered this question for a while. "I haven't worn that suit," he said, "since last August." This didn't seem to make his wife any happier. So he said, "Why are you worrying about when I last wore that suit?" His wife burst into tears. "I found a blonde hair on your coat," she said, sobbing bitterly, "and now I can't remember whether it was last July or last August that I was a blonde."

When did you last have:

1 cup crabmeat, fresh cooked or frozen or canned (frozen and
    canned are already cooked)
½ stick butter
4 tablespoons flour
¾ cup milk
¼ cup dry white wine
¼ teaspoon salt
⅛ teaspoon cayenne pepper
⅛ teaspoon curry powder
1 teaspoon Worcestershire sauce
3 eggs, separated
½ cup grated cheese (parmesan, swiss, any kind you like)

Flake the crabmeat. Chop it fine. (If it is canned crabmeat,
of course you'll drain it first; if it is frozen, you'll thaw it and
then drain it.) Dry the crabmeat. Now melt the butter and stir in
the flour, stirring for 2 minutes until it is smooth, and golden.
Add the milk and then the wine, stirring, stirring, stirring, over
low heat. Add the salt, cayenne, curry powder, and Worcestershire sauce, and stir some more, and remove it from heat. Let it
cool a bit and while it cools, stir, but don't beat the egg yolks,
but do beat the egg whites until they are stiff. (Lay off the wine,
or you may get likewise.)

When the mixture is somewhat cooled, stir in the egg yolks
and then the crabmeat and grated cheese. When everything is
thoroughly combined, fold in the stiff egg whites. Butter a casserole, put it all into the casserole, and bake it in a 350 degree
oven until it is firm, which will take maybe 25 to 30 minutes.
And of course, you can substitute chopped shrimp or lobster,
cooked, for the crabmeat. This is nice with hot garlic bread,
French fried onion rings, a salad, oh, anything you like.

SERVES THREE OR FOUR.

I have a friend who collects useless facts. He sent me the following, and I pass it on to you: Human fingernails grow an average of one thirty-second of an inch a week, or about one and one-half inches a year. When a human is sick, the growth of the nails is lessened. Nails grow faster in the summer than they do in the winter. The nail that grows fastest is the one on the middle finger; the slowest growing nail is on the thumb. A human who reaches the age of seventy without ever clipping his nails would have fingernails 77 feet, 6 inches long.

When I asked my friend where he got this stuff he just smiled a stupid kind of Mona Lisa-ish smile. Speaking of Mona Lisa, you know, of course, about all the speculation there always has been over whether she was actually smiling, and what was she thinking to make her smile like that. I have a theory which is at least as good as any I ever have heard. If you know a lady who is going to have a baby, sneak a look at her when she's not aware that anyone is looking at her, and I would bet you dollars against doughnuts that she will have the same kind of expression as Mona Lisa, if it were not for the fact that I already have two whole rooms full of doughnuts already won on bets.

How would you like to make some:

BAKED CURRIED CRABMEAT (Kind of Indian)

1 pound (approximately) cooked crabmeat
one stick butter
4 tablespoons flour
1 tablespoon curry powder (use *cautiously*)
½ teaspoon salt
¼ teaspoon pepper
2 cups milk or half-and-half
¼ cup bread crumbs
¼ cup grated cheese

Crabmeat is obtainable in cans of 6 to 7 ounces and it comes frozen. Both are already cooked. Flake the meat and pick it over very carefully eliminating all cartilage.

In a saucepan, hot up 6 tablespoons of the butter, add flour slowly, stirring constantly, and then about 1 tablespoon of the curry. Cook for about 2 minutes, stirring constantly, sprinkling with salt and pepper, and then slowly add the milk or half-and-half, and cook until the sauce is smooth and thickened. Taste it. Curry powder is an unpredictable ingredient; if you have had it for a long time, it will have lost some of its strength, and then, too, curry powders of the various brands differ in strength. All I can say is that you should taste the sauce, and add more than 1 tablespoon if you think it isn't quite hot enough. Remember, however, that you should rely more strongly on the aftertaste rather than your first impression. So add it cautiously.

Add the flaked crabmeat to the sauce. Spoon it all into a buttered baking dish, sprinkle with bread crumbs and grated cheese, dot with remaining butter and bake in oven preheated to 375 degrees until the top is browned. Excellent with rice or pasta.

SERVES FOUR.

Little boy was having dinner at the home of a friend and his friend's mother was delighted with the kid, for not only did he eat well, but he also complimented her on her cooking, and thanked her for everything she served him.

There was a beautiful, rich, chocolate layer cake for dessert. When the lad finished his piece of cake, he asked, "Please, may I have another piece of that beautiful, rich chocolate layer cake?"

His hostess regarded him dubiously. "Do you think you should have another piece?" she asked. "What would your mother say?"

The sturdy little fellow laughed. "My mother?" he said. "Why should she care, it isn't her cake."

Here is something everybody will care about:

CRABMEAT WITH A CHEDDAR CHEESE SAUCE (New England)

1 pound cooked crabmeat
1 can condensed cheddar cheese soup (11 ounces)
1 can beer (or water?)
1 tablespoon Worcestershire sauce
$\frac{1}{2}$ teaspoon hot crushed red pepper flakes
$\frac{1}{2}$ cup fine unseasoned bread crumbs

What I do with crabmeat is put it into a cloth kitchen towel and squeeze out all the water I can. Then flake it and toss away any bits of shell or cartilage or whatever it is that even the so-called "fancy" crabmeat occasionally has.

Combine, in a pan, the condensed cheddar cheese soup, the beer, Worcestershire and the hot red pepper flakes. Bring it to the boil and cook it, covered and just barely simmering, for 5 minutes.

Add the bread crumbs and crabmeat, and cook, simmering, for about 2 minutes. Taste it, and if you think it needs more salt, which I don't think you will, add a little more Worcestershire. This is a lovely dish for people who haven't got heartburn.

SERVES FOUR.

This politician was scurrying around the city, grabbing and shaking every hand in sight and clutching and kissing every baby who didn't flee quickly enough. He stopped dead in his tracks when he saw two small boys, both the same size, dressed in exactly the same clothes, one the image of the other. "Well, well, as I live and breathe," he said wittily, "twin brothers!" The two small boys looked at him repugnantly. "No," said one, "we are not twins!" The politician was rattled. "But you're the same size, and you look alike," he said, "and you must be brothers. How old are you?" One of the boys said he was five years old. "I'm five, too," said the other boy. "Well, if you're both five, and you're brothers, then you must be twins!" cried the politician.

The two boys sneered. "No, we're not twins!" one of them shouted. "Our brother is in the house! We're triplets!"

I always wish I was triplets, so I could have three times as much to eat when I have:

BROILED LOBSTERS (OR LOBSTER TAILS) (New England)

four 1¼-pound lobsters, or lobster tails (tell you how many
    lobster tails a little later on)
butter
lemon juice
salt and pepper

If you can get live lobsters, that's great! They are more delicate, of course, than the so-called lobster tails (which don't come from lobsters at all, of course, but are parts of crayfish), but lobster tails are better than no lobster at all. When I use lobster tails, I like the small ones, which are about the size of jumbo shrimp and come frozen from Iceland or Thailand, or Denmark. They are much sweeter and more delicate, I think, than the large frozen lobster tails. For each person there should be 2 large lobster tails—each about 8 ounces—or ½ to ¾ pound of the small lobster tails. (Shells make up the weight differences.)

If you're using frozen lobster tails, thaw them overnight in the refrigerator and then rinse and drain them well and dry them before broiling.

If you're using live lobsters, your fishmonger will slay and clean them for you. But if you want to do this yourself, do it like this: cross the claws and hold them securely. With a small, sharp knife, stab the lobster between the tail and the body; this puts the quietus on the beast immediately. Split the lobster open from the head to the tail, through the shell. Remove the spongy sac behind the head, and the dark vein that runs from the head to the tail. Leave the liver (green) and if it has coral (roe) you are lucky, because these two items are great delicacies. Crack the large claws.

Brush the meat of the lobster or tails with melted butter, sprinkle with a few drops of lemon juice, and dust with a little salt and pepper. Broil the lobster for 8 minutes, meat side 4 inches from source of heat. Turn the lobster, broil shell side toward source of heat for an additional 8 minutes. Large lobster tails are broiled for the same time; broil the small ones 6 minutes on each side. Best way of broiling lobster or tails over charcoal is in a large basket grill.

For each serving, have at least 2 tablespoons of hot melted butter into which a few drops of lemon juice has been stirred. I don't know anything better to have with lobster than lots of crisp French fried potatoes. And a green salad.

SERVES FOUR.

They had been to a party where the wife had worn a new dress, which had caused all the women there to be envious and all of the men had admired her extravagantly. And now they were driving home and she sat in the car with a happy, dreamy smile and she was humming softly. But her husband was glum.

"Do you know," he said, after a long silence, "that you danced with every man at the party all night long, but you didn't dance with me even once?" His wife smiled happily. "Yes, I know that, dear," she said. "It seems to me," her husband said, "that whenever there are other men around you seem to forget that you're married to me."

His wife laughed. "Oh no, dear," she said, "you're absolutely wrong; whenever there are other men around nothing makes me so aware that I'm married to you."

Are you aware of the fact that a lobster of 1½ pounds has only 150 calories? and that a dozen medium-sized shrimp have about 50 calories? and that ½ cup of cooked pasta has only about 60 calories? So even if you are a weight-watcher, you can have a delicious:

CURRIED LOBSTER (OR SHRIMP)
SPAGHETTI CASSEROLE (India)

3 tablespoons butter
3 medium-sized onions, chopped
¼ pound mushrooms, sliced
1 tablespoon (or more) curry powder
salt
1 pound thin spaghetti (spaghettini)
1 pound lobster meat, or shrimp or 1 pound lobster tails
1 bouillon cube plus 1 cup boiling water (or 1 cup hot milk)

Hot up the butter and fry the chopped onions and mushrooms until they are soft. Stir in the curry powder, taste the sauce and if you want it hotter, add more curry powder, and some salt. Cook the spaghetti in boiling salted water for not more than 6 minutes if the spaghetti is thin. (Start the timing when the water returns to boiling point after you have added the spaghetti to the boiling salted water.) This much cooking will make the spaghetti tender but chewable; if you like spaghetti softer, I think that's a shame.

In a dish like this, I think that using a lobster is an extravagance because lobster is so expensive I think it should be eaten whole, broiled, preferably, or maybe boiled, with some dill. Shrimp and lobster tails are wonderful, but less expensive.

If you are using shrimp or lobster tails, boil them, dropping them into boiling salted water, draining immediately when the water returns to the boiling point. Cut lobster meat or tails or large shrimp into 1-inch pieces.

Oil a baking dish lightly, pour in all the ingredients, including the bouillon or hot milk, cover, and in oven preheated to 350 degrees bake it for 30 minutes. I asked a scientific friend who is extremely conscious of calories (which I am not, have you noticed?) and she said that this would provide about 250 calories.

SERVES FOUR.

BEEF

PART SIX

The panhandler asked for a dime for a cup of coffee and the man he solicited stopped on the sidewalk and looked the bum over—an obvious rumdum. "Coffee?" the man said. "What a laugh that is! If I give you anything, you'll spend it on booze, won't you? Why, you're half-loaded right now!"

The panhandler smiled sheepishly. "Well, yeah, that's right, Mac, that's why I panhandle, to get money for booze." The man glared at him. "Why don't you quit drinking?" he asked.

The bum laughed sardonically. "Look Mac, if I didn't get boozed up," he said sardonically, "I wouldn't have the courage to stop jerks like you to ask for a dime."

I learned from a boozy chef how to make:

QUICK PAN-BROILED STEAK (Polynesian-Chinese)

1½ to 2 pounds beef (flank steak, shoulder, boneless chuck)
2 tablespoons lemon or lime juice
½ cup medium dry sherry or any slightly sweet wine
1 tablespoon soy sauce
¼ teaspoon pepper
4 tablespoons oil
½ cup scallions (green onions) with firm greenery, chopped
12 or more cherry tomatoes
1 cup peeled cucumber, chopped
2 tablespoons cornstarch
⅛ teaspoon cayenne pepper, maybe
maybe some salt

Cut the meat into strips about ¼ inch thick, throwing away any gobs of fat you come across. Put the strips into a bowl and pour over the meat the lemon—or lime—juice, the wine, and the soy sauce. Stir it around to get all of the meat coated, cover the bowl with foil or wax paper, and let the meat marinate for *at least* one hour, stirring at least once. In hot weather, let the meat marinate in the fridge.

After an hour take the meat out of the marinade—which save—and dry the meat on paper towels. Sprinkle with pepper. In a large pan, get 2 tablespoons of the oil very hot—when you see the first whiff of smoke, lift it away from heat for half a minute, reduce the heat, and set the pan down over the heat again. Put into the pan the scallions, cherry tomatoes and the chopped cucumbers. Fry, stirring, until the scallions begin to get soft. Add the rest of the oil, raise the heat, and add the dried meat strips. Fry—why this is called "pan broil" I don't know, but that's how it is—stirring over highest heat just until the meat is slightly browned on both sides if you like it rare; longer, of course, if you want it medium or well-done. Remove meat from pan.

Remember that marinade of lemon, wine and soy? Sure you do, it's right in front of you. Stir into it the cornstarch until the starch is thoroughly dissolved and pour it into the pan. Cook over high heat, stirring, until the sauce is thickened. Taste the sauce. Add the cayenne if you think the sauce needs it, and salt, too, if in your judgment it needs more salt than given to it by the soy sauce. Add meat long enough to heat it up. Serve on a bed of plain boiled rice or noodles.

SERVES FOUR.

Man running for Congress on the regular party ticket was called before his party's finance committee to explain how he was going to run his campaign and to give them an estimate of how much money he would spend on it. "I figure," he said, "that I should have about $1,000,000."

The committee members were aghast. "One million dollars?" said the chairman of the finance committee aghast. "Why, in your district you'd have trouble spending $250,000!" The candidate shrugged. "Yes, sure," he said, "but in case I lose the election I want to have something to fall back on."

Any time you're doubtful about what to give guests, you can always fall back on:

OVEN BROILED STEAK (Polynesian-Chinese)

2 pounds top sirloin, cut into 4 slices
1 tablespoon lemon or lime juice
½ teaspoon coarse black pepper
½ teaspoon dry mustard
2 tablespoons oil
½ pound mushrooms, sliced through caps and stems
¼ cup grated carrot
½ teaspoon salt
1 (or more) Bermuda or Spanish onion sliced
1 tablespoon soy sauce

Cut off fat on the meat and wipe dry. Combine the lemon or lime juice with the pepper, and mustard and rub some into each steak slice and let it stand.

In a large fry pan hot up the oil and fry the mushrooms and grated carrot, stirring often, until the mushrooms are soft. Add salt and stir well.

When the mushrooms are soft, cover the fry pan and remove from the heat.

Put a film of oil on a pan that will hold steaks side by side, put it into your broiler about 3 inches from the source of the heat, for not more than 1 minute. Put the steaks on the pan. If you want them to be rare, 3–4 minutes on each side will do it.

Cut into one of the steaks after 2 minutes and see how it looks inside. If you want it done more, you will broil it longer, but be sure to turn the steaks after each additional minute of broiling.

When the steaks have reached the stage of doneness that you prefer, take them out of the broiler and spread on each one some of the fried mushroom-carrot mixture. Put on top of each steak 1 thick slice (or more) of onion, sprinkle a few drops of soy sauce over all and put it back in the broiler for just 1 minute. French fries? A salad? Why not?

SERVES FOUR.

SCENE: A picnic at a picnic ground, with a long table holding food.

CHARACTERS: One tall young fellow, one short young fellow, and an extremely pretty girl. The young fellows are eating hot dogs, the girl is holding a hot dog in a bun.

Tall young fellow nudges short young fellow, and whispers: "Hey, look at that extremely pretty girl giving me the eye, and flirting with me."

Short young fellow looks at the extremely pretty girl and bursts out laughing. He says to the tall young fellow: "You tall dope you, that extremely pretty girl isn't giving you the eye, or flirting with you, it's just that you're holding the mustard."

You know what's good with mustard? What's good with mustard is:

BROILED STEAK WITH CHEESE-MUSTARD SAUCE

2- to 2½-pound shoulder steak, about 1 inch thick (see Note)
¼ teaspoon salt
¼ teaspoon pepper
1 clove (or more) garlic, pressed
2 tablespoons lemon juice or vinegar
2 tablespoons butter, oil, or margarine
½ teaspoon dry mustard
¼ cup strong cheese (cheddar? blue? Roquefort? Limburger?), crumbled

Cut all the fat off the steak. (Oh, yes, here's the Note: If you are rich, maybe you'll want to use a more expensive cut of steak than shoulder.) Rub the salt and pepper into the steak. Combine the pressed garlic with the lemon juice and rub it into the steak, put it into a bowl, cover the bowl, and let it stay outside the refrigerator for not more than an hour. In the fridge it can stay overnight. The lemon juice, you know, acts as a tenderizer, which is why I think it is not necessary to use a more expensive cut of steak, unless you are a show-off.

Broil the steak, in your broiler or over charcoal until it reaches the state of doneness you prefer. A steak approximately 1 inch thick, broiled 3 inches from the source of heat, will be rare if broiled for a total of 6 to 8 minutes and turned once. Cut into it after 6 minutes to see how it looks inside.

Cream together the butter—or oil or margarine—the mustard, and the crumbled cheese. One minute before serving the steak—with corn on the cob, or baked potato—smear the cheese mixture on the steak.

Way I cook corn, most times, is to strip the husks down to the bottom of the cob, without tearing it off. Remove the silk. Brush each ear of corn with melted butter. I have added minced or dried basil to the melted butter, and it is delicious, and does not overpower the delicate sweetness of the corn. Then I gather up the husks, enclosing the cob completely, and bind it together with a piece of string. Then dip the husk-covered corn into cold water, and broil it, turning the corn, until the husks are charred all over. Much better than boiling corn, because the husks add an indefinable, wonderful flavor to the corn.

SERVES FOUR.

Man told the bank manager that he wanted to borrow $1,000. "Are you regularly employed?" the banker asked. The man said yes, he was, and that his salary was $185 a week. "That's fine," said the banker. "Take this loan application, fill it out, have your employer endorse it right here, and bring it back to me and you'll get your loan with no trouble at all."

The man came back that afternoon and handed the loan application to the banker. He looked it over. Then he looked up at the man. "But," said the banker, "your employer didn't endorse it." The man nodded. "That's right," he said, "my boss said if you would endorse it, he'd lend me the thousand."

I endorse without reservations:

BATTER-FRIED STEAK SURPRISE (Italy)

2 pounds top sirloin or round (see Note)
$\frac{1}{4}$ teaspoon salt
$\frac{1}{8}$ teaspoon pepper
4 thin slices tongue or ham, cooked
4 slices of tomato
flour
2 eggs
4 tablespoons cheese, grated
2 cloves garlic, minced
fine bread crumbs
olive oil

(Many years ago, in a sleepy Mississippi town, when I asked a sleepy waitress what the menu meant by saying "Chicken-fried Steak" and she explained that it meant just what it said, a steak coated with batter and then fried, I shuddered and ordered a cheese sandwich and a glass of milk, and now, look, here I am, doing what I never in all my days thought I'd ever do—recommending a fried batter-coated steak, and, friends, learn a lesson from me, and don't knock it if you haven't tried it.)

Cut the beef into 4 slices, each about ½ inch thick. Now cut each slice of meat horizontally, but not all the way through. Open the slices, sprinkle with a little salt and pepper. Put a slice of tongue or ham and a slice of tomato on each of four of the pieces of meat, and close them up, as you would a book. Skewer them together with toothpick halves. Beat eggs, adding cheese and garlic. Now dip skewered steaks into flour, getting both sides coated. Dip each one into the egg mixture and finally into the bread crumbs. If you refrigerate these steaks for an hour, the breading will be more certain to stick to the meat during frying.

In a large fry pan, get 2 tablespoons of oil hot, and fry the steaks over medium heat until both sides are well browned. About 2 minutes on each side will leave the meat rare; 5 minutes will make them well done. Don't crowd the fry pan.

SERVES FOUR.

The powerful leader of a political party had gone to visit a colleague who had suffered a nervous breakdown, and just as he arrived at the psychiatric ward in the hospital where his friend was confined, he realized he had to make an important telephone call. The political leader kept getting wrong numbers and he became so exasperated that he jiggled the telephone hook exasperatedly until the operator came on and said, "Do you have a problem, mister?"

This infuriated the pol. "My name is" (I don't want to embarrass the fellow because for a political leader he isn't such a bad bloke, so I won't use it here) "and do you know who and what I am?"

The telephone operator giggled. "No sir," she said gigglingly, "I don't know who you are, or what you are, but I do know WHERE you are."

Where you are, indoors or out, a wonderful dish is:

MARINATED LONDON BROIL (Singapore)

1 to 1½ pounds flank steak
2 tablespoons each, peanut or corn oil; soy sauce, lemon or
     lime juice or vinegar; grated onion or onion juice
1 tablespoon sugar
1 tablespoon pressed or mashed garlic
⅛ teaspoon cayenne pepper
¼ cup fresh parsley, minced or 1 tablespoon dried flakes
4 cloves or ¼ teaspoon cloves, ground

Cut off some, but not all of the fat, most of which will be
down at the thin part of the hunk of meat. Put the meat on your
work counter, between 2 sheets of waxed paper or foil and beat
it unmercifully with a blunt instrument to make it more tender.

Combine all the other ingredients in an enameled or stain-
less steel pan—anything but aluminum which will be discolored
hellishly by the lemon, or lime juice or vinegar. Heat just long
enough, stirring, until the sugar is melted. Cool it. Put the meat
into the cooled marinade, turning it to coat it all over, and marinate it for several hours. In warm weather, marinate it in the
fridge. Turn it a couple of times, spooning marinade all over the
meat.

Over charcoal, broil it about 2 inches from the bed of coals
for 3 to 4 minutes on each side for rare, brushing the top with
marinade before you turn the meat, and then brushing once
more, on top, after you have turned it. The same timing goes for
indoor broiling, and if you don't want it rare, broil for another
minute or two.

SERVES TWO TO THREE.

A couple of college men I know met for the first time after more than 30 years had elapsed. One of the men worked for a salary and just about got along on his earnings. The other had become extremely rich. The conversation would have been extremely dull, for they were reminiscing about old acquaintances neither of them cared a farthing—whatever that is—for, except that the rich man said dreadfully shocking things about each name that came up. "You know," said the working man, "you haven't changed a bit in all these years! All your great wealth hasn't changed you at all!"

The rich man sneered. "Yes," he said, "that's true; I haven't changed at all, but everybody else has. Before I became rich, everyone said I was a nut; now they say I am wonderfully eccentric. And before I made my fortune, everyone used to say that I was terribly rude and ill-mannered, and what they say now is that I am a great wit."

How would you like a very witty:

BARBECUED MARINATED STEAK (Brazil)

3 pounds sirloin, porterhouse or tenderloin, cut 1 inch thick
⅓ cup olive oil
1 medium onion, chopped fine
1–2 clove garlic, chopped fine
½ teaspoon cayenne
½ to 1 tablespoon chili powder
½ teaspoon salt
2 tomatoes, peeled and chopped
¼ cup wine vinegar

The steak should be taken out of the refrigerator at least an hour before you start all this, but remember: in the summer it may well be anywhere from 90 to 100 degrees in your kitchen, so for goodness' sake, don't let the meat reach room temperature! Hot up 2 tablespoons of the oil and fry the onion and garlic, stirring, until it is all slightly browned. Add all the other ingredients and cook slowly over low heat, stirring all the while, for about 5 minutes. Now let it cool to room temperature. Put the steak in a large bowl, pot, whatever is handy, and pour the marinade over it. Let it stand for an hour or so, turning the steak at least once.

If you are charcoal-broiling, place the steak 3 inches from the firebed—after a gray ash has formed over the coals—first lightly greasing the grill on which the meat rests, and broil for 4 to 5 minutes on each side for rare, 6 to 8 minutes on each side for medium and as long as you like for well-done. Brush top of the meat with the marinade when you turn it. Serve it, maybe, sliced, on buns, with some of the marinade. This can be done indoors, too, of course.

SERVES SIX TO EIGHT.

It used to be a secret that politicians employ specialists whose job it is to write their speeches. Some of these speech writers earn large sums through their political savvy, a gift for invective, and artful phrase-making. A famous contender for political office was handed a copy of a speech he was supposed to give, and all the time he read it, he looked confused.

"There's something wrong with this," he said when he finished the speech. "I don't know just what it is, but something isn't right about this speech." It was explained to him that perhaps it seemed different because his regular speech writer had suddenly become ill, and a substitute had written this one.

"Ah, so that's it!" he cried out. "I knew it wasn't up to my usual high standard!"

If you want to raise your standards try:

BARBECUED STEAK MAITRE D'HOTEL BUTTER SAUCE (U.S.A.)

6—steaks, at least 1 inch thick and about ½ pound if
    boneless
2 tablespoons olive oil
4 tablespoons lemon juice (juice of one medium lemon)
1 stick butter
1 teaspoon parsley, chopped
1 teaspoon salt
¼ teaspoon pepper

A couple of hours before you are ready to barbecue the steaks, combine the olive oil and 2 tablespoons of the lemon juice and rub the meat with it. Have the grill about 3 inches from the bed of coals, which should have a film of gray ash over them before you put the meat on. Grease the hot grill with some of the excess fat you've trimmed from the steaks, and hold on to some of the fat for use later. Now make the maitre d'hotel butter.

Cream the butter with the remaining lemon juice, the chopped parsley and salt and pepper.

For a steak 1 inch thick, you should allow 4 to 5 minutes of broiling for each side if you like it rare; up to 6 to 8 minutes for medium and if you like it well done, well, let your conscience be your guide. Keep a water pistol handy for flare-ups, because if you like steak charred you shouldn't let this happen during the cooking, but wait until the meat is done to your satisfaction. If you are uncertain about how the steak is doing, cut into one of them and see; that's the surest way of finishing the steak the way you like it best.

Now, if you want it charred, drop onto the coals a piece of the fat you trimmed from the meat and let the flare-up touch each side of the steaks for about 10 seconds. Serve the steaks with generous dollops of the maitre d'hotel butter smeared all over the tops. Have salt and a pepper mill handy for those who like more seasoning. This amount of butter will be enough for 6 to 8 steaks. This can, of course, be done indoors, in your oven broiler, on a broiler pan.

SERVES SIX TO EIGHT.

No matter where you live, if your town has a daily paper it is bound to have a syndicated column written by someone who works in New York, in which case it is called a "Broadway column," or one that emanates from Los Angeles, in which case it is called a "Hollywood column" and many newspapers carry at least one of each.

I like to read them for only one reason. It amuses me vastly to see old jokes, anecdotes, so forth, rewritten and attributed to some actor, actress, athlete, political figure, or some sort of other so-called "celebrity." One of these I saw the other day had a certain theatrical producer tell an anecdote about an actor to several other theatrical people in a New York restaurant, which shall be nameless here, right after the producer debarked from a jet plane belonging to an airline which also will be nameless here. In other words, this anecdote mentioned the names of six "celebrities," one restaurant, and an airline. These are called, in the newspaper business, "plugs." This anecdote originated, actually, with Mark Twain.

Seems that Mr. Clemens used to infuriate his wife by visiting friends and neighbors in his shirtsleeves, without a collar, tie, and jacket. Once, she scolded him so severely that he hired a young boy as a messenger to take a note, and other things, to a neighbor. The note said: "I just visited with you for about 30 minutes without my collar, tie, or jacket. Here are the missing articles of clothing. Will you please look at them for about 30 minutes and then give them back to the boy who will return them to me."

Today I'd like to go back to my boyhood when I first had:

SWISS STEAK (Switzerland?)

2 pounds beef (top sirloin, or round, or shoulder), cut into 4
    slices
½ teaspoon salt
¼ teaspoon pepper
flour
2 tablespoons oil, or butter
1 clove garlic (if you don't like garlic, don't)
½ cup onion, chopped
one 1-pound can whole, peeled tomatoes, well mashed
½ cup dry red or white wine (if you don't like wine, don't)

If you buy a whole hunk of beef and cut it into 4 slices yourself, you'll save some money. Rub the salt and pepper into the meat. Sprinkle flour over each side of the meat, pounding the flour into the meat with the edge of a heavy plate. Don't be afraid of breaking the plate, it won't break unless it is already cracked. Shake off excess flour. This pounding in serves two purposes. It pounds in the flour, right? *And* it helps to make the meat more tender by breaking down the tendons or whatever.

Get the oil or butter—or a combination of both—hot in a large fry pan. Cook the garlic and onion in it until the onion is soft. Push the onion and garlic to side of pan. Over high heat, sear each slice of beef on both sides, loosening it from the pan with a spatula. Don't crowd the pan, and don't bother to keep hot the seared meat you take out of the pan, because it's going to be cooked some more.

When all 4 beef slices are seared, add the mashed-up tomatoes to the pan, scrape the pan to get up the goodies stuck to it, stir the onion-garlic mixture in, and return the beef slices to the frying pan, spooning the sauce over each slice. Now, if you are going to use wine, pour it into the pan. (If you're not going to use wine, that's none of my business.) Bring the sauce to a boil, reduce the heat so it simmers, and cook, covered, for 30 minutes. Or longer. As long as you want.

SERVES FOUR.

The newspaper reporter on a big city paper had always dreamed of owning his own paper and while vacationing in the country he paid a call on the owner and publisher of the weekly paper. "You're the only publisher in the county, aren't you?" he asked. "That's right," said the publisher. "What's the circulation?" the reporter asked. "About 600, give or take a few," was the reply. "Six hundred! why, you can't be making any money on that kind of circulation!" the reporter exclaimed, and the publisher agreed with him. "The paper is terribly thin, you can't be making any money on advertising," said the reporter, and again the publisher agreed. "Oh, I guess how you make money is by job-printing?" the reporter said, and this time the publisher disagreed. "You don't make money on circulation, you don't make anything on advertising, or job-printing, so how do you get by?" the reporter asked. The publisher shrugged. "I make out okay," he said, "because in each issue I purposely print some typographical errors with double meanings and the national magazines and big city newspapers pay me a lot of money for them."

What won't cost a lot of money to make is:

WINE MARINATED POT ROAST (France)

2 to 3 pounds boneless beef (chuck or round, etc.)
1 cup onion, minced
1 cup celery, strings scraped off, and chopped small
1 bay leaf
1 tablespoon cracked peppercorns
4 cloves
2 cups dry red wine
1 can (about 10 ounces) condensed beef broth
2 cups cubed potatoes
½ cup carrots cut into thin rounds
one 10-ounce package frozen peas, thawed
perhaps salt and pepper

Cut off all the fat you can get at on the meat. In an enameled saucepan or Dutch oven, melt down enough of the fat to leave a film of melted fat and in it cook the onions and celery until they are soft. Remove the pieces of fat that don't melt down. Remove pan from the heat and allow it to cool.

Tie into a small cheesecloth bag the bay leaf, cracked peppercorns and the cloves. Put the beef into the cooled pan, add the cheesecloth bag. Pour over the meat the 2 cups of wine, cover the pan and let the meat marinate, turning it from time to time, outside the refrigerator for a couple of hours, or overnight in the fridge.

Two hours before you are ready to serve, take the meat out of the marinade and dry it thoroughly. In a large, dry frying pan, sear the meat all over, turning it with two large kitchen spoons or other utensils, but do not prick the meat. When the meat is well browned all over, add to the marinade the can of condensed beef broth. Bring it to the boil and put the meat back in. Cover the meat and let it simmer for one-and-one-half hours. Add the cubed potatoes and sliced carrots. After 25 minutes of cooking, taste the sauce. Potatoes absorb a good deal of seasoning when cooked like this, so add salt or pepper if you think it needs some. Add the thawed peas just a few minutes before you serve this dish with the sauce poured over all.

SERVES FOUR TO SIX.

Each child in the class walked up to the teacher's desk and put his report card on it. When young Sam put his report card in front of the teacher, she picked it up. "Is this your father's signature? Did he notice that you failed in every subject including cleaning the blackboard?" she asked. "Yes, Ma'am," said young Sam, "he seen it and he signed it." The teacher leaned over her desk. "And did he have anything to say about it?" she asked. "Yes," said the stupid boy. "And what did he say?" the teacher asked. "Well, I wasn't gonna tell you because I didn't want to scare you," said the lad, "but he said if my marks weren't better next month somebody was gonna get what for."

What is better for to come home to on a cold winter night than:

A GREAT POTTED BEEF (Austria)

2 pounds beef (bottom or top round, or shoulder or boneless
    chuck)
2 tablespoons melted fat, or oil
1 pound onions, chopped
2 ribs celery, strings scraped off with knife, and chopped with
    greenery
1 tablespoon garlic, minced
¼ teaspoon powdered bay leaf
¼ teaspoon powdered cloves
1 can condensed cream of mushroom soup
1 can beer or ale, or, alas, water
Note: 2 whole bay leaves and 2 whole cloves tied in a
    cheesecloth bag may be substituted for the powdered
    ingredients

Cut off all the fat you can from the meat into small pieces and in a large pot melt down as much of it as can be melted down, over low heat. In the hot fat, over high heat, quickly sear the meat all over, getting it well browned. Throw away the pieces of fat that didn't melt down. If you haven't got about 2 tablespoons of melted fat in the pot, which, most likely, you won't have, add a little oil to the pot after taking out the meat. Over low heat, cook the chopped onions, celery, and garlic, stirring with a spatula, to get all of this stuff coated, scraping the bottom of the pot to get up the lovely burned meat particles stuck to it. Cover the pot and cook over low heat for 15 minutes.

Add the powdered spices—or the spices in the cheesecloth bag, and stir. Put the seared meat into the pot, on top of the vegetables, spooning some of the vegetables over the meat. Combine the mushroom soup with the beer, or whatever, and pour it over the meat. Put a piece of foil over the top of the pot, put the cover over the foil, and seal it with the overhanging foil as best you can so that no steam, or very little escapes. Cook over very low heat for 1½ hours.

After the meat has cooked for 1½ hours, take it out of the pot, cut it up into thick slices, and put the meat back into the pot, spooning the lovely sauce over the meat slices. Cook over low heat for an additional 30 minutes. Mashed or boiled potatoes are what to have with this, but if you don't think so, have whatever you like. Maybe some warm, garlicky French or Italian bread?

SERVES FOUR.

His wife finally agreed that her mother, who had come to stay with them for a weekend, had overstayed her welcome after two months. In fact, the wife, too, would be much happier if the meddlesome old lady went back home, especially because she had consented to marry the guy principally because he lived and worked on the opposite coast, so she would have a whole continent between her and the old lady.

"But how," she asked despairingly, "can I tell her to go?" Her husband kissed her on the brow. "I've got it figured out," he said. "When we have dinner tonight, I'll get very angry and bawl you out because I'll say the soup is so salty it's impossible to eat it, and you say that I'm crazy, and that what's wrong with it is that it needs a little more salt. And if she agrees with you, I'll start hollering at her and tell her to go pack her things, and if she agrees with me, you get mad and tell her to go." His wife grabbed and hugged him and cried out, "Oh, you are wonderful! You are a genius!" So that evening they played out their little charade, which was kind of wild and noisy. "Now how about it, Ma?" he asked. "Is it too salty or does it need more salt?" The old lady took another spoonful and said, "I think you're both stupid, this soup is just right, and I'm staying another month!"

Right about now how's about some:

2 pounds boneless beef (shoulder, top sirloin, top round)
½ teaspoon salt
¼ teaspoon pepper
1 tablespoon lemon or lime juice or vinegar
4 tablespoons oil
1 cup onion, chopped
½ pound mushrooms, sliced
1 cup beef broth
1 cup sour cream
¼ teaspoon paprika

Cut the meat up into strips or cubes, throw away fat you come across, or any tough membranes. Put the beef into a bowl, sprinkle with salt, pepper, and lime juice (or whatever), stir the beef around and let it stand in covered bowl for at least 1 hour outside fridge, longer inside.

In a large deep fry pan, get 2 tablespoons of the oil hot and in it fry the onion and mushrooms over high heat, stirring, until the onion is soft and is beginning to turn golden. Add the rest of the oil, and then the meat, and cook, stirring, until the meat is well browned.

Add the broth, stir and bring to the boil, and cook, covered, for 30 minutes. Taste a piece of the meat and a little of the sauce. The meat should be tender; if not, cook longer. Correct the seasoning of the sauce if necessary. Do you know, if soup or a sauce is too salty, you can remove some of the salty taste by adding to the liquid some slices of raw potatoes, and cook them for about 10 minutes. You can leave the potatoes or you can throw them away.

About 10 minutes before you want to serve the dish, stir in the sour cream and cook over extremely low heat; don't let the liquid boil. Sprinkle with paprika. Serve with mashed potatoes to glop up the gravy.

SERVES FOUR.

Two fathers were discussing their children. "It's fantastic" one said, "how my son takes after me. Not only does he look like me, but he also acts like I did when I was his age, and he's picked up a lot of my mannerisms, like the way I walk, and talk. It's wonderful!" "Yes, I know what you mean," the other father said. "My daughter looks like her mother, and she talks like her mother, and she thinks like her mother, and it's terrible."

The father of the boy asked why that was terrible. "Well," said the father of the girl, "I don't know if all wives think alike, but in our house, every time my wife and I have an argument about something she's done, somehow she's always able to twist it around so that I wind up being guilty, and yesterday my daughter showed unmistakably that she's just like her mother."

What happened, he said, was that his daughter came home eating a licorice stick, and crying.

"So I asked her what was the matter, and she told me that the kid next door, a boy her age, had broken her doll. When I asked her how the kid did it, she told me. He'd been eating this licorice stick, she said, and when he wouldn't give her a piece, she grabbed it from him, and when the kid tried to grab it back from her, she hit him on the head with her doll and the doll broke, and how do you like that for reasoning?"

You don't need a special reason to make:

BEEF AND CHICK PEAS IN MUSHROOM SAUCE (Near East)

2 pounds top sirloin or eye of round
1 tablespoon lemon or lime juice
3 tablespoons oil (olive, preferably, but peanut oil is fine)
1 cup scallions (green onions) with some greenery, chopped
½ pound mushrooms, sliced through stem and cap
¼ teaspoon cracked pepper, or peppercorns crushed
2 tablespoons tomato paste
1 cup beef broth (or 1 bouillon cube dissolved in boiling water)
½ cup dry wine, red or white
salt? maybe ¼ teaspoon
2 tablespoons instant mashed potatoes
1-pound can chick peas (garbanzos), drained

Cut the beef into 4 equally thick slices. Rub a little lemon juice on each side of each slice, and, in summertime, let stand in covered bowl outside your fridge for 30 minutes. (Juice acts as tenderizer, standing takes off chill.) In a large fry pan, get 1 tablespoon of oil hot and over high heat, sear each slice, without crowding pan, for not more than 1 minute on each side, if you like beef rare. Add a little more oil, if necessary. When beef slices are cooked, remove them from pan, but don't bother to keep them warm.

Get the rest of the oil hot in the same fry pan, scraping to get up the good stuff stuck to the pan. In it cook the scallions and mushrooms, stirring constantly over medium heat until the vegetables are soft. Sprinkle with pepper. Dissolve the tomato paste in the broth and add to the fry pan, stirring. Add the wine. Bring to the boil and taste. The broth is salty, but add some if your taste tells you to. Stir in the instant mashed potato until it is dissolved and the sauce thickened. Add the drained chick peas, the beef slices, cover and cook for 2 minutes until beef and chick peas are hot. If you don't have crisp Italian or French bread to glop up gravy, that's a shame.

SERVES FOUR.

Man in the plane had been trying to get his seatmate, an utter stranger, into a conversation, but all he got were grunts. Then, looking down at the man's crossed legs, he said, "You know what I find strange?" The other fellow shrugged. "What I find strange," the persistent bore said, "is the peculiar pair of socks you're wearing, one blue and the other red." This gambit finally got his fellow traveler talking. "You're right, that is peculiar," the man said, rising to go and sit in solitude in the lounge of the plane, "but what's even more peculiar is that in my valise I have a pair of socks that's just the same."

There are beef rolls and there are beef rolls, but in our house we always have the same:

BEEF ROLLS (Italy)

2 pounds boneless beef (top sirloin, top round) cut in equal slices

4 tablespoons oil, or butter

1 cup onions, minced

¼ pound mushrooms, chopped (or 1 four-ounce can mushroom pieces, drained and dried)

½ teaspoon dried oregano or thyme

½ teaspoon salt or 1 small can anchovies, drained of oil and minced fine

½ teaspoon pepper

½ cup fine bread crumbs

1 egg, beaten

flour

1 can (10½ ounces) beef broth

½ cup dry wine, red or white, or applecider for abstainers (or water?)

Buy the beef in one chunk, and if your butcher will slice it for you, that's fine; if he doesn't, chide the churl severely and do it yourself. Throw away any fat or tendons you come across. Put each slice between sheets of waxed paper and bludgeon it severely with a blunt instrument, working your way from the center of the meat slice to the outer edges. This serves two purposes: 1) it makes the meat more tender, 2) it spreads it out.

In a large fry pan, get 2 tablespoons of oil hot and in it fry the onions and mushrooms, sprinkled with oregano or thyme, until almost all the liquid in the pan has been cooked away. If you are going to use anchovies, don't add salt—I'll tell you pretty soon what to do with the anchovies—but sprinkle with pepper. Put the mixture into a bowl, combine with bread crumbs and the beaten egg. If you are using anchovies, now is the time to add it to the mixture. (If you aren't using the anchovies, you've already added the salt, haven't you?)

Now, let's see. We have the pounded beef slices? Sure we have. Spread some of the onion-mushroom-etc. mixture on the edge of each piece of beef and roll it up, and fasten with a toothpick. Dust each beef roll with flour. In the large fry pan you used for the onion-mushroom, get the remaining oil hot, and, over high heat, brown the beef rolls all over. Pour into the pan the broth and wine or whatever, cover the pan, bring the liquid to the boil, and simmer at lower heat for 20 minutes.

If you want to thicken the sauce, dissolve 2 tablespoons of flour or cornstarch in $\frac{1}{4}$ cup wine or whatever, stir it slowly into the gravy, and bring it to the boil and stir until it is thickened.

Would you like a salad and Italian or French bread toasted and wonderfully fragrant with garlic butter? Good. That's what I like, too.

SERVES FOUR.

The farmer was suing his neighbor for stabbing his dog with a pitchfork. "Why did you stab the dog?" the plaintiff's lawyer asked the defendant. "Because he was going to bite me," said the defendant. "But why didn't you jab at him with the other end of the pitchfork?" the lawyer asked. "I would have," the man said, "if he had come at me with *his* other end."

For a party or weekend dish, it would be hard to beat:

STUFFED BEEF STEAK (Italian)

$\frac{1}{4}$ pound spaghetti, broken up and cooked
1 flank steak, $2\frac{1}{2}$ to 3 pounds
4 tablespoons olive oil, or butter
1 tablespoon dried oregano
1 cup onion, chopped
garlic cloves minced to make 2 tablespoons
1 cup chopped celery, including top leaves
$\frac{1}{4}$ pound fresh mushrooms, sliced, or canned, drained and dried
$\frac{1}{4}$ cup carrot, grated
1 egg, beaten
$\frac{1}{2}$ teaspoon salt
$\frac{1}{4}$ teaspoon pepper
1 can (about 10 ounces) condensed cream of mushroom soup
$\frac{1}{2}$ cup strong brewed black coffee

Break up the spaghetti and pour it into boiling water to cover, with a little salt and a couple of drops of oil. Cook for 8 minutes, and drain it in a colander. While the spaghetti is cooking put the meat between 2 pieces of wax paper on a chopping board. Flank steak is narrow at one end and thick at the other. Pound the thick part until it is approximately as thin as the other end. This will not only tenderize the meat, but will spread it out so it will be easier to roll up, which you're going to do later on.

In a large frying pan, hot up 2 tablespoons of the oil and in it fry the oregano, chopped onion and garlic cloves, until the onion is browned, but not burned. By this time, the spaghetti will have been cooked and drained. Put the spaghetti and the onion mixture into a bowl.

Hot up the remaining 2 tablespoons of oil and in it fry the celery, mushrooms, and grated carrot until the mushrooms are browned, and a good deal of the moisture has been cooked out of the pan. Add this to the bowl, stir the beaten egg into the mixture, with $\frac{1}{4}$ teaspoon salt, and $\frac{1}{8}$ teaspoon pepper.

Spread this mixture on the broad end of the flank steak, tuck in the ends to cover the mixture, and roll up the meat. Fasten it with skewers, or tie it up with string. Rub the remaining salt and pepper into the rolled-up steak. Put the stuffed steak into a baking pan, combine the condensed soup with the coffee and pour it over all. Bake in oven preheated to 350 degrees for $1\frac{1}{2}$ hours, spooning sauce over the meat every 30 minutes. If the sauce thickens too much, and it seems to be drying out, add a little dry wine, or, alas, water. Have mashed, and a salad.

SERVES SIX, MAYBE EIGHT.

When little Sammy came home for dinner from the neighborhood park where he had spent the afternoon, he had a black eye. "Oh Sammy dear," his mother exclaimed, "what happened to you? How did you get that black eye?"

Sammy shrugged. "I had a fist fight with Max," he said.

Next morning, before he went to the park, his mother gave him two pieces of cake. "Here's a piece of cake for you, and another piece for Max, and then you'll be friends again," said his mother. When he came home for lunch, he had only the original black eye.

"See, I knew he'd be your friend again if you gave him the cake," his mother said.

But when he came home for dinner, Sammy's other eye was blackened, too. "My goodness!" his mother exclaimed, "who did that to you?"

Sammy shrugged. "It was Max," he said. "He wants more cake."

Everyone will want more if you give them:

CHINESE BEEF AND VEGETABLES

1½ to 2 pounds top sirloin or round
4 tablespoons (¼ cup) peanut, soy or vegetable oil
1 cup scallions with some of firm greenery chopped
2 cloves (more?) garlic, minced
2 sweet green peppers, cut into strips about 1 inch long, ½ inch wide
1-pound can peeled tomatoes, or equivalent peeled and squashed fresh ones
2 teaspoons soy sauce
½ cup water chestnuts, dried, sliced thin horizontally
1 tablespoon cornstarch
¼ cup dry red wine (or water?)

Slice the beef into strips about ½ inch thick, 1 inch wide, and 2 inches long, throwing away any fat you find. Get 1 tablespoon of oil hot in a large fry pan. Fry the beef strips just until they are browned on each side. If you're going to serve this dish to people who like their meat on the rare side, remove from the pan, at this point, enough to serve the rare ones. Add oil as you need it.

When all the meat has been browned, add the scallions, garlic and cut-up green peppers, and fry, stirring constantly, until the vegetables are soft. If you do this over really high heat, stirring all the while, it will take only 3 to 4 minutes to get the vegetables soft.

Add the mashed tomatoes—canned or fresh—and cook, stirring for about 2 minutes. You know, of course, that if you plunge tomatoes into boiling water for 1 minute and run cold water over them, they'll peel easily. Add the soy sauce and pepper, stir, and taste the sauce, adding either more soy sauce—which is quite salty—or salt. And pepper, too, if you think it needs some. Add the dried, sliced water chestnuts and stir. Dissolve the cornstarch in the wine, or water, add to the sauce, and stir over high heat, until the sauce boils and begins to thicken. Add the rare strips of beef, and cook for half a minute just to get them hot. When you add the rare beef, push everything in the pan to one side so the rare and well-done won't get mixed up, and you'll be able to give the rare people what they prefer.

Plain boiled rice is good with this. So are noodles. So is crusty French or Italian bread.

SERVES FOUR TO SIX.

Their minister had come with the family for Sunday dinner and everyone was on his best behavior. "Just before you came in," said the mother, "when I told little Willie here that you were going to have dinner with us, do you know what he said, Reverend?" The mother beamed. "He said that when he grew up," she said beamingly, "he was going to be a minister just like you."

The minister was astounded because he'd never seen the slightest indication that Willie was interested in religion. "Is that so?" said the minister. "And just why do you want to be a minister when you grow up, little Willie?"

Little Willie shrugged. "Well, the way I see it, I'm going to have to go to church every Sunday, all my life, and I figured that as long as I have to do that, I might just as well have the fun hollering at everybody for being miserable wretches, like you do."

The main course of a Sunday dinner can be ready in 25 minutes, with all work, except the final baking, done beforehand if you make a:

BEEF AND VEGETABLE PIE (Kind of Italian)

$1\frac{1}{2}$ pounds beef (top sirloin, round, or shoulder)
2 tablespoons oil
1 cup onion, chopped
1 small green pepper, chopped
4 to 6 black olives, pitted and chopped
$\frac{1}{4}$ cup pimiento or roasted red pepper, chopped
$\frac{1}{4}$ teaspoon oregano
$\frac{1}{4}$ teaspoon salt
$\frac{1}{8}$ teaspoon pepper
10-ounce package frozen tiny green peas, thawed
1 can (approximately 10 ounces) cream of mushroom soup
9- or 10-inch pie crust

Cut the beef into thin strips, removing and throwing away any fat. In a large frying pan, get the oil hot and in it cook the onion and chopped pepper until soft, add the chopped pitted olives, the pimiento or roasted red pepper. Add the beef strips and cook over high heat just until the meat loses its redness. Add the oregano, salt, pepper, and the peas and soup. Taste for seasoning.

Spoon it all into a deep pie plate or baking dish, cover with the pastry. This is where you can quit working until about 25 minutes before you want to serve dinner.

In oven preheated to 400 degrees, bake it for about 20 minutes or until the pie crust is browned and the pie is all hotted up nicely.

SERVES FOUR.

Tony Curtis was driving his silver Rolls Royce—I don't mean that it is merely silver-colored, I mean it is solid silver—through a disreputable part of Los Angeles one afternoon when he saw a sign over a saloon that said: "Tony Curtis's Bar & Grill." Furious, he stopped the car and went into the joint. "Where's the owner?" he demanded truculently of the man behind the bar. "I'm the owner, what's your problem, sport?" said the man. "Do you know who I am?" asked Tony. "Sure, you're that actor, whatsisname?" said the man. "My name is Tony Curtis, and if you don't take that sign right down I'm going to sue you," said the actor. The man behind the bar laughed, and took out his wallet. "Look," he said, "here's my birth certificate and it says my name is Anthony Curtis. Let's see your birth certificate, Bernie Schwartz."

No matter what your birth certificate says, you'll like:

BEEF (OR ALMOST ANYTHING) AND TOMATO-RICE AND EVERYTHING NICE (Universal)

4 tablespoons oil
1½ to 2 pounds cubed lean beef (shoulder, round, etc.), or
    lamb, veal, or pork
1 cup scallions (green onions) with some of firm greenery,
    minced
1 cup (approximately) green pepper, minced
1 cup celery, green strings scraped off, chopped with leaves
½ teaspoon salt
¼ teaspoon pepper
1 cup rice (uncooked)
2½ cups tomato juice
½ cup dry red wine
maybe some cayenne pepper?

In a large frying pan with an ovenproof handle, or in a flameproof baking dish, get 2 tablespoons of the oil hot and in it, over high heat, stirring all the while, fry the meat cubes until they are all well-browned all over. Remove meat to a bowl with a slotted spoon, but don't bother to keep it hot.

Add the rest of the oil and fry the scallions, green pepper, and celery until the onions are a golden color. Combine with meat, sprinkling with salt and pepper. Stir in the uncooked rice, add the tomato juice and wine, and if you know that everyone who'll eat this likes hot (read this "spicy") food, add cayenne as the spirit moves you. Stir well, cover the utensil first with foil and then with its own cover and cook in oven preheated to 350 degrees for 45 minutes.

The rice will have absorbed most of the liquid, and it will be a lovely dish to look at, pinkish-green-brown, and just as delicious as it looks. REMINDER: If you use pork, make certain that it has been cooked through before serving. You can do all of the work, up to the point of baking in oven long before, even the night before you plan to serve it.

SERVES FOUR.

Man was very ill. His doctor told his wife and children that there wasn't much hope for his recovery. But they loved him dearly so they sought out other doctors—maybe five or six—to get another, possibly more hopeful, prognosis. Last one they called in for a consultation beamed at them after he'd examined the head of the family. "How is he, Doctor?" asked the eldest son. "What are his chances?" The doctor kept beaming. "His chances?" he asked. "Why if I were a betting man I would give odds of 100 to one that he'll recover completely."

The family was astounded. "But all those other doctors," said the wife, "they all said there was no hope." The doctor laughed. "They are fools," he said. "Your husband is the tenth patient I've had with these complaints. Medical statistics show that nine out of ten people with these complications do not recover, and, by Jiminy, the last nine I had all cooled."

Hot or cold, what's wonderful are fried beef cakes which the Koreans call:

WAN-JAH JUHN (Korea)

4 tablespoons ($\frac{1}{4}$ cup) peanut or soy oil
1 tablespoon sesame seeds
bunch of scallions (green onions) with greenery, minced
2 (or more) cloves garlic, minced fine
2 pounds ground beef
$\frac{1}{4}$ teaspoon (or less) crushed red pepper flakes (see Note)
2 tablespoons soy sauce
2 medium-sized eggs, beaten
flour

In a large fry pan, get 2 tablespoons of the oil hot. Fry the sesame seeds, stirring until they are browned. Add the minced scallions and garlic and cook, stirring constantly, until the onion is soft. Put the stuff in the pan into a large mixing bowl, add the beef, the crushed red pepper flakes and the soy sauce. Pepper Note: this is very hot stuff, and if you haven't ever used it before, and are not familiar with its power, perhaps you should use $\frac{1}{8}$ of a teaspoon, but, if you like food real hot and know how hot these dried flakes are, why, just let your conscience guide you.

Combine thoroughly everything in the mixing bowl. You can, of course, use a fork to do this, but I like to use my hands because they are the best kitchen tools available.

Koreans form the meat mixture into small, thin cakes. I like them best when they are about $\frac{1}{2}$ inch thick, 2 inches long and wide.

Dip the cakes into the beaten eggs, and then into the flour. Add oil as needed in frying the cakes in the same large frying pan in which you cooked the sesame-onion-garlic mixture. Brown them well on both sides. Do not crowd the pan. To keep them hot, put them on a large, heavy platter set over a pot of very hot water, and invert a mixing bowl over the fried cakes. If any egg is left over, spoon some over the meat cakes as you fry.

Whenever Koreans eat fried food of any kind they dip the food into a sauce made of equal parts of vinegar and soy sauce, plus 1 teaspoon of sugar, and pine nuts that are chopped very fine, and very fine it is, too. Made into small cakes they make a marvelous hors d'oeuvre. If you want to call these meat cakes "patties" go right ahead. I don't like the word. If you serve them hot, rice or noodles are wonderful.

SERVES FOUR TO SIX.

Lady came into the fur shop, and, after telling the saleslady that her husband had told her she could pick out any fur coat she liked best and he would buy it for her as his anniversary present, she proceeded to try on every coat in the store. She tried on sable coats; she tried on mink coats; she tried on chinchilla coats; all kinds of fur coats. "This is terrible," she cried out, "just terrible!" The saleslady stared in amazement at her.

"What's so terrible?" she said. "My goodness, your husband says he'll buy you any fur coat you like best, and all the coats you tried on look beautiful on you, and then you start hollering 'It's terrible, it's terrible.' What kind of nut are you? Anyway?" The customer lady shook her head sorrowfully. "You just don't understand," she said, "because you don't know my husband. The coat I like best is that broadtail." She sobbed. "But I can't buy the broadtail because my husband thinks he's a funnier comedian than Jack Benny, Sam Levinson, and even Henny Youngman."

No matter how big a ham your husband may be, he'll get no laughs, but only pleasure out of this:

MISHMASH (Brooklyn)

4 tablespoons oil or butter
1 large onion, minced
2 cloves garlic, pressed or mashed
2 cups grated potatoes (non-baking ones)
1 to 1½ pounds ground beef
1 egg, beaten
½ teaspoon salt
¼ teaspoon pepper
¼ cup chili or tomato sauce or ketchup or catsup

In a large fry pan, get 2 tablespoons of the oil or butter—or 1 tablespoon of each—hot. In it, stirring all the while over medium heat, cook the onion and garlic until the onion begins to turn golden. Add the grated potatoes, and cook, stirring, until the mixture has lost most of its moistness. Remove the onion-potato mixture to a mixing bowl. In the bowl, combine the onion-potato mixture with the ground beef, the beaten egg, salt, pepper, and the sauce.

Form this mishmash into any kind of shape you like—ovals, rounds, squares, whatever. Fry them on both sides in the remaining oil—or butter—until they are browned all over, and cooked the way you like hamburgers, rare, medium, or well done. Serve with a green salad eaten before, during, or after the hamburgers. (Californians like to eat their salads before they tackle the main course.)

SERVES FOUR.

The barefoot young man was having an argument with his barefoot old father. Reason was he wanted to leave home in the hills of Kentucky and go to the big city. "But I got no chance here, Paw," he said. "In the big city I kin git me a job an' have a pair of shoes an' have a chanct to make suthin' of myself which I caint do heah." His Paw shook his head sadly. "Son," he said sadly, "you ain't thought this thing out very well, I'm afraid. Looka heah. Looka me. Why, when I come heah as a youngun thutty yars ago, I din't have nawthin, an' now looka me today."

His son looked at him sneeringly. "I'ma lookin' Paw," he said sneeringly, "but I see you ain't got nawthin, just like when you come heah thutty yars ago." His Paw laughed at him. "Why, you cretinous oaf," he said laughingly, "caint you see that now I have eleven kids an' twelve dawgs?"

What will satisfy 2 teen-agers or 4 grownups is:

JUICY CHINESE MEATLOAF

1½ pounds ground beef (chuck, preferably)
¼ cup peanut oil
1½ cups scallions (green onions) with firm greenery, chopped
6 water chestnuts, chopped
1 teaspoon sugar
1 egg, beaten
¼ cup soy sauce
2–4 drops hot sauce
1 tablespoon cornstarch
¼ cup dry wine, or broth, or, alas, water

Reason I say "chuck, preferably" is because chuck beef has just the right amount of fat in proportion to beef to make a juicy, tasty meatloaf or meatballs. In a large fry pan, over high heat, get 1 tablespoon of the peanut oil hot. When you see the first whiff of smoke, lift pan away from heat, reduce heat, add chopped scallions, and cook, stirring constantly until the scallions are soft. Remove fried scallions to a large bowl and add to the bowl the chopped water chestnuts.

Get the rest of the oil hot in the large fry pan and, over high heat, stirring all the while, cook the ground beef until it loses its redness and becomes well browned. Add this to the bowl with onion-water chestnuts.

Beat the sugar into the egg, and add this to the mixture into the bowl. Add the soy sauce and hot sauce. Combine all the ingredients thoroughly, using a fork, if you are dainty, use your hands if you mean business. Beat the cornstarch into the wine, or broth, or, alas, water. Add this to the mixture, and combine it well.

Spoon it all into an oiled baking dish or pan. What size pan? A pan large enough to hold all this stuff, that's how large.

If you like, you can quit right here, for the time being, and refrigerate it, covered. When you want to serve it, put the baking dish into your oven, preheated to 350 degrees, 30 minutes before serving time, after which the top should be nice and crusty. You want to put tomato sauce or ketchup or catsup on it? Go right ahead, put the sauce or whatever on it in last 10 minutes of baking. What I like is a poached or fried egg, with the yolk more than slightly runny, on top of my portion. Rice is good with this, so are potatoes, as are noodles. Have a green salad with this, will you? What should you drink with this? You should drink whatever you want to drink with this, that's what.

SERVES FOUR, MAYBE TWO IF THEY'RE HUNGRY.

The couple had been married for a score of years, which was evident by the fixed, strained smile on the wife's face as she listened to her husband pontificating all evening about politics, the baseball season, the younger generation, every subject that came up.

Finally, one of the other guests couldn't stand it any longer. "Tell me," he said to the husband, "you seem so sure about everything, haven't you ever been wrong in your life?" The husband frowned. "Well, yes," he said, "I remember one time when I was wrong." The wife sat up straight and looked amazed.

"Yes," said the husband, "one time I thought I was wrong about something, but I wasn't."

You can't go wrong with:

FRIED SPAETZLE AND MEAT BALLS (Germany)

2 cups flour
$\frac{1}{2}$ teaspoon salt
2 eggs
cold water

SPAETZLE

Sift the flour and salt together into a bowl. Make a well and drop the eggs into it. Work the flour with your hands until dough is formed, adding a little cold water at a time. Flour a board lightly and knead the dough until it is springy and smooth. Boil a couple of quarts of salted water, put the dough into a colander and force the dough into the boiling water through the colander. When the noodles—spaetzle, they're called—rise to the top, they are finished; drain them well. Now make the:

MEATBALLS

1 pound ground beef
$\frac{1}{4}$ cup bread crumbs
1 small onion, chopped
1 egg, beaten
1 can (10$\frac{1}{2}$ ounces) condensed cream of mushroom soup
$\frac{1}{2}$ cup water
salt and pepper

Mix together the meat, bread crumbs, onion and egg, shape into small, firm balls. Brown them in a heavy fry pan all over, and then add the soup and water, and stir contents of the pan. Cover the pan and cook over low heat for 15 to 20 minutes.

Taste the sauce and correct seasoning to suit yourself. In the last 10 minutes of cooking the meatballs, fry the spaetzle in 3 tablespoons of fat, butter or margarine in a separate pan, and serve in a large platter with the meatballs and sauce on a bed of the fried spaetzle.

SERVES SIX, MAYBE EIGHT.

Something funny happened to my wife and me on our way from Brooklyn. And I tell it to you folks, only because I think the experience we had has something, like maybe a moral, that may stand you in good stead. Well, maybe it isn't a moral, but it's something.

My wife and I moved from a large house in Brooklyn—well, not as large as, let us say, John Wayne's, or Tony Curtis', of course, but pretty large—to a small apartment—well, smaller than some. So there we were with some amenities like a fridge, a clothes dryer, a broiler, so forth that we couldn't use and which the Brooklyn Public Library said they couldn't use, either. So we offered them to a neighbor. Free. Gratis.

So when the men came to move the stuff we were taking, our neighbor asked the movers to move the stuff into their house, which led to a hot contretemps because they couldn't have a meeting of minds—or whatever it was they were using that day—on paying the movers, so they schlepped the stuff themselves and got all exhausted and irritable, and acted like we'd imposed something terrible on them, and wouldn't bid us a faretheewell or even talk to us. If there is a moral here, maybe it is: if you are going to give, give to organized charities.

What I give you here is:

CURRIED BEEFBALLS (Brooklyn)

2 pounds ground beef (chuck, preferably)
¼ teaspoon salt
1 tablespoon curry powder
4 tablespoons oil
1 cup onions, minced
1 large clove garlic, minced (about 1 tablespoon when minced)
¼ cup fresh parsley, minced, or 1 tablespoon dried flakes
10-ounce can (approximately) condensed beef broth plus 1
     canful water

I think chuck is best for this because it has just enough fat to make juicy beefballs or loaf, or whatever. Combine beef with salt and curry. You say you want more curry? You got a right. Go ahead, have more if you like. Hot up 2 tablespoons oil in large fry pan. In it, over medium heat, fry onion, garlic, parsley until onion is soft.

Combine fried stuff with meat. Wet your little hands slightly. Form meat mixture into balls. What size? Pingpong? Golf? Football? Any size your whim dictates is okay with me, folk.

Hot up rest of oil in that fry pan. Fry beefballs, turning gently with slotted spoon to brown them all over. When beefballs are browned, cover pan, cook over low heat 15 minutes, turning balls occasionally. Combine broth and water—or beer, which is what I sometimes do—add it to pan. Bring to boil. Taste. You think it needs seasoning, you go right ahead. You want the sauce thick? Dissolve 1 tablespoon cornstarch in ¼ cup cold water, stir it in, cook until thickened. Have a ball! Have many balls!

SERVES FOUR TO SIX.

Jimmy Durante is one of the few comedians who is a truly great wit, and here is some evidence.

Seems that Durante has loved golf for a long time, and though he's played it for many years, never has been able to get out of the duffer class.

One day he was playing a course that was next to a railroad. Good old Jimmy teed up his ball, took a mighty swing—and missed the ball completely. But he followed through on his swing, and looked up to the heavens, and stayed that way all the while a train was passing by.

"Well," said the friend he was playing with, "aren't you going to take another swing at it?" Jimmy glared at him. "Shut up, don't talk so loud, I want those people in the train going by to think I hit the ball for a mile." What is a hit in my house is:

OPEN FACE BEEF PIE (English)

9-inch pie pastry
$\frac{1}{4}$ cup oil or vegetable shortening
$1\frac{1}{2}$ to 2 pounds beef, chuck or round, chopped
1 bunch scallions (green onions), minced with white and
    greenery separated
1 sweet pepper, (red if you can get it), chopped
1 (or more) cloves garlic, pressed or minced fine
2 eggs, beaten
$\frac{1}{2}$ teaspoon salt, $\frac{1}{4}$ teaspoon pepper
$\frac{1}{4}$ cup bread crumbs

Have pie crust ready in pan, jab bottom all over with a fork. Preheat your oven to 425 degrees.

In 2 tablespoons of hot oil, in a large fry pan, fry the meat, stirring with a fork, until it is all well-browned. Pour off fat. Remove the beef to a large mixing bowl. Add the remaining oil to the fry pan and in it cook the minced white parts of the scallions, and the chopped sweet pepper and garlic until they are soft. Add this mixture to the beef in the mixing bowl.

Add the beaten eggs to the bowl, with salt and pepper. Combine the mixture thoroughly.

Spoon it all into the pie shell and bake for 25 to 30 minutes in oven which you have preheated to 425 degrees. In last 10 minutes, sprinkle with bread crumbs and the minced greenery of the scallions. The meat filling should not be dry. If it is, add a little hot broth to the filling, pouring it in slowly and evenly.

This, with a cooked vegetable, or a salad, will make a splendid dinner.

SERVES FOUR.

The drunken American tourist sitting at a sidewalk table of a cafe in Paris saw a long procession of automobiles, the first one carrying as passengers a beautiful young girl in a wedding gown and an elderly man in a high hat and cutaway, both of them brushing rice off their clothes and laughing gaily, their car dragging along the street several lengths of tin cans tied to each other, and all the cars behind them following with blaring horns. He grabbed the arm of a passing waiter. "Whozzat got married?" the drunken American asked.

"Je ne comprends pas," said the waiter, shaking himself loose.

Later on in the afternoon, the drunken American, somewhat more drunk by this time, was sitting at the same table when he saw a funeral motorcade pass by, going in the opposite direction. He grabbed the sleeve of a passing waiter—the same one, as it happened—and asked, "Whozzat died?"

The waiter shook himself loose and answered, "Je ne comprends pas."

The American drunk shook his head sadly. "Tsa shame," he murmured into his glass of Pernod, "poor old slob J. N. Comprawnpa sure didn't last long."

What won't last long before four people is:

BEEFBALLS WITH SWEET AND SOUR SAUCE

1½ pounds ground chuck
½ cup cracker meal
¼ teaspoon each, salt and pepper
1 egg
4 tablespoons melted fat (¼ cup), or butter, oil, or marge
½ cup chopped onions
¼ teaspoon oregano
¼ cup minced parsley
1 cup tomato or chili sauce
2 tablespoons (or more) sugar (brown if you have it)
2 tablespoons (more or less) lemon, or lime juice, or vinegar

I specified chuck beef because that cut of meat has just the right proportion of fat to the meat to make a juicy hamburger, meatloaf, or meatballs.

In a mixing bowl, combine the ground meat with the cracker meal, the salt and pepper, and the egg. In a large fry pan get 2 tablespoons of the fat hot and in it fry the onions until they are brown, over medium heat, stirring often, careful not to let the onions burn. Combine half the fried onions with the meat mixture.

Remove the rest of the fried onions to another mixing bowl and put all the other ingredients into this bowl and stir. Fry balls in the remaining fat until they are well-browned all over. The larger your balls, the longer you should fry them.

Now you have all the sauce ingredients combined thoroughly, haven't you? Of course you do. Pour all of the sauce ingredients over the meatballs, cover the pan, and cook for about 10 minutes, stirring often.

SERVES FOUR.

From his traffic post three blocks away, the cop could see the car careening from lane to lane as it approached him in the moving traffic. When it was about 29 feet away from him the car swerved and came to a full stop. The cop was enraged as he strode purposefully up to the car. In the driver's seat was a pretty gray-haired little lady who looked no more than 60, though she was pushing 70 pretty hard.

The cop clenched his teeth—he read bad novels where people were always saying things through "clenched teeth" to denote rage—and said: "Don't you know that this is a safety zone, lady?" he said. The little old lady said, "Officer, obviously you are a reader of bad novels where characters are always saying things through clenched teeth to denote anger, and if you and those bad novelists had the sense God gave a goose, you would know that it is impossible to understand anything said through clenched teeth. So unclench your teeth like a good boy, Officer, and say what you have to say."

So the cop unclenched his teeth and repeated, "Don't you know that this is a safety zone, lady?" The little old lady smiled sweetly. "Don't be stupider than is altogether necessary, Officer," she said sweetly, "of course I know this is a safety zone, why else do you think I stopped here?"

Don't let your unfamiliarity with okra stop you from making a splendid:

BEEF-TOMATO-OKRA BAKE (New Orleans Creole)

2 tablespoons melted fat, oil, butter, or marge
1 cup onions, chopped
1 cup chopped sweet pepper
1 tablespoon garlic, minced
1 to 1½ pounds ground beef (chuck, shoulder, or bottom round)
1-pound can whole, peeled tomatoes, well mashed
1-pound can or one 10-ounce package frozen okra drained
¼ teaspoon salt
⅛ teaspoon cayenne pepper
1 cup grated cheese, whatever kind you prefer (please see
    Note)

Get the melted fat, or whatever, hot in a large fry pan. In it cook the onion, sweet pepper, and garlic—stirring all the while —until the onion is golden and the pepper soft. Add the chopped beef, break it up in the pan with a kitchen fork or spoon, and cook over medium heat, stirring all the while, until the meat is all browned. Add the mashed tomatoes and okra, and stir it gently, to distribute all the ingredients thoroughly in the mixture.

Okra is a pod from a plant, African in origin, which is grown widely through the South.

Stir in salt and cayenne pepper. Taste the mixture, and add salt or cayenne to suit your taste. Remember, however, that cayenne is powerful stuff, and whenever using hot stuff like this, or curry, or chili, that you should judge the degree of hotness from the aftertaste.

Spoon the mixture into a casserole or baking dish, sprinkle with the grated cheese and bake in oven preheated to 350 degrees until the cheese is melted and bubbling.

Note about cheese: Kosher ladies constantly scold me for violating the precepts of kosher cooking, which forbid the use of dairy products with meat. To them I say, I'm writing for everyone, and if any recipe has an ingredient that makes the dish unkosher, or *traif*, just leave it out, or cook some other dish. This is good without cheese; but it is better with cheese.

SERVES FOUR.

The piano player, known as Scotch, because that's all he ever drank, was taking a break at the bar in the sleazy place he worked when the boss came up to him and told him to get back to the piano. He took his Scotch and water to the piano, took a long pull on it and began playing. When he finished his first piece one of the customers came over to him. "I don't know whether you realize it," said the customer, "but you are undoubtedly the worst piano player in the world." The pianist nodded. "Oh, I know that," he said, "but you see, I'm not really a pianist, I'm a violinist." The customer glared at him. "Then why don't you play a violin instead of a piano?" he asked. "Don't be stupid," said the musician, lifting his drink from the piano and taking a gulp, "if I played the violin, where would I keep my glass of booze?"

And, speaking of booze as I was, how about making:

ROAST OR CORNED BEEF HASH
WITH BOOZY SAUCE (Kentucky)

1 tablespoon melted fat, or butter, or marge
1 cup onion, minced
1 clove (or more) garlic, minced, fine or pressed
3 cups cooked roast or corned beef, cut into small cubes
1 cup potatoes, boiled and cut into small cubes
boozy sauce (ingredients below)
$\frac{1}{4}$ teaspoon each, salt and pepper
4 eggs, poached or fried

In a large fry pan, get the melted fat or whatever, hot, and in it cook the onion and garlic until the onion is soft and beginning to turn brown. You can do this very quickly if you use very high heat, and stir constantly. Stir in the cubed cooked meat—with all the fat removed—and then stir in cubed potatoes, gently so the potatoes don't get mashed. Add the

BOOZY SAUCE

1 tablespoon melted fat or whatever
1 tablespoon flour
1 cup boiling beef broth
$\frac{1}{2}$ cup bourbon
1 teaspoon commercial gravy coloring

Melt the fat in a small fry pan, stir in flour and stir for 2 minutes until flour is golden. Stir in boiling broth gradually, add the bourbon and gravy coloring and cook until slightly thickened.

Stir this sauce into the beef-potato mixture, with salt and pepper. Spoon the mixture into a baking dish, pack it down, and bake in oven preheated to 350 degrees until the top is crisp and browned.

Serve to 4 people, with a fried or poached egg sitting bravely on the top. The whites of the eggs should be well-set, but the yolks should be runny. Of course, if you don't want eggs, don't use them. And if, by some chance you don't want hash, serve 2 fried or poached eggs to 4 people. Or go out to a restaurant.

SERVES FOUR.

This fellow was a prominent freeloader and he constantly made the rounds of his friends' homes, always making sure that he arrived just as the family was sitting down to a meal. One Sunday, he arrived just in time at a friend's house for lunch. The family was having cold cuts, and not once did his knife and fork stop moving. Finally, the lady of the house noticed what he was doing.

"Why," she asked, "are you eating only the corned beef, and not any of the salami or the bologna?"

"Because," he said, "I like corned beef better."

The lady looked slightly irked. "You know," she said, "corned beef is much more expensive than the other meats."

The man smiled happily, and for the first time he stopped eating, but only momentarily. "That's right," he said, "and believe me, it's worth it!"

A fine thing for a party and much cheaper if you make it yourself is:

HOME-MADE CORNED BEEF (Jewish)

4 quarts water
1½ cups coarse, kosher salt
½ ounce saltpeter (obtainable only in drugstores)
1 tablespoon brown sugar
6 bay leaves, crumbled
2 tablespoons pickling spices
6 cloves garlic, slivered
5 pounds brisket of beef

For 5 minutes, boil the water with everything except the garlic and beef.

There should be streaks of fat in the beef, as well as some on the surface, otherwise the corned beef won't be juicy when it is finished. Let it get quite cool.

You must have a large glass or stoneware crock, or wooden cask. Put the beef into the crock, add the garlic and pour the spicy mixture over it. Put a heavy plate over the meat, to keep it all under the spicy water, and then tie a piece of muslin over the top of the crock. The muslin should be taut, and tied tight. Now put a cover on the crock, leaving a gap so there can be some circulation of air, and put the crock in a cool place and forget about it for 2 weeks.

At the end of 2 weeks, rinse the meat well, put it into a pot with enough water to cover it and about 1 inch more, add:

1 onion, chopped
3 bay leaves, crumbled
½ cup vinegar
2–3 cloves garlic, chopped

Bring the water to boil and then reduce the heat and simmer it until it is tender, about 2½ to 3 hours. Keep the meat in the pot, covered, for about 30 minutes before you drain it well and serve it. Corned beef, you know, is good hot or cold, or even lukewarm. Slice it thin and trim off fat before serving. Good with hot mustard. And pickles. And boiled potatoes. And beer.
SERVES A LOT OF PEOPLE.

For as long as he had been the minister in the rural area, he had received "offerings" from his parishioners in the form of farm products—a ham, a bushel of potatoes, corn, apples, like that. Then, one week, he was delighted beyond belief when one of the farmers gave him an envelope with a $1 bill in it. Following week, a couple of other farmers handed him envelopes with $1 bills in them. Finally, each one of his farmer parishioners did the same. "Don't misunderstand me," he said to one of the farmers, "because I am delighted to get the cash, because that way I can buy the things I really need, rather than depending on what kind of farm products I get. I merely want to know how come all you nice folks began giving me money instead of corn, and apples, and hams and like that?"

The farmer blushed. "Well," he said blushingly, "it's like this: the wife and I were talking about what to give you, corn, ham, or like that, and she came up with this idea: 'Hiram,' she said, 'you know how the price of corn, ham, things like that, that we get these days is much more than we used to,' and I had to agree with her, when she said it would be cheaper to give you money."

What won't cost much is:

FRANKFURTER, EGGPLANT AND MUSHROOM GRAVY CASSEROLE (U.S.A.)

1 medium-sized eggplant, peeled and sliced
¼ cup oil, olive or peanut
½ cup onion, minced
2 cloves garlic, minced
½ pound skinned or skinless all-beef frankfurters, sliced thin
¼ cup bread crumbs
1 can (10½ ounces) mushroom gravy
¼ cup grated cheese (Parmesan, any kind you like)

Peel the eggplant and cut it up into thin slices. In a large fry pan get 2 tablespoons of the oil hot and in it fry the eggplant on both sides until the eggplant is nicely browned. Remove it from the pan, but don't bother to keep it hot, because it is going to be baked.

Get the rest of the oil hot and fry the onion and garlic until the onion is soft. Combine the onion-garlic with the sliced skinned franks and the bread crumbs.

Put a layer of eggplant slices into a casserole, spoon some of the onion-frank-bread crumb mixture over it, spoon over that some of the mushroom gravy, and repeat until all ingredients have been used, with some of the mushroom gravy on the top.

Sprinkle with the grated cheese and bake in a 350 degree oven for about 25 minutes, when the gravy on top should be bubbling.

SERVES FOUR, MAYBE FIVE.

At first, when the man entered the European train compartment where she had hoped to remain alone, the lady traveler was nervous, but she soon got over that because he was not only polite, but also charming and witty. By the time they were nearing the border, she had relaxed completely and felt that not only did he not seem like a stranger, but rather like someone she'd known a long time, someone she could trust. "You know," she whispered, as the train slowed down and then stopped to allow the customs guards to board the train, "I'm terribly frightened, because this diamond-studded brooch I'm wearing is not on my customs declaration because the duty on it would be so high, I decided to smuggle it in, and I'm so scared I'm trembling."

Her fellow traveler smiled urbanely and assured her that he'd make sure she didn't get in trouble. The customs guard came into the compartment, smiled cynically, and said, "Of course, neither of you is possessed of anything on which a duty must be paid?" The gentleman passenger shook his head. "Oh, no," he said, "you are wrong. That brooch this lady is wearing was bought across the border and she's trying to smuggle it." The woman burst out crying and surrendered the brooch to the guard, who thanked the gentleman for his tip. When the train resumed its journey, the lady cried out, "How could you do such a thing after telling me that you'd see I didn't get caught?" The gentleman smiled gently, took his bulging suitcase off the overhead rack, and opened it. "Here, my dear lady," he said, "please stop crying and take any two of these diamond brooches you like, for without you I might have been in terrible trouble."

No trouble at all to make a:

LENTIL-FRANK CASSEROLE (Jewish)

2 cups dried lentils
2 tablespoons rendered fat or oil
1 cup onions, chopped
2 cloves garlic, mashed
2 ribs celery, chopped with greenery
1 green pepper, chopped
4 large frankfurters
1 can (10½ ounces) tomato soup

Soak the lentils overnight in slightly salted water to cover. Drain them the next day, and save the water. In a large frying pan, get the fat or oil hot and in it fry the onion, garlic, celery, and green pepper until the onion and pepper begin to turn brown, stirring often over medium heat.

Remove the vegetables to a casserole or baking dish. Dry the pan. Prick frankfurters with a fork, and fry them in the pan, and when they are browned and much of the fat has been drained off and thrown away, chop the franks up into small pieces.

Combine 1 cup of the water in which the lentils soaked with the tomato soup; combine, in the baking dish, the lentils, vegetables, frankfurters, and the tomato soup mixture.

Cover the dish and bake in oven preheated to 350 degrees for one hour, removing cover in the last 10 minutes.

Instead of frankfurters, sometimes try the Polish sausage called kielbasa, or knackwurst, or small breakfast sausages, all fried in dry pan, after pricking them with a fork, until most of the fat has been drained out. And, of course, you can do this same dish with any kind of beans you like.

SERVES FOUR.

VEAL

The man had just read a report from the nation's capital about a bill, submitted by the Republican leadership of Congress, which had been defeated because several of the Republican lawmakers had aligned themselves with the Democrats. He was denouncing those men.

"They should be read out of the party," he hollered. "They should be impeached, or something." When he was finished heaping maledictions on their heads, his son broke in. "But, old Daddy," the boy said, "after the last election when your candidate won, you praised all the Democrats who voted for him, because you said he couldn't have won without their votes, and you said they were intelligent, wonderful people because they came over to your side."

The boy's father nodded. "You are absolutely right, young son," he said, "and let that be a lesson to you which you should never in your life forget."

The boy looked puzzled. "And what, old Daddy," he asked puzzledly, "would that lesson be?"

His father said he was glad that the boy had asked that question. "Always remember, young son," he said, "that if you believe in a political party, or a religion, or whatever, the people who join the other side are terrible traitors, but those who come over to your side are wonderful converts who have seen the light."

If you want something light to eat, stay away from:

BREADED VEAL CHOPS WITH ASPARAGUS SAUCE (Sicily)

4 veal chops (about 1 inch thick)
oil
1 cup onions, minced
1 clove (or more) garlic, mashed
$\frac{1}{4}$ pound fresh mushrooms, sliced, or 4-ounce can pieces,
    drained and dried
$\frac{1}{4}$ teaspoon salt
$\frac{1}{4}$ teaspoon pepper
$\frac{1}{4}$ teaspoon oregano
flour
2 eggs, beaten
bread crumbs
1 can (10$\frac{1}{2}$) ounces, condensed cream of asparagus soup
$\frac{1}{4}$ cup bourbon, dry wine, or water, alas

Cut off as much fat as you can from the chops, without mangling them. Cut a slit in each chop, all the way through the meat, to the bone. Dry the chops thoroughly.

In a large frying pan, get 2 tablespoons of oil hot and in it fry the onion, garlic, and mushrooms, adding salt, pepper and oregano, until the onions and mushrooms are quite browned and most of the liquid is cooked away.

Put equal parts of the fried mixture into the pockets you cut in each chop. Coat each side of each chop with flour, dipping it into flour and shaking off excess.

Dip the chops into the beaten eggs, and then into the bread crumbs, coating them all over. Before I fry anything that's breaded, I like to refrigerate the stuff for an hour or longer, to make certain that the breading doesn't come off during frying.

Hot up 2 tablespoons of oil in the large frying pan and in it fry the breaded chops, until they are golden on both sides. Cover the pan and cook over low heat for 15 minutes, turning the chops once. At this point you can knock off work until 15 minutes before serving. Put soup into a pan, add bourbon or whatever, and slowly bring to a boil while you fry the chops, uncovered, in a little more oil, over high heat, until they are deeply browned. Serve with sauce on the side.

SERVES FOUR.

The rich bachelor came home late one night, well, early one morning probably would be more exact, and, to his great horror found that his "man servant," a middle-aged Englishman, was blind, roaring drunk. He didn't mind the fellow's having drunk his expensive booze, but he didn't like the idea of having to undress the man, clean up the mess he had made of the living room and all like that. So when he woke in the early afternoon he found his man, pale and shaky from his Bacchanalia.

"Look here," the bachelor hollered, "don't go trying to make believe nothing at all happened last night; it was disgusting to come home to find you in such a revoltingly drunken state."

His man shrugged (did I tell you that his man's name was Abercrombie?) and said, "Well that shouldn't have been much of a shock to you, sir, if I may say so." The rich fellow bellowed with rage. "What do you mean?" he bellowed, " 'it shouldn't have been much of a shock'?" Abercrombie smiled faintly. "Well, sir," he said, "if you don't know that I've been drunk every night since I've been working for you in the past 20 years, it can only be that last night was the first time you ever came home sober."

How, now, about some:

DRUNKEN VEAL CUTLETS (Italy)

1–1½ pounds veal cutlets, cut thin, Italian-style, from the leg,
     pounded thinner
½ teaspoon salt
¼ teaspoon pepper
1 cup onion, chopped fine (dried onion flakes are okay in dire
     emergency if soaked)
1 tablespoon garlic minced fine (ditto for dried minced garlic)
¼ teaspoon dried oregano
6 tablespoons oil (olive, preferably, but if you've got a thing
     about it, any oil)
½ cup dry wine, red or white
flour
red radishes, black olives, parsley sprigs, cucumber slices, and
     cherry tomatoes or tomato slices

The cutlets should be very thin. Rub salt and pepper into
them and let them stand while you make the marinade: combine
the onion, garlic, oregano, 2 tablespoons of the oil and the wine,
stir, and put the pounded cutlets into the marinade in a large
glazed earthenware, or enameled bowl or pot for at least one
hour.

Get a large fry pan very hot, put in 2 tablespoons of oil and
in it fry the cutlets quickly on both sides over medium heat.
When I say quickly I mean quickly, not more than 1 minute on
each side. Add oil as needed, and don't crowd the pan. When all
the cutlets have been lightly browned on each side, put them on
a hot serving platter, and pour the marinade into the frying pan.
Cook over high heat, scraping the bottom of the pan to get up
any burned bits—delicious!—from the pan. Pour the marinade
over the cutlets and serve.

SERVES FOUR.

The boy, dressed in a schmatteh (gown) generally worn by college graduates and carrying a mortarboard, sat down next to a large elderly man in the bus. "It isn't difficult to guess," said the man, "that you have just come from, or you are going to your commencement ceremony, right?"

The young man smiled. "You are absolutely correct, sir," he said.

The elderly man sighed sadly. "Ah me, lackaday, how well do I remember my own commencement ceremony when I was graduated so many years ago, and commenced to climb the ladder of life, rung by rung, rung by rung, just as the president of the university advised us all to do."

The boy looked with added interest at the elderly man and said, "And so, now these many years later, after having climbed the ladder of life rung by rung, rung by rung, as I am about to do, you are a rich, successful, and, undoubtedly, a happy man?"

"Don't you be getting smart with me, kiddo," the man said, snarling threateningly. "Who said anything about being rich, successful, and happy? What I am is the best climber of ladders on the East Coast, south of Boston, is all."

East or west, north or south, one of the best hot weather meat dishes I've ever eaten is:

VITELLO TONNATO (VEAL WITH TUNA SAUCE) (Italy)

2 pounds (approximately) boneless veal (leg, shoulder or rump) in one piece
chicken soup
1 large onion, chopped
1 clove
1 bay leaf
¼ cup parsley (maybe more), chopped (if no fresh available, 2 tablespoons dried)
2 ribs celery, chopped
6 peppercorns
1 teaspoon salt
1 can (approximately 7 ounces) tuna fish, drained, dried, and minced
3 or 4 anchovies, drained, dried, and minced fine
2 tablespoons lemon juice
approximately ½ cup olive oil (you can use other oils, of course, but it won't be the same)
2 teaspoons capers, minced

Leg is, of course, the most expensive cut of veal, and since this dish is going to be cooked for an hour, the cheaper cuts are just as good. Put the meat, tied up by the butcher into a compact chunk, in a pot and add chicken soup to cover. Put into the pot the chopped onion, clove, bay leaf, parsley, celery, peppercorns and salt. Bring to the boil, reduce the heat and simmer for 1 hour.

Chop the drained, dried minced tuna fish and anchovies, adding just a little lemon juice and olive oil, until the mixture is like a paste. Put it into a mixing bowl, and add the minced capers, and add lemon juice and oil carefully, tasting the mixture as you add the juice and oil. It should taste slightly salty, faintly of the tuna flavor, and very, very smooth and somewhat oily. When the mixture pleases your palate, put it, in a tightly sealed container, into the refrigerator.

When the veal has simmered for 1 hour, remove it from pot, put it into a large bowl, cover the bowl and let it cool. When it is quite cool, cut it into very thin slices, removing the butcher's cord. Put a thin layer of the tuna sauce in the bowl, cover it with slices of veal, put a thin layer of sauce over that, and repeat the process until everything is in the bowl, with a thin layer of tuna sauce on top. Strain broth and keep in fridge for sauces.

Refrigerate it for hours and hours, preferably overnight. When you serve it, put the veal slices, covered with the sauce which will be stiffened, on a large, chilled platter, arranged as tastefully as you can, have a garnishment of sliced red radishes, cherry tomatoes if they are available, and pimiento-stuffed green olives, drained and dried, all over the platter. If you can't get cherry tomatoes, use chopped strips of drained, dried pimiento or roasted red pepper slices all around the platter, and over the meat. Serve this with pumpernickel, corn, or rye bread, a mixed green salad and what I like with this is a good beer, chilled, but not icy-cold, for overchilling a good beer destroys the flavor, and you might as well be drinking sarsaparilla. You say you like sarsaparilla? Well, this is the U.S.A., and you got a right.

This is, as I said at the outset, an ideal cold meat dish for a hot summer day; the veal marinated in the tuna sauce has a wonderful, subtle flavor that is unique and not known to many people, and all the work—what little there is—can be done in the cool of the evening the day before it is to be served.

SERVES SIX TO EIGHT.

These two friends came back by plane to New York after a long stay in California and one of them rushed for a telephone to call his girl friend. He was in the phone booth for quite a while, and his friend, who was waiting outside the booth, could see that he was having some sort of difficulty, because he kept making excited motions with his free hand. Finally, he hung up, and came out of the booth. He looked quite worried.

"What's the matter?" asked his friend. The fellow shook his head sadly. "She says," he said, "that she's getting married next week."

"So what?" said the friend, laughing. "You know a lot of other girls, call one of them up." The fellow shook his head. "No, no," he said, "you don't understand. She says she's marrying me."

Two ingredients that make a perfect marriage, as do spaghetti and meatballs, cheese blintzes and sour cream, and ham and eggs, are:

VEAL AND KIDNEYS (England)

1 pound veal steak
1 veal kidney
1 teaspoon salt
½ teaspoon pepper
2 tablespoons oil or butter
1 cup bouillon
6 large mushrooms
¼ cup port wine

Wipe the veal with a damp cloth and cut it into bite-size cubes. Cut the fat off the kidney, scald it for a few minutes in boiling water and then slice it into small pieces, discarding the core. Dry it. Sprinkle the veal and kidney pieces with the salt and pepper. Hot up the oil or butter and brown the veal and kidney pieces all over, stirring it. When the meat is well browned remove it from the pan, and put it all into a casserole and preheat your oven to 350 degrees.

Wash the mushrooms, slice them, and fry them gently in the pan in which you browned the meat. Bring the bouillon to the boil and add it to the meat in the casserole. Bake it, covered, for 30 minutes. Now add the mushrooms and stir, and cook until the meat is tender, which should be another 10 to 15 minutes. In the last 5 minutes, add the wine and stir. This is a total cooking time of 40 to 45 minutes in the oven. Mashed potatoes are good with this.

SERVES FOUR TO FIVE.

When the burglar's wife woke in the morning she was furious to see, right in the middle of the living room floor, a large safe. She went back to the bedroom and furiously woke up her husband.

"What's the idea," she hollered, "bringing that safe home with you? Why didn't you open it where you found it?" Her husband made quiet shushing noises designed to soothe her, but it didn't work, and then, when she paused to take breath for another outburst, he said, "Look, honey, I tried everything to open it up in the office I robbed last night—I used nitro; I used the acetylene torch; nothing worked." His wife glared. "Then why did you bring it here?" she hollered.

The burglar shrugged. "Well," he said, "you know how that kid of ours is? Breaks every toy he gets his hands on? I figured I'd bring it home and let him play with it for a half-hour or so."

A half-hour or so of preparatory work is all you'll have to do, with just an occasional peek to see how it's coming along, to make a wonderful:

TOP OF THE STOVE VEAL ROAST (U.S.A.)

3 pounds boneless veal roast
4 tablespoons oil (or 2 tablespoons each oil and butter)
1 pound onions, chopped
1 large clove garlic, minced (approximately 1 tablespoon)
2 cups celery with leaves, chopped
1 cup carrots, chopped
$\frac{1}{2}$ cup parsley, minced (2 tablespoons if dried flakes)
$\frac{1}{4}$ teaspoon ground bay leaves or 1 large leaf, crumbled fine
1 can (approximately 10 ounces) condensed chicken soup
$\frac{1}{2}$ soupcanful vermouth or dry wine (red or white)
salt and pepper

The roast will be tied when you get it from the butcher. Put 1 tablespoon of oil into a large, heavy pot and hot it up. Brown the roast, over high heat, all over. When it starts to smoke, turn the heat down—take the pot off the burner if you're using an electric range because it will take quite a while before the coils lose their red-hotness. When the meat is nicely browned, remove it from the pot. Don't bother to keep it hot.

Add the rest of the oil to the pot and in it, over low heat, fry the onions, garlic, the celery, and parsley, scraping the pot with a flexible metal spatula to get up the good burned stuff from the meat. Add the bay leaf and stir. Make a small hollow in the vegetables and put the meat into it. Pour the soup over the meat and add half of the wine, which will leave you $\frac{1}{4}$ canful.

Bring the liquid to the boil, cover the pot, and reduce the heat so that it simmers slightly. The tighter the cover fits the pot, the better it is. If much steam escapes right at the start, cover the top of the pot with aluminum foil and set the cover down on the foil. Some steam will escape, inevitably, but not as

much as would were you to use no foil. Cook for 2 hours, turning the meat every 30 minutes, adding a bit of wine each time. The onions and the celery will liquefy, but if too much of the liquid escapes, add a little boiling water so that there is about 1 inch of liquid in the pot at all times. In the last 30 minutes of cooking, taste the sauce and add salt and pepper to suit your taste, also add the carrots. Before serving, cut string off the roast. If you have a blender, puree the vegetables, cut enough thin slices off the roast to allow for 1 serving per person, pour the sauce over all. With a cooked veg or green salad.
SERVES FOUR TO SIX.

All the ladies at the coffee klatch laughed when one of them declared, smugly, that in 11 years of marriage she had never had even one argument with her husband. They didn't believe her. They posed particular situations and asked if those had caused a fight between them. The woman said "No" to each one. They'd never fought about money; their respective in-laws; who should close the windows on cold mornings; her cooking; who should answer the phone; his going out "with the boys"; her going out "with the girls"; or any of the things most married people argue about at some time or other.

"You mean to say that you never had a difference of opinion about anything?" one of them asked, finally. The lady laughed. "Oh, I didn't say that," she said laughingly. "I just never let him know about my difference with his opinion."

What is your opinion of:

VEAL WITH HAM AND MUSHROOM CAPS? (Spain)

1½ pounds veal cutlets, sliced thin
½ teaspoon salt
½ teaspoon pepper
4 tablespoons oil, butter, or margarine
8 large mushrooms (or a lot more button mushrooms),
      discolored tips of stems cut off and thrown away
1 tablespoon parsley, chopped
¼ pound boiled ham
½ cup pitted black olives, sliced

Rub into the veal cutlets the salt and pepper and put them aside. Hot up the oil, or butter or margarine in a large fry pan, and in it fry the mushrooms. With large mushrooms, it is always good to cut off the stems and save them in your fridge to use them, chopped, in soups, stews, and stuffings.

But if you can't get the big ones, several small ones for each serving will do fine. With spatula, remove the mushrooms from the fry pan when they are tender, which will take about five minutes over medium heat, to a large platter placed over pot of very hot water, and cover with bowl.

Add parsley and fry the veal cutlets—this amount of meat should serve 4 people, so there should be two pieces of veal for each serving—for not more than 2 minutes on each side, over medium heat. Put cooked veal on bowl-covered platter to keep hot. Veal is toughened by overcooking, especially when it is cut or pounded thin. Fry the ham slightly in the same pan, with sliced olives. Put 2 pieces of veal on individual serving plates, put a slice of ham on each piece of veal and top with mushrooms. Pour pan juices over each serving.

SERVES FOUR.

The part owner of the shoe store was teaching a young fellow the business, and the new clerk watched and listened carefully while the partner sold, wrapped the shoes, and collected the money from the customer. When the customer left the store, the partner beckoned to the new clerk. "Did you watch, and listen all the time until the customer left the store?" he asked.

The young man nodded. "Yes, sir," he said. "And did you hear me tell the man that the price was $10, including the tax?" he asked. Again the young man nodded. "And did you see the man pay me?" the partner asked. The young man nodded again. "And did you notice that the man gave me this $20 bill and then walked out without waiting for his change?" asked the partner. "No, sir, I didn't notice that it was a $20 bill," the clerk answered.

"Well, never mind that, what I want you to know is that there is a question of business ethics involved here, and I want you to tell me what that question is," the partner said. The new clerk did not hesitate. "You should have run after the man with his change," he said unhesitatingly.

The partner howled with rage. "No, no, you cretinous oaf," he howled ragingly, "the ethical question is: should I tell my partner?"

What I'm going to tell you now is how to make:

ROAST STUFFED BREAST OF VEAL (Jewish)

1 breast of veal (they average about 5 pounds, much of it bone)
2 large cloves garlic
flour
1 cup onion, grated (see Note)
2 medium eggs, beaten
4 large potatoes, grated
¼ cup rendered chicken fat or vegetable shortening
¼ pound fresh mushrooms, sliced, or one 4-ounce can pieces,
    drained and dried
¼ cup parsley, minced
1 teaspoon salt
¼ teaspoon cayenne pepper

Almost always now, veal breasts are sold in supermarkets with a pocket already cut in it. If there is no pocket, ask the meat cutter to make one, or, if he's surly about it—and there are too many surly ones around—just cut a deep slit between the meat and the bones all the way to the back, but don't sever the flap of meat from the bones.

Cut small slits in the meat, cut one of the garlic cloves into thin slivers and put them into the slits. Mince the other garlic clove for use later. Rub about 1 tablespoon of flour into the meat.

Onion Note: Undoubtedly, peeling, slicing, chopping, and, especially grating onions make your eyes water. If so, put your hands, with the onion and knife, into a plastic bag, peel it; throw away the peel; now put the grater or chopping board into the bag, and chop, slice, or grate, and weep no more my lady.

Beat the eggs into the grated onion, in a large bowl. Grate the potatoes into the bowl with the onion-egg mixture, and the potatoes will not become discolored. Use the coarse side of the grater.

In a large fry pan, hot up the fat or whatever, and in it fry the mushrooms and parsley until the mushrooms are soft. (Canned mushrooms are already cooked, of course, but frying makes them taste better.) Add the potato-onion-egg mixture to the pan, sprinkle with ½ teaspoon salt, and ⅛ teaspoon cayenne pepper, and stir in just enough flour to make the mixture hold together. Stuff the mixture into the veal breast pocket. Rub the meat with the remaining salt—½ teaspoon—and cayenne—⅛ teaspoon.

Put the stuffed breast on a lightly oiled pan. Bake it in oven preheated to 350 degrees for 25 to 30 minutes per pound, basting often with pan juices, or melted fat, or both. The stuffing can, of course, be varied by adding chopped meat, chicken, or hard-boiled eggs.

SERVES FOUR.

The neighbor lady asked if her husband ever complained about the food she serves him. "Once in a while," she said.

"What do you do about it, what do you give him when he doesn't like something you cooked for him?" the neighbor asked.

"I give him," she said, "his hat and coat."

Hang up your husband's hat and coat and give him:

HOT SAUSAGE-EGG-MUSHROOM STUFFED VEAL ROAST (Spain)

boned veal rump, about 3 to 3½ pounds
2 tablespoons rendered fat, or butter, oil, or marge
¼ pound mushrooms, sliced
½ cup scallions (green onions), minced
2 hot Italian or Spanish sausages
3 hard-boiled eggs
1 cup chicken broth, boiling

Almost always these rolled roasts are to be found in the meat markets, already tied. Get some butchers' cord—what they tie up rolled roasts with. When you get home, cut the twine off and unroll the meat. You are going to stuff it and then you will roll it up and tie it up yourself. You say you can't do it? How do you know you can't, if you've never tried it? Get the fat hot in a large fry pan; in it fry the mushrooms and scallions until they are soft and browned well.

Cut open the casings of the sausages and combine the meat with the fried mushrooms and scallions. Spread this mixture on half of the unrolled roast. Place the hard-boiled eggs in a row across the roast so that, when it is rolled up, the eggs are in a line as close as possible to the middle of the meat. Put the roast into a pan. Pour the boiling broth over the roast and cook in oven preheated to 350 degrees for 30 minutes to the pound. Baste the roast from time to time with the pan juices.

Cut it into thin slices and put them on a hot platter. Pour pan juices over all, and accompany with mashed potatoes, or crisp Italian or French bread with which to glop up the wonderful sauce. And have a green salad.

SERVES FOUR TO SIX.

Small boy came home from school and, as usual, his mother asked him what he had done that day. "I learned how to write today," he said. "That's wonderful! What did you write?" she asked. The boy shrugged. "I think it was 'cat'," the small boy said, "but I ain't sure, because we don't study reading until next week."

When the weather is coolish, warmish, hottish, coldish, any day, any week, to make me moan low with pleasure, serve:

OSSO BUCO (Braised Veal Marrowbone) (Italy)

eight 3-inch pieces of shank of veal (see Note)
2 tablespoons each, oil and butter or 4 tablespoons oil
1 teaspoon salt
$\frac{1}{2}$ teaspoon pepper
1 medium carrot, grated
1 large onion, minced
1 rib celery, chopped with greenery
$\frac{1}{2}$ teaspoon each dried rosemary and sage; or thyme and
    oregano
2 cloves garlic, pressed
1 cup dry wine, red or white
2 tablespoons tomato paste
1 cup chicken broth
2 tablespoons grated lemon rind (no white pith)
$\frac{1}{4}$ cup parsley

Note: You should be able to get the veal shanks in any butcher shop or meat department of supermarket, sawed to your specifications, and, if they don't have it always, they can order it for you, and don't take "no" for an answer; make a scene; kick butcher in shin; or go to another butcher, or take all three courses of action.

In a large heavy pot, get the butter and oil—or all oil—hot, and in it brown the meat on the bones all over. Each section of bone should have a nice layer of meat, in the center of which is the marrowbone.

After the meat has been well browned, turn each piece so the bones are standing up, which will keep the marrow inside the bone.

Sprinkle with salt and pepper, add the carrot, onion, celery, and herbs. Reason I like the thyme and oregano is that these herbs give any dish a distinctly Italian flavor.

If you go into any restaurant that claims to be Italian and if you are not made aware immediately that oregano has been used, march right out again. Add the garlic, the dry wine, red or white, stir the tomato paste into the broth, and add it to the pot.

Bring the liquid to the boil, reduce the heat to let it simmer gently, cover the pot and cook for 2 hours. From time to time, look into pot. If liquid has cooked off, as it will, add small amounts of liquid (I suggest wine and broth, mixed) at a time. In last half hour of cooking, sprinkle grated rind and minced parsley over all.

Have small spoons with which to scoop marrow out of bones. Delicious!

Serve this on a bed of rice, the kind of rice that produces about 3 cups of finished rice when 1 cup raw rice is cooked in 2½ cups of water. When the water boils, add 1 teaspoon of turmeric instead of the usual, wildly expensive saffron, before adding rice. Gives it a beautiful golden color, and a slightly warm flavor that is beautiful, too. This spice can be found in any supermarket.

SERVES FOUR.

VARIETY MEATS

The tramp knocked on the back door of the farmhouse and when the farmwife came to see what he wanted, he doffed his raggedy hat, bowed low, and said, "Lady, could you tell me how I might happen to get a bite to eat?" The lady glared at him. "Yes," she said coldly, "just go right over there to the woodshed and take a few chops."

Maybe you never in your life chopped wood, but did you ever try:

CHOPPED CHICKEN LIVER (Jewish)

1 pound chicken livers
2 large onions, chopped (about 2 cups)
chicken fat
3 hard boiled eggs
1 teaspoon salt
¼ teaspoon pepper

You can use calves' liver for this, too, but chicken liver is better. Wash the livers in cold running water, separate them and remove all fat and membranes. Dry them. Brown the chopped onions in 2 tablespoons of hot fat, and remove them from the pan. Now fry the chicken livers gently, don't overcook them or they'll get tough, in 2 tablespoons of fat, over low heat, maybe 3 minutes on each side. Cut one of them in half; if it is just barely pink they are all done.

Now, if you have an electric blender, the rest of this is a cinch. What you do is first put the browned onion into the container, run it on high for 30 seconds, then add the fried chicken livers and all the other ingredients—except the hard-boiled yolk—running the motor on high, and pushing the stuff down into the blades with a rubber spatula. (When you use the spatula with the motor running, you are careful, of course, not to touch the blades, because chopped rubber doesn't go well with chopped liver or anything else.)

It will take about 2 minutes in the blender to get the smoothest, tastiest chopped chicken liver you ever had; smoother than my Mama or any other pre-blender Mama ever made.

In case you don't know how to eat chopped chicken liver, what you do is refrigerate it, then put a big hunk on a piece of lettuce, spread it with a little cold rendered chicken fat, and sprinkle crumbled hard-boiled egg yolk and go to it. Or you can put some on a hunk of rye, corn or pumpernickel bread, and smear it with a little chicken fat.

If you haven't got a blender, which my Mama didn't have, what you do is chop, chop, chop, until you have as smooth a mixture as you can get. You'll know when to stop—when you feel as though your arm is going to fall off, that's how. Putting the stuff through a grinder just doesn't work right; needs chopping after grinding. Most of the time, chopped chicken liver is an appetizer, but one pound, especially in hot weather, makes a splendid main course for 4 people, with lettuce, scallions, cucumbers, white or red radishes, etc.

About that chicken fat. If your supermarket doesn't have it, demand to see the manager and make a scene until he promises to get it in stock. And, of course, you can make your own. Every time you get a chicken, take off the excess fat, melt it down over low heat and store it in your refrigerator. It will keep indefinitely. Chicken fat—next to goose fat—is just about the greatest stuff to use for frying anything, even eggs!

SERVES FOUR.

"But most of all, the kind of man we are looking for to fill this job is a man who is responsible," said the head of the employment office to a job applicant. The job-seeker jumped up and slapped the employment man on the back. "If that's the case," he shouted, "this is your lucky day, because all my life, for the last twenty years, every place I worked people said I was responsible whenever anything went wrong."

Only if you tried very hard could you make anything go wrong with:

ITALIAN CHICKEN LIVER

6 tablespoons rendered chicken fat (3 tablespoons each, butter and olive oil)
½ pound mushrooms, sliced through stems and caps, or one 4-ounce can, drained
1½ cups onion, minced
2 cloves (or more) garlic, minced
1 pound chicken livers, separated, fat removed, washed and dried
1 quart chicken soup (canned is okay)
1 envelope brown sauce mix
1 teaspoon turmeric
one 5-serving instant mashed potatoes
½ cup pimiento-stuffed olives, cut in half

Get hot, in a large fry pan, 2 tablespoons of rendered chicken fat or 1 tablespoon each of butter and oil. In it fry the sliced mushrooms and one cup of the minced onions until the mushrooms are soft. Push to the sides of the pan.

Add to the pan 2 more tablespoons of rendered chicken fat (leaving 2 tablespoons)—or butter and oil—and when it is hot sprinkle pan with garlic and fry the chicken livers on both sides until they lose color. I like chicken livers best when they are slightly underdone, with some pink showing inside.

But I must admit that most people like them fried until no blood shows when they are pricked with a fork, but, don't cook them so long that they become tough, for it is shameful to mal-treat such tender little things. Cover the frying pan and remove it from the heat.

We will now make the sauce for the chicken livers, thus: Pour one cup of chicken broth into a pan, shake the brown sauce mix into the broth, stir well and slowly bring to the boil, stirring all the while. Cover the pan and remove from the heat.

Pour another cup of broth into another pan. Stir into the broth the teaspoon of turmeric, the remaining rendered fat—or butter and oil—bring it slowly to the boil, remove from the heat, add the contents of one 5-serving envelope of instant potato granules, and whip with a whisk, away from the heat. Stir into the mashed potatoes some of the halved pimiento-stuffed olives, save the rest for garnish, and ½ cup onion.

Now then. We have in a large frying pan the fried chicken livers and the mushroom-onion mixture. Put this into the center of a large well-heated serving platter after combining the mixture thoroughly. Pour some of the brown sauce over it. (There's no salt or pepper listed anywhere because the soup and gravy mix are well-seasoned.)

Around the sauced chicken liver mixture, arrange the golden mashed potatoes. You can, of course, just plunk the mashed down around the borders of the platter, but I prefer to form balls with an ice cream scoop, or a large-cupped ladle.

Put a slice of pimiento-stuffed olive on the potato balls, pour the rest of the sauce over the potatoes and serve it to people you love. Don't waste this beauty dish on people you don't love.

SERVES FOUR.

The men were having a heated argument about the economic condition of the country and one of them said the main thing wrong was that banks had very little money available for starting new business and the expansion of existing enterprises. "That's how much you know," the other fellow said, "why, just the other day I went to my bank for a loan to expand, and when the manager said he couldn't lend it to me, I asked him why? Didn't the bank have any money to lend? And he said, 'Sure, the bank has millions to lend, but you don't have enough collateral.' So, you see, what's wrong with the country is not a shortage of money, it's a shortage of collateral."

You won't have to float a loan—I hope—to make a marvelous:

BEEF AND CHICKEN LIVER PIE (Midwestern U.S.A.)

1 pound chicken livers
1 pound top sirloin or round
12 or more small white onions
1 large carrot, cut into thin rounds
4 tablespoons melted chicken fat or oil
$\frac{1}{2}$ pound mushrooms, sliced
1 can condensed beef broth
2 tablespoons cornstarch or flour
$\frac{1}{2}$ can dry red wine, or, alas, water
salt and pepper
1 envelope (supposedly "5 portions") instant mashed potatoes

Wash the chicken livers in cold water, separate them, and remove and throw away any fat, or black spots. Dry the separated chicken livers thoroughly on paper toweling. Cut each liver half into halves. Cut the beef into cubes about the same size as the liver pieces, removing and throwing away all fat on the meat. Dry the meat cubes.

Put into a pan enough water to cover the small white onions and bring the water to the boil. Drop the onions, unpeeled, into the boiling water for about 30 seconds, remove them with a slotted spoon and run cold water over them. Now the onions will be a cinch to peel. If you try to peel these small white onions without plunging them into boiling water you will have a hellish time. After you've peeled the onions make 2 crosswise slashes in the root ends, which will prevent them from popping apart when they are cooked further, which you do right now, in fresh simmering salted water to cover, along with the sliced carrot. Simmer for 10 minutes and drain the onions and carrot slices.

In a large fry pan, melt 2 tablespoons of fat, or hot up oil, and in it fry the mushrooms until they are soft. Remove mushrooms from pan with a slotted spoon. Add the rest of the fat, fry the chicken livers quickly, over low heat, just long enough to brown both sides lightly. Remove the chicken livers. Now raise the heat and fry the beef cubes until they are browned all over. Add the beef broth, bring to the boil, then lower the heat so it simmers slowly.

Dissolve the cornstarch or flour in the wine, or, alas, the water. Add the cornstarchy wine or water, bring to the boil, and stir until it begins to thicken somewhat. Taste the sauce, add salt and pepper if needed. Put into the pan the chicken livers, the onions, carrot slices, and mushrooms, and stir until the sauce is thickened. Spoon it all into a baking dish or casserole. Prepare the mashed potatoes according to the directions on the package, and pile the mashed potatoes over everything in the baking dish. Bake in oven preheated to 350 degrees until potatoes are slightly browned.

SERVES FOUR TO SIX.

This city fellow, spending his vacation in a hotel near a small village, found a peculiar way to amuse himself. Instead of tennis, horseback riding, running after girls, or playing gin rummy and drinking, he hung out in the general store and pestered the denizens of the area with questions, trying to ferret out local folklore, and chuckling over their quaint folkways. He plagued everyone who dropped around to the general store with cretinous questions about their courtship habits; how they amused themselves during the long winter nights; how often they went to the movies; what newspapers, magazines and books they read, and tried to argue with them about their politics. The last question he asked before slinking away was, "And what is your death rate?" The general storekeeper looked at him with deep loathing and snarled, "About one to each person."

Each person at your table will be happy if you give them:

BAKED EGGS WITH CHICKEN LIVERS (Mexican)

12 chicken livers
4 tablespoons oil
2 cloves garlic, minced
1 small onion, minced
½ cup bread crumbs
½ cup chili sauce
1 cup chicken broth
salt and pepper
8 eggs

Separate the chicken livers, wash and dry them and remove any fat or membranes. Heat 2 tablespoons of the oil in a large pan and brown the garlic and onion slightly. Add the bread crumbs, and stir-fry for a couple of minutes over medium heat. Add all the other ingredients except the eggs and chicken livers, and stir. Remove from pan. Now heat the remaining oil and brown the chicken livers gently, over low heat, for about 2 minutes on each side.

Chicken livers are delicate little things, you know, and they mustn't be overcooked, and these are going to have some more cooking done to them, in the oven, which should be preheated to 375 degrees.

Now the best utensil to bake this dish would be individual baking dishes, 4 of them. But if you don't have any, don't worry about it; any baking dish will do. Whatever you use, grease it lightly. Pour in the sauce, then distribute the chicken livers, either in the individual baking dishes or the large one. Break 2 eggs into each dish, or distribute them evenly over the surface of the large one. Bake until well set.

If you've been using individual baking dishes, you've got no problem; serve one to each of 4 people. If you've been using a large baking dish you must be careful that you don't break the eggs in serving. What you should do is take up the eggs carefully with a spatula and set them aside. Now in each of four plates put some of the sauce, one set of chicken livers, and place on top of it all 2 baked eggs. See?

SERVES FOUR.

The civil defense group had just finished its course in first aid, and they were being given an oral examination. "Now, suppose," said the instructor, "that your patient had a broken leg, and that you had put splints on it, and the patient complained of terrible pain, and you had no anesthetic. What would you do, Miss Wunderkind?"

Miss Wunderkind thought, and thought and thought. Then she smiled brightly. "Oh, I know!" she cried out happily. "I'd give him a pint of whiskey!" The instructor frowned. "But suppose," he said, "that you didn't have any whiskey?" This time Miss Wunderkind frowned, and then her face brightened. "Oh, I know!" she cried out happily. "Then I'd promise him some!"

Promise your family a fine:

BAKED LIVER LOAF (England)

2 pounds beef or calf's liver
3 tablespoons shortening
4 hard-boiled eggs
½ cup bread crumbs
2 medium onions, chopped
1 teaspoon salt
½ teaspoon pepper

Remove membranes from liver, wipe it with a damp cloth and dry it. Fry it on both sides over medium heat, about 3 minutes on each side if the liver is 1 inch thick, a little longer if it is thicker. Put the meat through a grinder, using the finest blade. Cut the eggs into thin slices. Now mix together the ground liver, along with the shortening in which it was fried, with the bread crumbs, chopped onions and salt and pepper. Put half of the mixture into a greased baking dish, put the sliced hard-boiled eggs over this, and cover with the rest of the liver mixture.

In oven preheated to 350 degrees, bake it for 25 to 30 minutes. This is good with a sauce made quickly with a can of condensed cream of mushroom soup, or a homemade:

MUSHROOM SAUCE

¼ pound mushrooms
2 tablespoons shortening
2 tablespoons flour
1 cup beef stock or chicken consomme
salt and pepper to taste

Slice the mushrooms and fry them gently in the hot short-ening. Remove the mushrooms from the pan and hold on to them. Dissolve the flour in cold stock or consomme and cook, stirring until it is thickened. Season to taste, return the mush-rooms to the pan and cook until reheated. Pour over baked liver. This dish will make a delicious sandwich, cold, if there are any leftovers.

SERVES FOUR TO SIX.

The two men were discussing their boss. "The thing I most detest about him is his conceit; he thinks he knows everything about every subject that comes up," said one of them. "Well, it's hard to find fault with him for that, because he's a multimil-lionaire, and he's a self-made man," said the other. "I know, I know, he's always telling everybody that self-made jazz," said the first one, "but I think he's carrying much too far his adoration for his maker."

How would you like to make:

BEEF AND LIVER LOAF (Midwestern U.S.A.)

1 pound beef, ground
1 pound beef liver, chopped fine
2 eggs
2 cups beef broth
1 cup rice
2 tablespoons peanut oil
1 large onion, chopped
1 green pepper, chopped
2 cups tomato sauce or ketchup

You can, of course, get ground beef at the store, but I doubt that the butcher there will grind the beef liver, because it will make his meat grinder pretty messy. It used to be that every household—those I went into, anyway—had a hand-powered meat grinder that was clamped to the kitchen worktable and now there are, of course, electrical meat grinders.

But I know only a few people who have either. Hardware stores and utensil departments of department stores sometimes have the hand-powered ones, or will get one for you if you are persistent. They are wonderfully useful and remarkably cheap.

If you don't have a meat grinder, chop the liver fine, removing any ligaments you come across. Combine the ground beef and chopped liver in a mixing bowl. Beat the eggs into the beef broth in a saucepan; bring it to the boil, and cook the rice in it, covered, at a low simmer, until all but about ½ cup of the liquid is absorbed.

Heat the oil in a fry pan and in it fry the chopped onion and green pepper until they are soft. Put all of the ingredients except 1 cup of the tomato sauce or ketchup into the mixing bowl with the meat and combine the mixture thoroughly. You can do it with a fork, but your hands, moistened with water, are much better tools for mixing this. Pack it into a loaf pan, baking dish, or casserole.

Spoon remaining tomato sauce or ketchup over all, cover— foil makes a good cover—and bake for 1½ hours in oven preheated to 375 degrees. Uncover in last 10 minutes.

If there is some left over, it makes a wonderful sandwich, cold.

SERVES FOUR.

The man and wife were sitting despondently on the sidewalk amidst their meager belongings in front of the house from which they had been evicted for non-payment of their rent. Passersby turned their heads in embarrassment as they walked past the miserable-looking couple. Suddenly the woman burst into loud, happy laughter. This startled a man passing by. "You are a brave little woman," he said to the woman, "but tell me, how can you laugh in a terrible situation like this?" The woman grinned, "I'd always heard," she said, "that every cloud had its silver lining, but now for the first time in my life I see that it's true." The passerby looked at her wonderingly. "Tell me?" he said. "This," the woman happily hollered, "is the first time in twelve years that my husband and I have gone out of the house together."

Together with three other people, try some:

CALF'S OR BEEF LIVER WITH
ONION-MUSHROOM SAUCE (English)

1½ to 2 pounds calf's (expensive) or beef liver cut into 4 slices
⅛ teaspoon each, salt and pepper
flour
4 tablespoons oil
1 cup onion, minced
½ pound mushrooms, sliced
¼ cup parsley, minced
1 cup chicken broth

Almost always you will find in calf's or beef liver circular pieces of gristle or cartilage, not sure what it's really called. Anyway, cut them out, because they are tough and inedible, and don't add at all to the delicacy of this lovely, sadly neglected meat. Everybody has heard that it is health-giving to eat liver, so maybe that's why a lot of people profess to dislike it.

Rub salt and pepper into each liver slice, dust with flour, shaking off excess. In 2 tablespoons of oil, in a saucepan, cook the chopped onion, and sliced mushrooms, and parsley until the onion and mushroom pieces are beginning to brown. Pour the chicken broth into the pan, and cook over high heat, uncovered, to reduce the broth to a considerable extent while you cook the liver.

In a large fry pan, get the remaining oil—2 tablespoons— hot, and in it, over low heat, cook the liver until the meat loses its color on both sides.

Before you pour the mushroom-onion sauce over the meat, taste it. Doubt you'll need more salt, and maybe a little pepper will help. Will serve 4 people who like liver. Will serve thousands who don't. One reason many people don't like liver is because they never have had it properly cooked. Overcooking makes it tough and dry. Pink juices should flow from properly cooked underdone liver.

SERVES FOUR.

She was telling her lawyer about all the terrible things her husband had done to make valid her suit for divorce on the grounds of cruelty. ". . . and from the first night we were married," she wound up, "he never once talked in his sleep."

The lawyer looked up from his notes. "What's that you said?" he said. "Don't you mean that he has kept you awake every night by talking in his sleep?"

The woman shook her head testily. "No no," she said testily, "I mean what I said: he never talks in his sleep."

Now the lawyer shook his head testily. "How can you claim cruelty with something like that?" he asked testily.

The woman sneered. "Look," she said sneeringly, "how would you like it if your wife, from the first night you were married, kept laughing out loud all night long, never saying a word about what she was laughing about?" What I keep laughing about, with tears in my eyes, are the stupid directions printed on packaged foods which direct you to spoil products that are excellent, like spinach, which you will almost always find in a dish called "Florentine" as, for instance:

CALF'S LIVER FLORENTINE (Italy)

2 pounds calf's liver (or beef liver), sliced a little more than
    $\frac{1}{4}$-inch thick
$\frac{1}{4}$ teaspoon each, salt and pepper
flour
1 teaspoon powdered sage (if you can possibly get fresh sage,
    use 1 tablespoon, minced)
1 package (10 ounces) frozen chopped spinach
olive oil
1 tablespoon sesame seeds
1 egg, beaten with 2 tablespoons melted butter
salt and pepper to taste
lemon wedges, sliced tomatoes, parsley sprigs

You will notice that in this Italian recipe there is no garlic, or oregano, because the people of Tuscany, the hilly region of which Florence is the principal city, traditionally have employed a cooking style that is mild, subtle, delicately seasoned, unlike the more robust southern Neapolitan, or Sicilian style which is best known by United Statesers. The Tuscan cuisine is the basis for the French style of cooking, introduced to the French by Catherine de Medici, of Florence, who married King Henry II of France. Until then the French ate like the English, and their food was terrible.

Dry the liver slices thoroughly. Calf's liver is, of course, more tender and delicate than beef liver, so, of course, it costs more. What you must remember about either calf's or beef liver (or chicken) is that it must *not* be overcooked, or it will get tough. It is best, indeed, in my judgment, when the inside is still pink. Rub some salt and pepper into each slice and dust the slices with a very little bit of flour, shaking off excess. Dust the slices with sage.

At this point, start cooking the spinach. Pay *no* attention to the stupid directions on the package which tell you to cook it in a pan with ¼ or ½ cup of water. The spinach already has more than enough water in it to enable it to be cooked thoroughly, and if you add water, you must drain it, and so you lose a fantastic amount of valuable vitamins and good tasting stuff. Put the frozen cake of spinach into a pan, cover it and cook for 5 minutes over very low heat. Turn the cake over and cook for 5 minutes more. Now you can break it up with a fork. Now, in a large fry pan, heat 1 teaspoon of oil or whatever and in it brown the sesame seeds. When most of the moisture has been cooked out of the spinach, stir in the seeds, the egg beaten with melted butter or whatever, and add salt and pepper to taste. Cover pan. Add more oil to the fry pan and in it cook the liver slices over medium heat for 1 minute on each side. Serve with the fried liver sitting on the bed of spinach. Have wedges of lemon, and tomato slices, and parsley sprigs for garnishment—and use.

SERVES FOUR.

Woman was talking to her lawyer because her husband had started a suit for divorce. The lawyer listened to her story and elicited, though she didn't realize it, the complete story about her marriage. "Madame," said the lawyer, "I think that the best advice I can give you is not to fight your husband's suit for divorce, but, instead, to let him have his way." The lady was furious. "What do you mean 'let him have his way'?" she shouted furiously. "After being married to that beast for eight years, now I should start making him happy?"

Happiness for me is a dish called *oo-sul kui*, which is:

FRIED BEEF TONGUE-RICE (Korea)

1 ready-to-eat beef tongue, from 1½ to 2 pounds
¼ cup peanut oil
1 tablespoon sesame seeds
2 tablespoons soy sauce
⅛ teaspoon pepper
5 or 6 scallions with greenery, chopped
1 clove garlic (two cloves? maybe 3?), minced fine
1 tablespoon sugar

Cut the tongue into thin slices, and then cut the slices into quarters, once up-and-down, once across. In a large frying pan, in hot oil, fry the sesame seeds, stirring, for 2 minutes.

Add all the other ingredients and fry over high heat, stirring constantly with a fork, until the tongue is slightly browned, and the scallions are soft. Plain boiled rice is good with this, but what I like better is:

FRIED RICE

1 cup raw rice
2½ cups water, boiling
¼ cup peanut oil
1 teaspoon soy sauce
2 eggs, beaten
½ cup unsalted peanuts broken up

It is best, I think, to boil the rice the day before you fry it, because the rice gets fluffier when refrigerated overnight. One cup raw rice simmered slowly in 2½ cups of water will make about 3 cups of cooked rice. When all the water is absorbed, fluff and put the rice into a bowl and refrigerate. Next day, get the oil hot in a large frying pan, add soy sauce, and the cooked rice. Do this over very high heat, stirring constantly. Add the beaten eggs, stir rapidly, add the peanuts. When the rice is well-browned, combine it with the fried tongue mixture. Good? Ah yes, indeed it is.

SERVES FOUR.

The two ladies hadn't met for a long time, so, of course, they had a lot to talk about. "Tell me," said one of them, "how is your son the doctor?" The mother of the doctor beamed. "Oh, he's wonderful, that son of mine the doctor," she said. "That's nice," said her friend. "How is his practice? He has a good practice?" The doctor's mother beamed. "Has he got a practice?" she said. "He has such a good practice that now he can even tell a patient that there's nothing wrong with him."

One of my favorite dishes is chicken Tetrazzini, but when I tried it I found just as good:

TONGUE TETRAZZINI (kind of Italian)

4 tablespoons oil or butter
½ cup onions, minced
½ pound mushrooms, sliced
1 pound ready-to-eat beef tongue, sliced into thin strips
1 can (approximately 10 ounces) condensed cream of
    mushroom soup
1 cup grated Parmesan cheese
¼ cup dry sherry or vermouth (but if you don't want it, don't use
    it)
1 pound cooked spaghetti
¼ teaspoon salt
⅛ teaspoon (or more) cayenne pepper

In a large frying pan, get 2 tablespoons of the oil or butter hot and in it cook the onions and mushrooms until they are soft. Push onions and mushrooms to side of pan. Add the tongue and fry on both sides over medium heat until the tongue is slightly frizzled. Add the can of condensed cream of mushroom soup, and cook over low heat, stirring, adding ½ cup of the grated Parmesan cheese, until the cheese is melted.

Reason I said, about the wine, "but if you don't want it, don't use it," is because it irritates us to read in recipes the word "optional" after any ingredient. (Just saw one recipe in which four out of nine ingredients were followed by that word, "optional." Why do I find it irritating? Don't know why, just do.)

Bring salted water to the boil, add spaghetti, and start timing when water returns to the boil. For the thinnest spaghetti—vermicelli, linguini, or spaghettini, 6 minutes is just right, cooked through but chewy. For thick forms of pasta taste a small piece every minute after 6, then drain immediately when it is cooked.

In a large buttered casserole or baking dish, combine the tongue and sauce with the spaghetti, sprinkle with salt, the remaining ½ cup of grated cheese, dot with remaining 2 tablespoons of butter or oil, sprinkle with cayenne pepper, and bake uncovered in 350 degree oven until cheese is bubbling. Have chopped hot red pepper flakes and more grated cheese at the table.

SERVES FOUR TO SIX.

When Calvin Coolidge left the White House, refusing to run for another term as president of the U.S. of A., a syndicate signed him to a contract to write a column which would be distributed to newspapers all over the country. (In one column he wrote, if I remember correctly, "When large numbers of people are out of work, unemployment is the result.") When he signed the contract, every newspaper in the country printed the fact that he was going to be paid $5 a word. This astounded everyone. A group of fraternity brothers at a university chipped in and collected $5 which they sent to the former president, saying: "Send us a word." President Coolidge wrote back: "Thanks."

Let us give thanks for:

GINGERY TONGUE BALLS (kind of India-Jewish)

1 pound ready-to-eat tongue, minced
5-serving envelope instant mashed potatoes (made according to
    package instructions, but omit seasoning)
$\frac{1}{2}$ teaspoon salt
$\frac{1}{4}$ teaspoon pepper
2 eggs, beaten
cracker meal
about 6 gingersnaps, crumbed
peanut oil or vegetable shortening for frying

Mince the tongue fine, discarding any fat you come across. Make the mashed potatoes, omitting seasonings, according to package directions. In a mixing bowl, with a fork, combine the minced tongue and the mashed potatoes.

Season the mixture judiciously, starting out with $\frac{1}{4}$ teaspoon salt and $\frac{1}{8}$ teaspoon pepper. Taste the mixture and if you think it needs it, add the rest of the salt and pepper, or as much of it as you think is necessary.

Stir the beaten eggs into the mixture and then add just enough cracker meal so that it is stiff enough to hold together when you shape it into small balls. If you refrigerate the mixture for about an hour that will help to stiffen the mixture.

With moist hands, form the mixture into balls and then roll in the crumbed gingersnaps.

Suggest you garnish the serving platter with sprigs of parsley, cherry tomatoes or tomato slices, and have at the table some chutney, maybe sweet cucumber slices, unsalted peanuts, coconut flakes, or any or all.

SERVES FOUR.

Later on in life he was to have a great deal of experience in courtrooms, but this was his first time. He stood in front of the judge when his name was called and stood there, a not very pre-possessing-type fellow at all, because he was threadbare and shifty-eyed, while the clerk read the charge.

When the clerk finished reading the charge he asked the defendant, "How do you plead? Guilty or not guilty?" The prisoner burst out laughing. "Say, that's rich, that is," he said laughingly, "that's the funniest thing I've heard all day, isn't that the precise thing we are all gathered here to find out?"

Would you like to find out how to make a lovely old-timey kind of:

STEAK AND KIDNEY PIE (England)

1 pound beef kidney
1 pound top sirloin or round
¼ teaspoon each, salt and pepper
flour
rendered fat
12 small white onions
½ cup thin rounds of carrot
10-ounce package frozen small peas, defrosted and drained
1 can (about 10-ounces) condensed beef broth
1½ cups flour
⅓ cup shortening
¼ teaspoon salt
water
1 egg yolk

Cut the kidneys in half. Cut out the tubes and membranes and throw them away. Put the kidneys into a bowl of cold water, slightly salted, and let it stand, covered, in your fridge for about 30 minutes—changing water at least once. Cut the steak into cubes large or small, depending on how you like them, removing and throwing away any fat you come across. Drain and dry the kidneys, cut them into cubes.

In a large frying pan, hot up whatever fat you are using—about 3 tablespoons will be all you'll need for this—and in it fry the beef and kidney cubes until they are well-browned, stirring almost constantly, over medium heat.

While this is going on, plunge the onions, unpeeled, into boiling water, let them boil for 1 minute, drain and run cold water over them, and peel them and make 2 cross-cuts in the root end of each onion.

Add the onions to the fry pan, the thin rounds of carrots also, and the defrosted and drained peas. Add the broth and bring to the boil. Spoon it all in a baking dish. Taste the sauce for seasoning. You know how to reduce saltiness? Peel a large potato, slice it, add to the dish, cook 10 minutes, and it will absorb the excess salt. If the mixture comes almost to the top of your baking dish, that's fine; if there are a couple of inches to the top, form a ball of foil and put it into the baking dish, so it reaches the top. Combine the flour with the shortening, cutting the fat in, add salt, and add water by the drop until you form a dough which is manageable. Roll it out and cover the baking dish with the dough. Combine 1 teaspoon water with the egg yolk, brush the dough with it, make several gashes in the dough and bake in oven preheated to 375 degrees until the dough is browned, about 25 minutes.

SERVES FOUR.

The judge was astounded by the ineptitude of the young lawyer. He called him up to the bench. The judge leaned over the bench. "Young man," he whispered, "have you ever before appeared in a suit in this court?" The young lawyer nodded. "Why yes sir, Your Honor," he said, "just last week." The judge frowned. "Which suit was that?" he asked. The young lawyer replied, "My blue suit."

If you like chicken livers, what will suit you is:

A CHICKEN LIVER MAIN COURSE, OR FANTASTIC STUFFING

6 tablespoons melted chicken fat, oil, or butter, or marge
2 cups raw rice
3½ cups chicken broth, boiling
chicken giblets
1 pound chicken livers, fat and cartilage removed, separated, washed and dried
4 cups onions, chopped
1 pound mushrooms, sliced
garlic cloves minced fine to make 1 tablespoon or more
¼ cup parsley, minced, with stems
1 teaspoon dried thyme
1 teaspoon salt
¼ teaspoon pepper

In a large saucepan, hot up 2 tablespoons of the fat or whatever. Pour in the 2 cups of raw rice, and cook, stirring with a large kitchen spoon, until all the rice is coated and turns brown. While this is going on, bring to the boil, in another pan, the 3½ cups of broth. When the rice is browned, pour the broth, slowly, over the rice. Add the broth carefully, because the fat in the rice will make it froth up high in the pan. Cover the pan and let the broth simmer very slowly until all of it is absorbed by the rice.

While this is going on cook the giblets—heart, gizzard, and neck—in water to cover, with a little salt and pepper. In a large fry pan, hot up 2 more tablespoons of fat and in it fry the chicken livers, which you've prepared as described in the list of ingredients. Cook for no more than 5 minutes, stirring constantly with a large fork, or the livers, gentle creatures, will get tough. If a little pink shows when one of them is pricked, that's fine. While they're in the pan, away from heat, cut each piece of liver into 2 or 3 pieces. Put them into a large bowl.

By this time, the rice should have absorbed all of the broth. Add the rice to the bowl with the fried chicken livers. In the pan in which the rice was cooked, hot up the remaining 2 tablespoons of fat. Spoon in the chopped onions, mushrooms, garlic, parsley, and thyme. Stir to get everything coated with fat, and cook over high heat, stirring constantly, until the onion is quite brown, and most of the moisture has been cooked away. Be careful not to let the onions burn. Drain the giblets and let them cool. Cut the tough, outer cartilage from the gizzard, tear the meat off the neck, and chop the heart, gizzard and neck meat. Combine all the ingredients in the bowl. Sprinkle with salt and pepper, taste, and add seasoning to suit your taste.

This amount will be enough to stuff any sized chicken, duck, goose, or a turkey of about 16 pounds, with enough to be baked separately for second helpings.

SERVES SIX TO EIGHT AS A MAIN COURSE.

PORK, HAM, BACON, ETC.

PART NINE

Young fellow was urging his shy friend to go to a party with him. "Look," he said, "You just stick with me, and as soon as we get there I'll walk over to the prettiest girl at the party and you listen to what I say, and then you go over to another girl and say to her what you heard me say, or something approximately the same."

So they went to the party. The brash one quickly glanced around the room, nudged his friend, and they walked over to a very pretty girl. "You know," said the brash one, "it's astounding how beautifully cool you look." The girl smiled, patted the fellow on the cheek, and said, "What a sweet boy you are." The brash boy whispered to his friend, "Beat it."

So he beat it and picked out the second prettiest girl, said something to her, and got slapped in the face. Abashed, he rejoined his friend who was deep in conversation with the prettiest girl. "Why did she slap you?" asked the brash one. "What did you say to her?" The shy one shrugged and said, "I said: 'What amazes me is you don't look so hot.'"

If you like hot, I commend to you these indoor or outdoor

BARBECUED SPARERIBS (Mexican)

4 pounds spareribs
1 can condensed chili beef soup
1 can (or bottle) beer or ale
1 tablespoon or more chili or curry powder
1 teaspoon salt

First cut off as much fat from the ribs as you can. Cut the ribs into sections that will fit into a large Dutch oven or some other utensil for which you have a cover. Combine the chili beef soup, beer and whichever hot spice you like. Put some into the Dutch oven, or whatever. Put some ribs in.

Spoon some of the marinade over it, and keep putting stuff in like that. Let it marinate for an hour outside fridge, or for as long as you like inside fridge, spooning marinade over ribs from time to time.

If you are going to do this over charcoal, outdoors, I suggest you use a basket-type, hinged grill, which can be raised from grill instantly when flare-ups occur. Turn the ribs from time to time, and before turning, baste with a little of the marinade.

A total of 40 minutes or so, over coals, depending on how deep a bed of coals you have, should do it. One hour turning once, in 350 degree oven broiler. Pour off fat frequently.

SERVES FOUR.

Man was awakened by the loud, uncontrolled sobbing of his wife. He peeked at her out of one eye from under the covers and waited for her to stop crying. But she didn't. She just went on sobbing and sobbing. When he couldn't stand it any longer, he sighed, sat up in bed, and said: "What's the matter?" She just sobbed. "What are you crying for?" he asked. She sobbed. "Honey," he wheedled, "why are you crying? What's wrong, darling?"

"Oh, it's just terrible!" she cried out. "It's just too awful! I woke up and went to the window to close it, and I looked outside, and it was absolutely beautiful! The sun was shining! There wasn't a single cloud in the sky! The birds were singing! It was marvelous! And then I thought to myself, 'Now I've got to wake him up just so he'll be able to mess up this beautiful day!'"

A beautiful dish that would be difficult to mess up is:

INDOOR CHINESE ROAST PORK

2- to 2½-pound fresh pork tenderloin, boneless
¼ cup soy sauce
1 tablespoon honey
¼ cup chili sauce
3 or 4 (or maybe more) cloves garlic, pressed
hot mustard

The pork tenderloin will be kind of fat, and if you think it has too much fat on it, trim some off with a small knife. But don't trim off too much, because a bit is wonderfully good when it is roasted. Combine all of the other ingredients, *except* the mustard, in a bowl or some other vessel large enough to hold the pork flat on its bottom.

Put the pork into the marinade and spoon the marinade over the pork, cover it securely, maybe with some foil and let it stand for several hours or overnight in the refrigerator, turning the pork and spooning the marinade over it several times. If you've kept it in the fridge overnight, take it out of the refrigerator several hours before you're going to cook it, to take off the chill.

I'm not going to tell you to bring it up to room temperature because some time of year it may very well be 90 degrees or more in your kitchen, you poor thing you.

Put meat on foil-covered roasting pan and in oven preheated to 350 degrees roast it for 1½ to 2 hours, basting it with large kitchen spoon several times. Slice it thin and serve with plain boiled rice and hot mustard. Leftovers make wonderful sandwiches.

SERVES FOUR, MAYBE SIX.

Two ladies met in the supermarket. "My goodness," said one of them, "did we ever have an exciting time last night. In the middle of the night—must have been about 3 A.M.—I heard a noise downstairs. It was a great big crash, like somebody had knocked over a chair. So I jumped up out of bed, and you know the first thing I saw?" The other lady said how could she know when she wasn't there?

"Well, the first thing I saw was a man's feet sticking out from under the bed," the first lady said. "You mean to say there was a burglar under your bed?" asked the second lady. "No, no," said the first lady, "it wasn't a burglar, the burglar was downstairs. My husband had heard him first, and it was *his* feet sticking out from under the bed."

Your husband will be stronger, if not braver, if you give him:

ROAST STUFFED PORK LOIN (Pennsylvania)

1 loin of pork, 4 to 5 pounds
$\frac{1}{2}$ teaspoon each, salt and pepper
foil
your favorite stuffing, or see below
2 tablespoons gravy maker
2 tablespoons bourbon
1 tablespoon honey

Ask your butcher to saw through the chine bone of the loin, which will make carving the roast easy. Even the surliest butcher will do this, but, of course, the butchers in the stores where you buy meat are pleasant, and obliging, and charming, aren't they?

Rub salt and pepper into the meat. Line your roasting pan with foil, make deep cuts between each bone and in oven preheated to 350 degrees roast the loin for 30 minutes, fat side of roast up. Pour off fat. Put your stuffing between each chop. Combine the 2 tablespoons of gravy maker, the bourbon, and the honey. Smear this mixture on top of the roast.

Now, you have foil under the roast on the pan, don't you? Sure you do. Now cover the roast with foil, and put it back into the oven, still preheated to 350 degrees. A loin of pork should be roasted for 35 minutes to the pound. When you figure out the roasting time, remember to take into account the 30 minutes it was roasted before being stuffed. This is done, of course, to get rid of some of the fat. In the last 35 minutes, take the foil off the top of the roast.

If you don't like your favorite stuffing (some joke, hey?), how about this?

STUFFING

1 tablespoon bacon drippings or oil
1 large onion, chopped
2 cloves garlic, minced
¼ cup parsley, minced
1 teaspoon oregano
4 to 6 slices bread, crusts removed and thrown away,
    moistened with water or any other liquid you like, like,
    maybe, some beer? and crumbled

In hot fat or oil fry the onion, garlic, parsley, and oregano until onion is soft. Combine with crumbled moistened bread. Stuff it. Mashed potatoes, with grated cheese sprinkled on top of the potatoes, and melted butter drizzled over the cheese is real good. Have a green salad. And maybe a cooked vegetable that isn't overcooked.

SERVES SIX TO EIGHT.

The man was a very good worker and he was stupid, minded his own business and caused no one any trouble. Only thing his boss objected to was his continual tardiness in getting to work in the morning. Finally his boss asked him why he didn't get his alarm clock fixed. "Alarm clock?" asked stupid, "why, I never had an alarm clock." So the boss told him to buy one after work that night. Next morning he was late, as usual. "Didn't you do what I told you? Didn't you buy an alarm clock?" his boss asked. "Sure I did," said the dope, "but it's no good, it went off while I was asleep."

After you have done the preparatory work, you can take a nap while you cook:

MARINATED ROAST PORK LOIN (France)

    3 to 4 pounds boneless pork loin
    ¼ cup each, lemon or lime juice, and oil
    1 cup dry wine, red or white
    1 cup onion, minced
    1 (or more) clove garlic, pressed or mashed
    1 teaspoon dried rosemary, or parsley, or thyme
    1 tablespoon cracked pepper
    1 teaspoon salt
    1 large carrot, cut into thin rounds
    2 ribs celery, chopped, with greenery

Winter is almost always the best time of year for pork, because it is plentiful, and, therefore, cheaper. Cut off as much surface fat as you can, or ask your butcher to trim it completely before he rolls and ties it.

In a large non-aluminum bowl or pot, combine the lemon or lime juice, oil, wine, minced onion, garlic, rosemary—or whatever—and cracked pepper and salt. Put the pork into the marinade and spoon some over it, turning the meat and pricking it with a fork as you turn. Cover the pork. This may be left outside of the refrigerator for several hours if temperature is 70 or below, or kept in the refrigerator for as long as two days. Turn the meat and baste with marinade from time to time.

When you are ready to cook it, take the meat out of the marinade, put the pork on a foil-lined roasting pan, and pour the marinade into an enameled pot or non-aluminum flameproof utensil. Cover the marinade and keep over very low heat.

In oven preheated to 425 degrees, roast the pork for 10 minutes. Pour off fat, spoon some marinade over the pork, lower the heat to 350 degrees, and roast at that heat for 35 to 40 minutes per pound, basting with marinade from time to time.

The foil on the roasting pan prevents a hard-to-clean crust from forming on the pan. Lemon juice, vinegar, and acidy wines leave a hard-to-clean stain in aluminum vessels.

Strain the marinade before serving and spoon some over the meat, have the rest on table for those who want more sauce. To thicken it, dissolve 2 tablespoons of flour in 4 tablespoons of water—or wine—add it to the marinade and cook at high heat, stirring until the sauce thickens. Boiled, parsleyed potatoes are fine with this.

SERVES SIX TO EIGHT.

Every travel writer will tell you that the question asked most often of him is about the subject of tipping in foreign countries. What they all tell people is that tips should range between ten and fifteen per cent of the bill, whether it is in a restaurant, in a hotel, a ship, or a taxi. I know a travel writer who gives his readers this answer (though he himself follows a system that is altogether different): "Take, for instance," he told me, "a cab driver in Paris. I always give tips in coins. When the cabbie holds out his hand I put in one coin after another. Just as soon as he begins to smile, I can take back the last coin, because they only smile when they're overtipped."

If you want to see smiles on the faces of your loved ones, give them:

PORK CHOPS BAKED IN ONION SAUCE (France)

4 double pork chops
1 clove garlic, pressed
1 can (approximately 10 ounces) condensed onion soup
$\frac{1}{4}$ can dry red or white wine, or water
2 tablespoons lemon juice
salt and pepper to taste

Cut off as much fat as you can, without mangling the pork chops. In a large fry pan, over medium heat, melt down some of the fat in order to get just a thin film of fat all over the pan. Throw away all of the unmelted fat. Raise the heat in the pan and in it, over medium heat, brown the chops on both sides, turning with spatula, adding the pressed garlic when you turn the chops. Combine in a bowl the soup, wine (or water), and lemon juice. If your fry pan has an ovenproof handle, pour off the fat and add the combined condensed soup, wine—or water —and lemon juice, and bring to the boil, and taste the sauce for seasoning, adding salt and pepper if you think it needs additional seasoning. Cover the pan, and bake for 1 hour in oven preheated to 350 degrees, removing the cover in the last 10 minutes.

If the handle of your fry pan is not ovenproof—made of a material that won't be affected by high heat—transfer the chops after they are browned to a baking dish, and follow the steps described in the foregoing instructions after bringing the liquid ingredients to the boil in a saucepan, and tasting it for seasoning.

With this dish there should be at least one cooked green vegetable, or a salad, or both.

The salad should be made earlier, and allowed to chill in the refrigerator. In different parts of the U.S., salads are eaten at different times. In the West, salads are served before the main dish is put on the table. In the East, salads are served at the same time, or after the main course is brought to the table. Don't be bound by the prevailing custom wherever you may live; try it the other way and you may find you prefer it.

SERVES FOUR.

The leader of the Boy Scout troop was lecturing his charges on all of the points in the Scout Law, which goes, as you probably know, "I will be trustworthy, loyal, helpful, friendly, courteous, kind, obedient, cheerful, thrifty, brave, clean and reverent." He had already spoken about "trustworthiness," "loyalty," "helpfulness," "friendliness," and was now discussing the "courteous" law. When he thought he had covered that point well he paused, as he had on the preceding ones, and called on one of the troop for an answer. "Pincus," he said, "will you please stand and describe what 'courteous,' means to you, by telling us when you say: 'Thank you.' " Pincus, a sturdy lad, rose. "We say 'thank you' " he said sturdily, "when we have company."

• When I have company I sometimes give them chops in wine, which sounds much fancier when you give it its Italian name:

COSTATELLE DI MAIALE CON VINO (Italy)

4 double loin pork chops (pork is "maiale")
½ teaspoon salt, ¼ teaspoon pepper
4 tablespoons olive oil
1 large onion (really large), chopped
1 large clove garlic, minced
1 large carrot, minced
1 rib celery, chopped
¼ cup parsley, minced
3 tablespoons tomato paste
½ cup vermouth or dry white wine (maybe a little more)
1 cup chicken broth

Loin chops, of pork, veal, or lamb, are the most expensive, of course, but you can use other cuts of chops if you like. Whatever kind you get, get doubles, because a single chop, veal or pork, I think is a meager little thing. And, of course, you *know* that pork must be cooked thoroughly.

Cut fat off chops. Rub salt and pepper into them. Hot up 2 tablespoons of oil in a large fry pan, and in it fry the chops over high heat, browning them on both sides, turning with spatula. Remove them from pan and keep them hot on a platter set over a pot of very hot water, with a large bowl covering the chops. Add the rest of the oil to the pan, scrape it with spatula to get up the good brown particles, and then cook the onion, garlic, carrot, celery, and parsley until the vegetables are soft. Stir almost continually over medium heat.

Stir tomato paste into the vermouth or dry wine. Put the chops into the pan, over the vegetables, and pour the wine-tomato paste mixture and broth over all.

Cover the pan and cook over medium heat until meat is thoroughly cooked, about 40 minutes, turning chops occasionally. Cut into one of the pork chops at end of 40 minutes to see if it is cooked through. You may want some more broth or wine in the dish if you think the sauce is too thick, or if it cooks off too quickly.

If you don't have crisp Italian or French bread with which to glop up the sauce, have mashed potatoes.

SERVES FOUR.

Little girl was picked up by her father after her first Sunday school class and on the way home he asked her what she had learned. "The teacher read to us," she told him, "how God created the world, and how on the first day, He said: 'Let there be light!' and there was light! And then on the second day, He made Heaven. And on the third day, He made the Earth, and trees, and grass, and fruits, and everything, and on the fourth day, He made the sun and the moon and the stars, and on the fifth day, He made the birds and chickens and whales and all the animals, and everything."

The little girl stopped talking and her father asked her to go on. "That's all we learned today," she said, "next week we learn about the sixth day and the seventh day." Her father asked her how she liked Sunday school.

"Oh, it's wonderful!" she cried out, "it's exciting! You never can tell what God will do next!"

What you should try to do sometime is:

BAKED PORK CHOPS IN TOMATO SOUP (U.S.A.)

8 thick pork chops, fat cut off and saved
1 large onion, sliced
1 green pepper, seeded and chopped
1 can (approximately 10 ounces) condensed tomato-rice soup
$\frac{1}{2}$ soupcanful water
$\frac{1}{8}$ teaspoon sage or thyme
$\frac{1}{4}$ teaspoon pepper

In a large fry pan melt some fat cut from chops. Fry chops on both sides, turning with spatula. In the fat from chops fry the onion and chopped green pepper until they are soft. Put chops into baking dish, cover with the onion and green pepper. In bowl, combine the soup with the water. Add the sage or thyme and pepper, stir it, and pour over chops. Bake for 1 hour in oven preheated to 350 degrees, basting chops several times. Taste the sauce and add salt and pepper if you think it needs more seasoning.

This will serve 4 to 6 people, who knows? If I say it will serve 6 people, someone will write and say everybody didn't have enough to eat; if I say it serves 4 people, someone will say they had too much to eat. Serves 4 to 6, hear?

Look, you want to use any other kind of soup, go ahead: onion soup (leave out onions); pepper pot (cut down on seasoning); homemade or boughten chicken soup or chicken noodle soup; cream of mushroom soup; anything you like.

SERVES FOUR TO SIX AS I SAID.

Two actors whom we will call Lionel Shlepper and J. Aubrey Mitnick because those happen to be their names, were sitting at the bar in a New York restaurant frequented largely by theatrical people, and a newspaper columnist came by and eavesdropped on their conversation. The next day the columnist printed this gossip item: "Sitting at the bar of Yenem's Restaurant yesterday afternoon were actors Shlepper and Mitnick deep in conversation—about themselves, of course." This caused Shlepper deep anguish, and he called the editor of the paper to complain. "Your columnist," he said, "printed a lying statement about me; he said Mitnick and I were talking about each other, and that is simply not true. We were talking only about me."

What I'm talking about here is:

PORK IN SOUR CREAM (Russia)

2 pounds boneless pork butt
flour
2 to 4 cloves garlic, minced fine
½ cup sour cream
1 small crumbled bay leaf, or ¼ teaspoon powdered bay leaf
1 tablespoon sugar
1 tablespoon vinegar or lemon or lime juice
¼ cup water
¼ teaspoon salt
⅛ (or more) teaspoon pepper

Cut the pork into cubes about 1 inch, cutting off and saving the fat—there will be some—and put meat into a paper bag with ¼ cup of flour. Bounce the bag up and down, holding the bottom securely so it doesn't tear. Take the meat out of the bag, and shake off the excess flour.

In a large frying pan, melt down the fat until you have about 3 or 4 tablespoons of fat. Throw away the pieces of fat that don't melt down. In the hot fat in pan, fry the garlic until it begins to turn golden, then add the flour-coated pork.

Over medium heat, stirring all the while, fry the meat until the cubes are quite browned all over. Put all the remaining ingredients into a baking dish, stir to combine thoroughly, then add the browned meat.

Cover the baking dish and in oven preheated to 350 degrees, bake for about 45 minutes. Taste the sauce and add salt or pepper if necessary.

Serve this with mashed potatoes with which to glop up the lovely sauce, and a green salad or cooked vegetable.

This will serve 4 people adequately. Adequately? No, beautifully.

This rich man, a very rich man, was scheduled to fly to several foreign countries for his company and he was distraught because the young fellow who had worked for him for several years as a combination assistant-chauffeur-linguist-bodyguard had quit on him. So he advertised for someone to take his place, asking in the ad for a tall, strong, young man, preferably a former college football player, who could fill all these requirements.

The advertisement ran for four days without any response at all, but on the fifth day his secretary came into his office to say there was an applicant for the job.

"Sir," she said, "I don't think he's the right man for the job, because he's only about 5 feet 2, and he has gray hair, and he's dressed like a slob." The rich man sighed. "Well," he said, "send him in anyway, he's the only response we've had to the ad."

So the secretary showed the man in. He was just as she'd described him. The rich man was dubious, but even so, he asked: "Can you take shorthand and type?" The applicant laughed. "Who? me? Who knows from shorthand to typing? Not me!" he said. "Can you drive a fast sports car?" the rich man asked. The applicant laughed again. "Drive? Who knows from driving sports cars? Not me!" The rich man asked, "Can you speak any foreign languages?" Again the applicant laughed. "Foreign languages? Who knows from foreign languages? Not me! I talk only good English."

The rich man sighed. "Well, do you know karate? Are you good with guns?" he asked. The applicant laughed hysterically. "Karate I wouldn't know if I fell over him, and guns I'm afraid of," he said.

The rich man was pretty angry by now. "If you don't know shorthand and typing, and you can't drive a sports car, and you don't know languages or karate or guns," he shouted, "why the devil did you apply for this job?"

The applicant shrugged. "For five days I saw your ad," he said, "so I figured I should tell you that on me you couldn't depend."

What you can depend on is:

BAKED PORK CHOPS IN SOUR CREAM (Poland)

8 pork chops (preferably loin chops)
flour
4 cloves garlic, pressed
$\frac{1}{2}$ cup sour cream
1 tablespoon each, sugar and vinegar
$\frac{1}{2}$ teaspoon each, salt and pepper
1 bay leaf

Trim fat off chops, and melt some down in a large fry pan. Rub a little flour into both sides of trimmed chops. Throw away unmelted fat in pan and in hot fat, over high heat, brown chops on both sides, turning with a spatula. Brown pressed garlic, stir it, with the sour cream, sugar, vinegar, salt and pepper in a large bowl. Put chops into baking dish or casserole, spoon cream mixture all over chops, add the bay leaf.

Cover the dish or casserole and bake it in oven preheated to 350 degrees for 1 hour, when they will be done, and is it ever good!! Throw away bay leaf, and serve with mashed potatoes to glop up the lovely sauce. Or crisp French or Italian bread.

SERVES FOUR.

Man was brought before the judge, charged with driving a car while drunk. The judge asked the cop, "What caused you to stop him?" The cop replied, "Well, Your Honor, he was zig-zagging all over the road." The judge asked, "Was there anything else that convinced you he'd been drinking?" The cop nodded. "Yes, Your Honor, his breath smelled of alcohol," said the cop. "And what had he been drinking, beer, wine, or whiskey?" the judge asked. The cop shrugged. "Your Honor, I really can't be sure, but his breath smelled of alcohol." The judge frowned. "You mean to tell me you can't say whether the defendant had been drinking beer, wine, or whiskey? Can't you judge?" The cop shook his head. "No, Your Honor," he said, "for I am only a humble cop."

In my humble opinion—if you think I really am humble, you certainly got another think coming—a wonderful quick dish is:

BROILED HAM AND YAM (Virginia)

2 pounds ready-to-eat ham steaks, cut into 4 portions
1 can (approximately 8 ounces) yams in light syrup (save syrup)
2 tablespoons lemon juice
1 tablespoon dry mustard
1 bunch scallions, chopped

Cut the fat off the ham steaks, mince the fat and put it on a baking sheet that will fit into your broiler, about 3 inches from the source of heat. Scrape the pan after about 1 minute, with a metal spatula, to unstick the pieces of fat, and to turn them. Don't for goodness sake throw away the unmelted bits of fat because they are delicious—not as delicious as the bits left over when chicken fat is rendered, but delicious—and put the ham steaks on the pan, turning them to get them coated on both sides. Broil them until the steaks get slightly browned, about 3 minutes on each side.

Meanwhile, away from the range, combine the yam syrup with the lemon juice and mustard, and cut each yam in half.

Turn the ham steaks, pour the syrupy mixture over them, and put yam halves on top of each piece of meat. Put some chopped scallions over all and broil until the yams are slightly browned, and the ham steaks are slightly glazed. Delicious. And a nice change, I think, from the usual pineapple that's generally cooked with ham steaks.

SERVES FOUR.

The young bride was quite dissatisfied with the woman she had hired to clean house for her three days a week, but she was a kindhearted chick, and she was very unhappy because she didn't know what to say to the woman about her slipshod methods. She confided her troubles to her husband, a young gung-ho junior executive who had a solution, he thought, for every problem and his bride, being deeply in love, believed him implicitly. "There, there," he said, comfortingly, "don't you worry your pretty little head about that, I'll take care of that dame for you." So next time the cleaning woman came, he took her by the arm and led her over to the piano. "Look here," he said sternly, "the next to the last time you were here, right after you left, I took my finger and wrote your name on the piano, and it's still here."

The cleaning woman looked and saw spelled out in the dust, "Mrs. Finerty." She glared at the smartalecky young fellow. "I saw it last time I was here," she said glaringly, "and I meant to talk to you about it, but I forgot. I spell my name with two Ns."

What I mean to talk about now is:

GLAZED SWEET AND SOUR HAM (Puerto Rico)

2 cups cubed potatoes
1 large onion (about the size of a baseball) sliced
one 2-pound ready-to-eat ham steak
$\frac{1}{2}$ teaspoon dry mustard
2 tablespoons lemon juice
2 tablespoons dark rum (or light rum)
4 tablespoons molasses (or honey)

I hear someone asking: how large should the potato cubes be? and I answer: how about 1-inch cubes? And when I say the onion should be about the size of a baseball, I mean a regulation league ball, not a softball that's used in indoor gyms. Separate the onion rings. Put the potato cubes and onion rings into boiling, salted water to cover and boil until potato cubes are cooked through but not mushy. How to tell? Taste a cube after 10 minutes. Drain the potato cubes and onion rings and hold on to them, friends, until I tell you GO.

While potato and onion are cooking, cut fat off ham steak, leaving a little on the meat, and make gashes all around the ham to prevent curling, unless you happen to like curly ham. Stir the mustard into the combined lemon juice, and rum, and molasses. Hold on to this mixture until I say GO.

Put the ham steak on a broiler pan, put the pan about 3 inches from source of heat, add pieces of fat you cut off around meat, and broil until the top of the ham is lightly browned. How long should you broil it to achieve that? Look at it, friends, look at it; when it is lightly browned, turn the ham steak to the other side. Spoon the mustard-lemon juice-rum mixture over top of the ham steak. Remove the bits of fat. Put the potato cubes and onion rings into pan, turn them to get them coated all over with pan juice, and put the pan back under the broiler and broil until the top of the ham steak is slightly glazed, with the potatoes and onion rings drained on paper toweling. If you want to get slightly glazed, have a few gulps of rum, but be wary of getting overglazed.

SERVES FOUR.

The middle-aged husband and wife were fishing in a lake, sitting in a rowboat. The fish weren't biting, so they both leaped into the water and swam.

The husband climbed back into the boat first. Then his wife came back to the boat and she tried to climb in, which was quite difficult, for she was not only not a spring chicken, but another thing she was not was a sylph. Matter of fact she was downright fat. When she finally did get back in, she sat and panted and glared at her husband, who had watched impassively while she'd been struggling so hard.

"You know," she said between pants, "when you were a boy courting me, and I was a gal, you were much more gallant and you would have helped me into the boat before you climbed in."

Her husband nodded. "You are absolutely right, my dear," he said agreeably, "but you must remember that when I was courting you when you were a gal and I was a boy, you were much more buoyant."

How about all us boys and girls having some:

BAKED HAM AND CHICK PEAS (GARBANZOS) (Mexican)

2 pounds ready-to-eat ham steak, cut into two ½-inch slices
1 or 2 tablespoons oil
1 cup onions, chopped
1 small green pepper, chopped
1-pound can chick peas (garbanzos) drained
1 teaspoon dry mustard
1 cup cream sherry (sweet)
1 cup orange juice, or pineapple juice
2 tablespoons brown sugar

Cut all the fat off the ham and melt it down in a large fry pan. In the hot fat—if you haven't got 2 tablespoons of melted fat, add oil to augment it—fry the chopped onion and pepper until they are soft and the onions begin to turn golden. Fry the ham slices over high heat until they are browned on each side.

Put one slice of the ham into a baking dish or casserole and sprinkle the ham with the fried onion and pepper. Mash up the chick peas with the dry mustard and spread it over the onion and pepper over the ham slice. Cover it with the second ham slice. Pour the sherry and juice over all.

Bake it uncovered for 30 minutes in oven preheated to 350 degrees, basting with juices several times, then sprinkle with brown sugar. If you don't have brown sugar, do you have molasses? That's fine, too.

Baked, honeyed sweet potatoes or yams are all the time served with ham. That's fine once in a while. What I like better is creamed spinach with sesame seeds browned in a little bit of oil. Uncreamed spinach is wonderful with sesame seeds, too.

Speaking of ham—we were, were we not?—recalls a story that is attributed to almost every old-timey lawyer and once I heard it credited to Patrick Henry. Seems the lawyer had a client who was accused of stealing a pig. "Did you steal that pig?" he asked. When his client said yes, he did, the lawyer told the man to give him half of it. So well known was he for his probity that when he arose in court and declared, "This man has no more of that pig than I do," his client was acquitted. Do you believe this story?

Well, I don't.

SERVES FOUR.

"This," said a Mr. J. Wagner in a note to me, "happened to me the other day. A man stopped me and asked for a nickel for a cup of coffee. 'Where can you get a cup of coffee for a nickel?' I asked. 'For another nickel I'll tell you where,' he said." Very funny story, J. Wagner of West 83rd Street, very nice.

What is also nice is:

HAM CASSEROLE (U.S.A.)

1½ to 2 pounds ham steak sliced into ½-inch thick pieces
5 large peeled potatoes, sliced thin into a bowl of cold water
¼ teaspoon pepper
1 can (10½ ounces) cream of mushroom soup
½ cup milk
½ cup fresh bread crumbs

Cut fat off ham, and in large fry pan melt down fat and throw away the browned pieces that do not melt. Fry the slices of ham on both sides until they are lightly browned. Remove the ham steaks and hold on to the fat in the pan.

Coat the sides and bottom of a large casserole or baking dish with a little of the ham fat. Take ½ of the sliced potatoes out of the water (water protects potato from discoloration), dry them on paper towels and put them into the casserole. Sprinkle the potatoes with half the pepper and cover them with half the ham steaks.

Put half the remaining potato slices, dried, on top of the ham slices, sprinkle with the rest of the pepper, put into the casserole the remaining ham, cover with the remaining potato slices. In bowl, combine the mushroom soup with the milk, pour it into the casserole, and top with the fresh bread crumbs.

Sprinkle the crumbs with the remaining melted down fat. Bake, covered, in oven preheated to 350 degrees for one hour. After an hour of baking, remove the cover from the casserole and bake for another 15 to 20 minutes until the top is browned. Canadian bacon can be used as a variation on this dish, and you might sometimes try adding some chopped green sweet pepper, and substitute sweet potatoes for the white ones. Serve this dish with a nice green salad.

SERVES FOUR TO SIX.

Man went to his doctor and he was quite vague about what his trouble was, so the doc gave him a real thorough examination.

"You are in fine shape," the doctor told him when they were seated in his office after the examination. "Can't you tell me just what it is that's troubling you?"

The man hemmed and hawed. "Hem, haw," he said, "well, it's when I kiss my wife is when strange things happen. Sometimes when I kiss her, I get very warm and uncomfortable, and other times when I kiss her I get a terrible chill and I'm uncomfortable."

The doctor was forced to confess that he was stumped and the man left his office unhappily. The doctor thought and thought and finally, he called up the man's wife. The man's wife snorted derisively when the doctor told her about her husband's peculiar complaint.

"Tshah," she snorted, "what's so peculiar about that? The only time he kisses me is in August and then in February!"

Summer or winter, what's good is:

TOMATO PIE WITH HAM, BACON OR TONGUE (Canada)

Biscuit dough mix for 2 layers, 8–9 inch pie
3 large tomatoes, peeled
½ pound ham, bacon or tongue
1 cup sour cream
1 tablespoon parsley, chopped (or 1 teaspoon dried flakes)
¼ teaspoon black pepper

Cover an 8- or 9-inch pie pan with biscuit dough pressed out on waxed paper with your fingers to about ¼ inch thick. Peel the tomatoes by dropping them into a pot of boiling water for a few seconds, then into some cold water, and with the aid of a small knife the skin will come off easily. Fry the ham, bacon, or tongue the way you like it. (Canadian bacon is great with this.) Put the meat over the pie crust, cut the peeled tomatoes into slices about ½ inch thick and put them over the meat. In bowl, with small fork, mix the sour cream with the parsley and spread it over the tomatoes. Sprinkle it all with the black pepper, cover the pan with the second layer of biscuit dough pressed out, and sealed, with wet fingers, to bottom layer of dough. Prick the dough with a fork so steam can escape. Bake it in oven preheated to 350 degrees until the dough is nicely browned. This is a lovely main course for dinner or lunch, and a great late breakfast for a Sunday.

SERVES FOUR.

Donald Culross Peattie, whose writings I have long admired, once said: "The time to hear bird music is between four and six in the morning. Seven o'clock is not too late, but by eight the fine rapture is over, due, I suspect, to the contentment of the inner man which comes with breakfast; a poet should always be hungry or have a lost love." Well, I know a couple of poets pretty well; well, these two fellows eat like stevedores any time of the day or night, but they write pretty terrible poetry, anyway.

Two ladies went to the downtown shopping district together. "Oh, look," said one of them, "my husband's office is in that building across the street. Come on up there with me, and I'll get him to buy our lunch." So they went across the street, and sure enough, the husband took them both out to lunch in a nearby restaurant.

After lunch, when the husband had left to go back to his office, the friend said: "My goodness, I had no idea, your husband seems to be an awful important man in that company, what is he, a vice president, or something?" The man's wife laughed hysterically. "No-no-no," she said hysterically, "he's just an assistant bookkeeper, but you're absolutely right, he sure makes it SEEM like he's important."

What is important to keep in mind when using ready-to-eat ham is that you should always taste it before adding seasoning, because saltiness can vary greatly, so do as we say when making:

HAM AND NOODLE CASSEROLE (Italy)

1½ to 2 pounds ready-to-eat ham steak
probably some oil
2 cloves garlic
2 medium-sized tomatoes, peeled and cored
1 small green sweet pepper, chopped
1 rib celery, strings scraped off, and chopped
¼ teaspoon oregano or thyme
1 can condensed cream of mushroom soup
½ can milk
½ pound green noodles, cooked
¼ cup each, bread crumbs and grated cheese

Cut off all fat from the ham steak, and put the fat into a large frying pan. Taste a piece of the ham. If you find it more than just mildly salty, parboil it for 5 minutes, dry it thoroughly and cut it into cubes. Reason we say you should parboil it if it is more than slightly salty is because the condensed soup which will be used is very well seasoned, and if the ham is more than slightly salty this dish will be *too* salty. See?

Melt down as much fat as you can in that large frying pan. If you don't have at least 2 tablespoons of melted fat as a result, augment it with some oil. In the hot fat, fry the minced garlic until it is slightly golden. Add the cubed ham, and peeled, cored tomatoes to the frying pan. Tomatoes are peeled easily if they are plunged into boiling water for 30 seconds, and cooled quickly in running cold water. Mash the tomatoes in the pan. Add the chopped green pepper, the chopped celery, and sprinkle with oregano or thyme. Cook covered for 10 minutes. Add the condensed cream of mushroom soup, the milk and the cubed ham. Stir, cover the pan, and cook over very low heat until noodles are finished.

Bring to the boil enough water to cover the noodles, add 1 teaspoon salt and 1 tablespoon oil. Break the noodles in 2-inch pieces, into the pot. Start timing when the water returns to the boil. Taste a piece of noodle after 6 minutes, then taste again every minute until you find that the noodles are cooked through but still chewy. Drain immediately when the noodles have reached the state you like. In a large mixing bowl, combine the noodles and the ham-sauce mixture and spoon it all into a large oiled casserole or baking dish. Top with the combined bread crumbs and grated cheese and bake in oven preheated to 350 degrees until the top is browned and crisp. Have grated cheese at the table. And have a salad with this.

SERVES FOUR TO SIX.

The doctor completed his examination of the ailing and aged multi-millionaire and came out into the hospital hallway where he was confronted by the beautiful teen-ager the sick man had married the week before. "Tell me, Doctor," the girl said, "how is my husband? Is there any hope?" The doctor looked at her reflectively. "Well, that's hard to say," he said, "unless I know just what you're hoping for."

Don't know what you're hoping for, but here I give you:

BAKED CHICKEN-STUFFED HAM SLICES (Singapore)

2 thick slices ready-to-eat ham, each approximately 1 pound
1 cup cooked chicken, chopped fine
$\frac{1}{2}$ cup chutney, chopped
$\frac{1}{4}$ teaspoon dry mustard
$\frac{1}{2}$ cup scallions with some greenery, chopped
$\frac{1}{8}$ teaspoon powdered cloves
1 cup wine, sweet or dry, whatever you prefer, red or white

Trim the ham slices of all fat. Taste the ham to see how salty it is. If it is too salty, parboil the ham for about 5 minutes, drain and dry the meat.

Put 1 ham slice into a baking dish. Combine the chopped, cooked chicken, the chopped chutney—plus some of the chutney liquid—the dry mustard, and scallions.

Spread the mixture over the ham slice in the baking dish. Put the second ham slice over the mixture. Stir the powdered cloves into the wine and pour it over the meat. In oven preheated to 350 degrees bake it uncovered until the top piece of ham begins to get frizzled, which will take about 30 to 35 minutes.

SERVES FOUR.

Man who was in the nation's capital on business dropped in to see his Congressman. Of course, he complained about the taxes he had to pay.

"Well," said the Congressman, "it is a worn-out cliche, of course, to say that death and taxes are inevitable, but that's why it's a cliche, because it's true."

The businessman snorted derisively. "Yeah, yeah," he said derisively, "but there's one thing you've got to say in favor of death. It doesn't get worse every time Congress is in session."

What I seem to like better each time I have it is a:

HAM OR TONGUE CASSEROLE WITH CHICK PEAS (Spain)

2 tablespoons butter or oil
1 cup chopped onion
1 medium-sized green pepper, chopped
$\frac{1}{4}$ teaspoon salt
$\frac{1}{8}$ teaspoon pepper
$\frac{1}{2}$ teaspoon thyme
$\frac{1}{2}$ cup tomato sauce
1 pound cooked ham or beef tongue, cubed
1-pound can chick peas (garbanzos), drained
2 thick slices cheddar, American, Mozzarella, any cheese you
    like

In a large fry pan, hot up the butter or oil and in it fry the chopped onion and pepper, stirring from time to time, over low heat until the vegetables are soft. Sprinkle with salt, pepper, and thyme, add half the tomato sauce, stir, and taste for seasoning. Add more of whatever you think it needs.

Stir into the mixture the cooked meat and the drained chick peas. Oil a casserole, spoon the mixture into it, cover with the remaining ¼ cup of tomato sauce and top it all with the cheese slices. Bake it in oven preheated to 350 degrees until the cheese melts and begins to brown, which should take about 20 minutes.

SERVES FOUR.

Man driving his car on a back road in Tennessee came upon a fellow who was herding a drove of hogs slowly in the same direction he was going. The hogs and their drover paid no attention to the car. Finally the man got out of his car and walked up to the hog drover. "You gonna be turning off the road soon?" he asked. The pig man nodded. "About half a mile more down the road," he said. The automobilist kept pace with the drover.

"I'm a farmer myself, in New Jersey," he said, and I keep pigs, too." The Tennesseean just nodded. "Where you taking these hogs?" asked the Northerner. "Gonna turn 'em loose in the woods, so they'll fatten up on acorns," said the Tennesseean.

"That's pretty inefficient," said the Jerseyite. "What we do up north is put them in a pen and feed them corn, and if you did that, your hogs would get fat much quicker."

The Tennesseean laughed. "That's pretty stupid," he said. "Who ever heard of a hog that was in a hurry?" (He said something else, but you'll have to wait until the end of this sermon before I tell you what it was, because otherwise it might be anti-climactic, or something.)

I commend to you something I call:

CANADIAN BACON HASH (Canada, where else?)

1 pound potatoes, peeled and cubed
1 to 1½ pounds Canadian bacon (get an unsliced roll if you can
    and slice it thick)
maybe some oil or butter
1 cup onion, chopped, but not too fine
¼ teaspoon powdered cloves
1 pound tomatoes, peeled and cubed
1 cup tomato sauce
½ cup chopped dill pickles or gherkins
4, maybe 8 eggs, poached or fried

Boil the cubed potatoes for 15 minutes in covering water, drain, and put into a bowl. Cut off as much fat as you can from the bacon and in a large fry pan, over low heat, stirring from time to time, melt down the fat. Don't throw away the unmelted bits, because they're delicious when fried crisp.

Canadian bacon comes sliced and unsliced. The unsliced is cheaper because it doesn't come in a fancy package, and I like it better, because it can be sliced to any thickness. Fry the sliced bacon, using a little oil or butter if necessary, then cut them up into cubes. Remove the bacon to a mixing bowl.

Fry the chopped onion until it is soft, put the fried onion and all the remaining ingredients—except the eggs, of course—into the bowl with the potato-bacon mixture and stir it well to combine all the ingredients thoroughly. Oil a baking dish or casserole, spoon the mixture into it and bake in oven preheated to 350 degrees until the top is browned and crisp. Put 1 or 2 poached or fried eggs on each portion.

You want to know what else the Tennessee farmer said to the New Jersey one about feeding corn to hogs? What he said was, "You might as well strew pearls before swine, because corn is too good for a hog, when you can make good drinkin' liquor from corn." That's what the Tennessee farmer said.

SERVES FOUR.

There was a long line at the bus station ticket window. A meek little man came up to the window and said, "Excuse me, do you remember me? I bought a ticket for Philadelphia and gave you a $20 bill, and you gave me the wrong change." The ticket seller snarled. "That's too bad," he said, snarlingly, "you should have counted it and told me while you were still at the counter." The meek fellow shrugged and started to walk away. One of the men in the line who had overheard this stopped him. "You don't have to take that kind of guff, you should have given him an argument," said the man in the line. The meek man shook his head deprecatingly. "Oh, no," he said in a deprecating way, "I'm accustomed to being treated like that, and I don't mind too much, but I did think he'd be interested in knowing that the change he gave me was $3 too much."

One per adult serving is not too much when you make:

BRAISED PIGS' KNUCKLES WITH SAUERKRAUT (Germany)

4 pigs' knuckles
2 cups onion, minced
$\frac{1}{4}$ cup parsley, minced
$\frac{1}{2}$ teaspoon dried oregano
1 bay leaf
10 peppercorns (approximately)
1 can (10$\frac{1}{2}$ ounces) condensed beef soup
$\frac{1}{2}$ canful water
maybe some salt, but not likely
1 pound sauerkraut

Cut rind and fat off the meat. Put the minced onions, parsley, and oregano into a pot and put the knuckles in over all. Cook over very low heat, covered, for about 10 minutes.

Tie the bay leaf and peppercorns into a small cheesecloth bag and add it to the pot, along with the beef soup and water. Spoon some of the onions over the pigs' knuckles and scrape the pot, making certain that any onions on the bottom of the pot, which may be browned, don't stick to the pot. Cover the pot and cook for 1½ hours, with the liquid just barely simmering.

Taste the liquid. If the salt in the soup hasn't seasoned it enough to suit your taste, add some. Fish out the cheesecloth bag with the bay leaf and peppercorns and throw it away.

Drain the sauerkraut and squeeze out as much liquid as you can. Add the sauerkraut to the pot and stir. Cook just long enough to heat the sauerkraut.

Serve knuckles with sauerkraut. I like a large boiled potato with this. And hot mustard. And dark bread. And beer.

SERVES FOUR.

LAMB

PART TEN

I was talking with some friends about the violence that is displayed every day and every night on the telly in great detail and in shocking natural color. One of them laughed and said that TV shouldn't bear too much of this kind of criticism because gory tales have always been popular as far back as prehistory. One of his examples was the Greek legend of Medea, a dame who helped Jason steal the Golden Fleece, then fled with him, had two children by him, killed them, as well as the lady that Jason wanted to marry, and also did away with sundry other citizens.

"The late Robinson Jeffers wrote a play about Medea," said our friend, "and a fellow I know had a secretary who went to see it one night. Next day her boss asked her what the play was about, and his secretary said: 'It's about a girl who is a very sore loser.'"

A dish that is a winner whether broiled indoors or outdoors is:

LAMB CHOPS WITH MEAT SAUCE (Italian)

4 double loin lamb chops, approximately 1 inch thick
2 tablespoons oil
1 medium onion, minced
2 (?) cloves garlic, minced
¼ cup parsley, minced
½ teaspoon dried oregano, or thyme
1 can meat sauce or steak sauce (preferably with mushrooms),
    approximately 10 ounces
maybe salt?
maybe pepper? or hot sauce?

Cut off as much fat as you can get at, without mangling the meat on the chops. Throw the fat away.

In a small fry pan, get the tablespoon of oil—any kind, olive, peanut, or vegetable—hot and in it fry the onion and minced garlic until the onions are just beginning to turn golden. Add the parsley and oregano, or thyme, stir, and cook over low heat for about 5 minutes, stirring often.

About that meat or steak sauce. Canners of food have to be careful in the use of seasoning, and such ingredients as garlic, for they try mightily to make their product pleasing even to those people who are chary about strongly flavored stuff. Which is why I put a "?" after garlic, salt, pepper, and hot sauce. All I can tell you to do, if you prefer blandness, is to taste the sauce before you put into it garlic, salt, pepper, or hot sauce. If you like it the way it is, without embellishments, why, then all you have to do is omit them. Right? But, as you may have noticed, I like to jazz sauces up somewhat.

If you are doing this in your oven broiler, put the sauce—jazzed-up or not—on a pan about 3 inches from the source of heat after adding onion-herb mixture, for 5 minutes. Put the chops into the sauce, turning them to get them coated all over, and broil them for 3 minutes on each side, basting when you turn them, for somewhat rare chops.

If you do it over charcoal, outdoors, coat the chops with the sauce and broil for the same length of time, at same distance from heat, for somewhat rare. In both cases, serve the chops, with a mixed green salad, with the sauce poured over the chops.

SERVES FOUR.

The husband was reading the evening paper and, because there was nothing on the telly that she cared to watch, his wife just sat there looking pensive, which alarmed him because whenever she had time to be pensive he was bound to get into trouble. "Please, dear," he said plaintively, "isn't there something you could do, like maybe read a book?" His wife shook her head. "No, I've been thinking. I think we should sell this house and move to another neighborhood." Her husband was aghast. "Why should we?" he asked. "We both love this house, and anyway, we've been here only a year." His wife nodded. "Yes, dear, I know," she said, "but we've gotten to know every family for a mile around so well that I'm tired of gossiping about the same people all the time."

I think I'd be happy even if all the time I had to eat:

SAUCED CHOPS (Kentucky)

8 lamb or pork chops
1 teaspoon salt
fat rendered from chops
$\frac{1}{4}$ cup onion, grated or minced fine
$\frac{1}{2}$ teaspoon dried thyme
$\frac{1}{4}$ teaspoon cayenne pepper (use *cautiously*)
2 tablespoons each, rendered fat and flour
1 can (10$\frac{1}{2}$ ounces) condensed cream of mushroom soup
$\frac{1}{2}$ can (same one) bourbon

Cut off the chops all the fat you can get at, without man-gling the chops. In a large fry pan, over low heat, melt the fat down. *Don't* for goodness' sake throw away the unmelted bits which too many recipe-putters-down say to do, because they are delicious. Have a pot of very hot water handy, cover it with a pretty, heat-proof platter, and on the platter place a large bowl. This is much better than a warming oven for keeping cooked food hot, without further cooking, which is what a warming oven does.

Rub each chop with a little salt. Fry them on both sides, until they are well-browned. You know, of course, that pork must be well-done. Do you like lamb to be pink inside? I do. Don't crowd the pan, put cooked chops on the hot platter, cover with the bowl, inverted.

When you are ready to start browning the last two or three chops, sprinkle the pan with onion and thyme after pouring out fat. Add cayenne pepper to onion and thyme, but do not sprin-kle any of it on the chops, for it will go into the sauce. I said "use cautiously" about the cayenne, for it is very hot, so, if you don't know its strength too well, maybe you'd best start with ⅛th teaspoon and work your way up.

There should be 2 tablespoons of fat in the large fry pan, along with the onion mixture. Get it hot, and sprinkle with flour. Cook for 2 minutes, stirring, and add combined soup and bourbon, stirring until the sauce boils and thickens. If you find that your strength has waned from standing over the hot stove, you may take a gulp or two of bourbon to revive your flagging spirits, but use cautiously, for the chops are supposed to get sauced, not the cook. You know of course, that the alcohol will evaporate from the bourbon? If this thought depresses you, why, just add a little more to the sauce, away from heat. Enjoy! Enjoy!

SERVES FOUR.

The traffic cop commandeered an empty taxicab and told the driver to catch up with the car just ahead. He waved the driver over to the sidewalk. Leaning out of the cab, he asked the driver, "Didn't you see me signal you to stop?" he asked angrily. The driver shook his head. "No, Officer," he said. "Didn't you hear me hollering at you when you started to pass me?" the cop asked. "No, Officer," the driver said. "And I suppose you didn't hear me blow my whistle, either?" the cop asked sarcastically. "No, Officer," said the driver. The cop sat back in his seat and shook his head despairingly. "I guess," he told the cabbie, "you might as well take me home, because I'm certainly not accomplishing much around here."

A fine dish you can accomplish without much fuss or trouble is:

LAMB (OR PORK) CHOPS WITH BANANAS OR PINEAPPLE OR BOTH (Polynesian)

8 loin or shoulder lamb (or pork) chops
½ teaspoon salt
¼ teaspoon pepper
flour
2 eggs, beaten
bread crumbs
¼ cup oil (approximately)
¼ cup parsley, minced
4 bananas or 8 canned pineapple slices or both
4 tablespoons honey

Cut off as much fat as you can from the chops, without mangling them too much. Rub the salt and pepper into them. (Of course, you won't make this mistake, but I feel constrained to tell you about something awful a beginning cook did with a recipe that had instructions something like this. She thought that each piece had to have the entire quantity of ingredients that were listed. That is, she rubbed ½ teaspoon salt, ¼ teaspoon pepper, and so forth, into each piece of meat, rarther than sharing all the ingredients equally between each piece. "It was a disaster," she wrote, and I told her I bet it was.)

Now let's see where we stand. We have the fat trimmed off the chops, and salt and pepper rubbed into each one, right? Okay. Dust each chop lightly with flour, dip them first into the beaten eggs, then into the bread crumbs, coating each side. It is a good idea at this point to refrigerate them for an hour or two, which helps keep the breading on the meat when the chops are fried.

Get 2 tablespoons of the oil hot, add the parsley, then fry the breaded chops, getting each side well browned over medium heat. I think that lamb tastes best when it is still pink inside, and if you do, too, 5 minutes of frying on each side should do it if the chops with the breading are approximately 1 inch thick, adding oil as needed. Pork, of course, must be well done, so if you are using pork chops, brown them slightly on each side, then cover the pan and cook them over medium heat for 20 minutes, turning once, then remove the cover and cook over high heat, to get both sides well browned. You will, of course, use a spatula to turn the chops. Keep the chops hot while you do the bananas or pineapple accompaniment, in a 300 degree oven, or on a large platter set over a pot of very hot water, with an inverted bowl covering the cooked chops.

Scrape your frying pan with a stiff spatula, adding a little oil, to get up the good stuff from the chops, and fry the bananas, sliced in half the long way, on each side. Serve 2 chops and 2 banana halves, or 2 fried slices of pineapple, or both spread with honey. Bananas and pineapple go beautifully with chops.

SERVES FOUR.

HE: "Will you marry me?"

SHE: "No, I'm sorry."

HE: "Why not? Why won't you marry me?"

SHE: "Because I don't love you."

HE: "Well, don't you think you could learn to love me?"

SHE, thoughtfully: "You might have something there, you know? After all, I did learn to love martinis."

Everyone will love it if you give them:

AN ENGLISH GRILL

8 strips bacon
8 small breakfast sausages
2 large chicken breasts, skinned, boned, and cut in halves
salt and pepper
4 tablespoons butter
4 baby lamb chops
8 large mushrooms, stems chopped
4 large tomatoes, peeled, cored and cut into thick slices
bread crumbs

First, get a pot of water boiling, take away from heat, cover it with a large, heat-proof platter, and put on that a large mixing bowl. Put the bacon into a cold large fry pan, cook slowly over low heat, turning bacon and pouring off fat as it accumulates, until the bacon is quite crisp; save 2 tablespoons of fat.

Drain on paper towel, put the bacon on the large hot platter, and invert the bowl over it, to keep it hot. Wipe the fry pan with paper towel, put ¼ inch of water into the pan, prick the sausages with a fork, cook until water evaporates, pour off fat and when sausages are browned, put them on platter with bacon.

Put back into the pan 2 tablespoons of bacon fat, and in it fry the boned, skinned, chicken halves sprinkling with a little salt and pepper, until they are well-browned on both sides and cooked through. Put the fried chicken on the hot platter with the bacon and sausages, cover with the bowl.

Pour off the fat in pan, wipe it dry, and in it hot up 2 tablespoons of the butter. The lamb chops should have very little, if any, fat on them. Fry the chops until browned on both sides, adding a little bit of salt and pepper. Don't overcook the chops. Put them on the platter with the bacon, sausages, and the chicken.

Add the remaining butter to the pan, fry the mushroom caps and stem bits, adding tomato slices when there is room in the pan, and fry until the caps are browned and tender. Sprinkle with the bacon, the sausages, and crumbs.

Now, what have we got on that hot platter? Eight rashers of bacon, 8 small breakfast sausages, 4 chicken breast halves, 4 baby lamb chops, 8 large mushrooms, 8 fried tomato slices. What's that you said? "And a partridge in a pear tree?" Wherever did that come from? If someone doesn't like bacon, omit; someone doesn't like sausage, omit. Mushroom and tomato haters? Well how about a slice of bread and butter, or, better yet, chicken fat?

SERVES FOUR.

The boy's mother was quite angry with him because his hair was wet, a dead giveaway that he'd been swimming though he had been warned about swimming without parental supervision. He denied, at first, that he had been swimming, but under her cross cross-examination he confessed.

"Yes, Mama," he said, "I did go swimming, but I couldn't help it, because I passed by the old swimming hole on my way to the store to get the groceries you sent me for, and I couldn't withstand the temptation."

His mother forgave him then and he promised not to do it again. But then she noticed that he was holding his hands behind his back. "What have you got there?" she asked, grabbing and turning him around. He was holding his wet bathing trunks.

"How can you say you were tempted?" she asked, "when you took your trunks with you knowing full well that you were planning all the time to go for a swim?"

The boy shook his head. "Oh, no, Mama," he said, "I didn't plan it, but when I left the house I thought maybe I'd better be prepared in case I did get tempted."

One of the most temptingly and spectacularly beautiful, and delicious dishes I've cooked is:

LAMB (OR PORK) CHOPS A L'ORANGE AND SOUR CREAM (French-Russian)

4 thick double lamb or pork chops
melted fat and perhaps some oil, butter or margarine
½ teaspoon salt
⅛ teaspoon pepper
¼ cup parsley, minced plus several sprigs
½ cup orange juice
1 pint (2 cups) sour cream
1 teaspoon orange rind

Use a large, heavy frying pan, and you'll need also: a small knife, a chopping board, large kitchen fork or spoon, spatula, measuring spoons and cup, and, possibly a grater, and we advise, a pot of very hot water, a large, heavy serving platter and a large bowl.

On chopping board, cut off as much fat as you can get at without mangling the chops. Melt the fat over low heat. Sprinkle the chops with salt and pepper. Do not crowd the pan with the chops, all of which must lie flat in the pan.

When the chops are browned, and if you have no room in your pan for 4 of them together, put the finished ones on the platter sitting on the pot of very hot water, and cover them with the bowl, inverted, of course. If you need more fat for frying add one of the ingredients listed.

Add minced parsley to the pan when frying the last chops. Have all the chops on the heavy platter under the bowl. Add orange juice to pan, and scrape the good stuff stuck to the pan.

Orange Note: If you want to be elegant, have ¼ cup orange liqueur warmed to ignite and pour over dish at table, as last step.

Stir in the sour cream, put the chops back into the pan. Cook for 1 minute. Sprinkle with grated rind. Serve with some crisp, warm bread or toast with which to glop up the beautiful sauce.

SERVES FOUR.

Several friends were discussing the recent marriage of an actress they all knew very well. The actress was no longer a young chick, but she was still a great beauty. She had been married twice before, and these friends had known her from the time she was still in her teens when she first started "going around" with men.

"You know what she told me?" one of the ladies said. "She told me that before they were married she told her husband that she wanted to be honest with him, and she told him about every single one of her affairs."

The other ladies expressed amazement. "That certainly took a lot of courage," said one of them. Another one laughed. "I don't admire her for her courage," she said, "what I find amazing is her fantastic memory."

You'll want to forget all other ways of cooking lamb once you've had:

LAMB SHISHKEBOBS, SHISHED OUT-OR-INDOORS (Middle East)

2½ to 3 pounds leg of lamb (bottom, shank half, preferably)
1 teaspoon dry mustard
¼ cup wine vinegar or dry wine
¼ cup olive oil
½ teaspoon salt
¼ teaspoon pepper
¼ cup parsley, minced
1? (or more?) cloves garlic, pressed or mashed
1 teaspoon each, basil and oregano
2 large green peppers
12 (or more) small white onions

Cut the meat off the bone in large chunks, throwing away all fat, and cut the meat into cubes. Dissolve the mustard in the vinegar in a large mixing bowl, and add the oil, salt, pepper, parsley, garlic, basil, and oregano. Put the lamb cubes into the bowl, swish it around until all the meat is coated with the mixture. In the summer it is advisable to let the meat stand outside the refrigerator no more than one hour.

After seeding the green peppers, cut them into pieces about the same size as the lamb cubes. Bring a pot of water to the boil, drop the small white onions in the boiling water for a minute or two, remove them, run cold water over them, and you will be delighted to see how easily these onions are peeled—a pesty business otherwise. Cut a cross in the root end of each onion—this prevents the onion rings from popping out—and simmer them and the pieces of green pepper for 10 minutes. Drain, run cold water over the onions and pepper pieces, and add them to the lamb marinating in the bowl. Swish it all around. You are now ready to shish the kebobs.

If you are doing this outdoors, over charcoal, a basket-type grill in which the food is enclosed is the best utensil. Oil the grill, hot it up over the coals, and then put into the grill the lamb, peppers and onions. Keep the food 3 inches from the bed of coals, and grill for a total of 10 minutes, turning the grill often, and basting with the marinade before each turn.

In your oven broiler, oil a pan, set it 3 inches from the source of heat, hot it up, and put the meat and vegetables on the pan. Broil for 5 minutes, then, with a spatula, turn the meat and vegetables, spoon the pan juices over all, and broil for 3 or 4 minutes longer.

You can, of course, add cherry tomatoes, mushrooms, or any other vegetable you like. Be careful, in oven broiling, to see that neither the meat nor the vegetables get charred.

SERVES FOUR.

When the lady returned to her suburban home by the last train, she found the baby sitter, a high school senior, fast asleep on the living room sofa, looking terribly worn out and disheveled. Furiously, she woke the girl. "What do you mean by falling asleep?" she hollered. "Did you give the children their dinner? Did you bathe each of them and then tuck them into bed?"

The girl rubbed her eyes, and said, "Yes, Mam," to each of the questions. "But I'll tell you, Mam, this is the last time," she said, "that I baby sit for you."

The lady wanted to know why. "Did you have a difficult time with them?" she asked.

"Yes, Mam," the young girl said, "all of them, except the big boy."

The lady looked startled. "What's that you said?" she asked.

"The three girls didn't want to let me bathe them or tuck them into bed, but the big boy couldn't be sweeter."

The lady howled, "But I have only three daughters! I don't have any big boy! That must have been my husband!"

The high school senior stretched and yawned and smiled sleepily. "Gee," she said, "and I just thought he was kind of precocious."

Once, a couple of decades ago a precocious, voracious baby sitter I had engaged ate up all by herself, an already cooked, meant for four, dish of:

TOP OF THE STOVE KIND OF ITALIAN LAMB STEW

1 cup chicken broth
½ cup raw rice
1½ pounds (approximately) boneless lamb
½ teaspoon salt
¼ teaspoon pepper
flour
2 tablespoons oil (preferably olive)
1 tablespoon garlic, minced
½ teaspoon dried oregano
½ cup tomato sauce
¼ cup dry wine, red or white

Bring the chicken broth to the boil, add the rice, DON'T add salt, reduce to simmer and cook until all the liquid is absorbed, which will give you about 1½ cups of cooked rice.

While this is going on, rub the salt and pepper into the meat, cut it up into cubes, sprinkle them with just a little flour. Get the oil hot in a large fry pan for which you have a cover and in it fry the meat, adding the minced garlic and oregano, until the meat is browned all over. Combine the tomato sauce with the wine and add it to the pan, add the cooked rice and stir.

At this point you can leave the dish, after cooling it, in the fridge, for hours, or overnight, and then, when you want to serve it, cook covered.

SERVES FOUR.

Fellow was a prominent chiseler and freeloader and he was also considered very unreliable. But his story of woe was so convincing that Sam Nitgedeiget, a notorious soft touch, loaned him $50. "I'll pay you back," the chiseler said with cheerful insincerity, "next Friday, at noon."

When Friday came around, Mr. Nitgedeiget was astounded, because the chiseler came to see him and returned the loan. Couple of days later, the chiseler asked for another loan of $50, promising to return it promptly. Mr. Nitgedeiget shrugged philosophically and gave him the money. Sure enough, when the appointed day arrived, the chiseler came around with the money. And then, a couple of days later, the chiseler asked for another loan of $50.

This time Mr. Nitgedeiget's reaction was different. His face grew red with rage. "Get out of here, you scoundrel!" he shouted. "Two times you fooled me by returning my money! You think I'm going to let you make a fool out of me a third time?"

In Arabic, the word for beans is "fool," and in Syria they have a lamb dish with beans that is called:

FOOLEEYEE (Syria)

½ pound lamb, cubed
3 tablespoons oil, butter or margarine
1 onion, chopped
1 clove garlic, minced
1 pound lima beans or chick peas
salt and pepper to taste
1 cup water

Brown the lamb in whatever fat you are using, and then take it out of the pan and hold on to it. Fry the onion and the garlic until they are soft. Now, if you are using canned limas or chick peas, add them to the pan, along with the meat, the cup of water and seasoning and simmer it for about 20 minutes, covered.

The Syrians, Egyptians and Greeks sometimes use in this dish a bean called fava, and it comes dried, and also in cans and in bottles, already cooked. But I don't think you can get it everywhere, maybe only in specialty food stores or in Greek, or Arabic food stores. But lima beans or chick peas are more than just adequate substitutes.

If you are using dried lima beans or dried chick peas you must soak them first in enough water to cover for about 12 hours, then drain them and boil them in salted water until they are tender, which will take 1½ to 2 hours.

SERVES THREE OR FOUR, EVEN FIVE.

This fellow was telling his friend that everytime he drove to his girl friend's house, he intended to ask her to marry him, but always, after he got there, he lost his courage.

"That's too bad," said his friend. "Doesn't she give you any encouragement at all?"

The fellow shrugged. "Oh, yes," he said, "as soon as I get into her apartment, she gives me a bourbon and water. But the trouble is, one isn't enough."

No one will think one is enough if you give them:

BAKED LAMB SHANKS (Australia)

4 lamb shanks
4 tablespoons (approximately) flour
1 teaspoon fat, butter or margarine
1 cup water
2 tablespoons Worcestershire sauce
2 teaspoons prepared horseradish
2 teaspoons lemon, lime juice or cider vinegar
salt and pepper to taste

Roll the lamb shanks in the flour and get them well coated. In a large, heavy fry pan—if you use a small, light one, it will just take you longer, that's all—melt the fat and brown the shanks well all over. Now get hold of a baking dish and preheat your oven to 300 degrees. Put the lamb shanks into the baking dish. Pour the cup of water into the pan in which you browned the shanks. Bring it to a boil, scrape the skillet, and add all the other ingredients, stirring it wildly. Be careful with the salt and pepper.

Pour this over the lamb shanks in the baking dish, put it in the oven and bake it for 2 hours, covered. As long as you've got your oven hot—well, 300 degrees isn't too hot, even for a July day, is it, now?—why not make with it some:

RICE AND PEAS

1 cup rice
3 tablespoons fat, butter, or margarine
2 cups peas
½ teaspoon salt
3 cups boiling water

Melt the fat in the pan in which you browned the lamb shanks, and pour in the rice. Cook-stir the rice until it is all nicely browned, over medium heat. Add the peas and salt, and then add the boiling water slowly. Stir it well, then let it cook, uncovered, for about 5 minutes. Pour it all into a casserole and during the last hour of cooking the lamb shanks, put the rice-peas casserole into the oven and they'll both be ready at the same time.

SERVES FOUR.

Her father had been wanting for a long time to ask his daughter about the intentions of the most persistent one of her many boy friends, but, knowing that it was a real square question to ask, or even think these days, he restrained himself until, on one of the rare evenings she spent at home with her parents, she herself began talking incessantly about the young man.

"Tell me, girl," said the father, "do you think he wants to marry you, or what?"

The girl laughed. "When I first started going out with him it was 'or what' but now I'm beginning to think he really wants to marry me," she said.

Her father frowned. "Tell me, girl, what makes you think now that he wants to marry you?" he asked.

The girl shrugged. "Well, last week he asked me what your yearly income is," she said, "and last night he wanted to know if you and Mama are easy to live with."

The living is much easier if you always have in your house an assortment of canned condensed soups which you can use as the bases for various sauces, such as:

MUSHROOMS WITH PRACTICALLY ANYTHING (Brooklyn)

2 tablespoons oil (or melted chicken fat, or butter, or
    margarine)
1 large onion, chopped
1 can, approximately 4 ounces, mushroom stems and pieces
    (see Note)
¼ cup parsley, minced
garlic, minced (as much as you like—or none)
pepper to taste, be cautious about adding salt
1 can, approximately 10 ounces, condensed cream of
    mushroom soup
¼ canful water (maybe some dry wine?)
2 cups or more cubed, cooked meat (chicken, beef, lamb, pork,
    cooked shrimp, or lobster tail meat)

LAMB   323

In a large fry pan, get the oil or whatever hot, cook the chopped onion until it is just turning golden. Mushroom Note: In hot weather, it is difficult to keep fresh mushrooms very long in the markets, no matter how good the air conditioning or refrigeration, so fresh mushrooms, where available in hot weather, are insanely high-priced, which is why I say "canned." Drain, dry, and chop the mushroom pieces, add to the pan, and stir. Add the parsley and stir. If you're going to use garlic, what I say is "hurray for you." Add a very little bit of pepper, but don't add salt until you have stirred in the condensed mushroom soup and other liquid, for the soup is seasoned, you know. Add the cooked meat, stir, and taste for seasoning

Who will know that it didn't take you more than 20 minutes, only about half that time spent at the stove, to make this superlative dish? Nobody. Have a mixed green salad. Always have a salad.

SERVES FOUR.

SALADS

PART ELEVEN

Did I tell you that I managed to find some very nice people who rescued me from the fell clutches of the Damocles Savings Bank of Brooklyn who had been dangling a mortgage over my head suspended from an alarmingly frayed string for years? Well, I did.

And now we are living in an apartment house from which, our law student friend tells us, it will take the landlord at least six months, if we don't pay the rent, to evict, or as this embryonic lawyer put it, "dispossess" us. It is very nice. It is much more private than living in a private house where the next-door neighbor tells you the next day precisely what time you came home and in what condition. What makes it nicer is that now the people who live nearby won't speak to us or even nod "good morning" to us.

They have five children and no carpets and they have a bowling alley, a skating rink, and a basketball court in their apartment. Suddenly one day, we realized we hadn't heard a peep out of them for the entire day. Next day we got a particularly ugly picture postcard from them on which they had written: "Sleeping under blankets having wonderful time wish you were here." To which we replied: "Enjoying your vacation tremendously stay as long as possible love . . ."

And now that they're back they won't talk to us, which is wonderful because now we can have any time we want to, without them all busting in on us exactly at our dinner hour, some wonderful:

JELLIED SHRIMPY CLAMMY SALAD A LA VYE (Greece)

1 pound cooked shrimp
8-ounce can canned clams, minced (maybe with some extra
 clam juice, let's see later?)
½ tablespoon (half of 1 packet) unflavored gelatin
2 cups lettuce, shredded
1 cup celery (strings removed by scraping with knife), chopped
 with greenery
½ sweet onion (Bermuda, Spanish, whatever they call it on your
 block), sliced thin and rings separated
enough tomatoes cut into eighths or sixteenths or whatever
green pepper, cut into very thin rings and if we have to tell you
 at this stage to cut away and throw away the seeds and
 pith sometimes we feel like a motherless child
pimiento or roasted red pepper strips, pitted black olives, whole
 corn kernels (fresh, uncooked, great; but canned are
 okay), raw, thawed and dried green peas (10-ounce
 package), mayonnaise, salt and pepper to taste

Put the shrimp, fresh or frozen, into boiling, salted water. As soon as the water returns to boil, drain it, cover pot of shrimp securely and let them sit there.

Drain the can of chopped clams. If you haven't got a full cup of clam juice, which you may not have, augment it with more clam juice (comes in 8-ounce bottles) or water. Into the cold clam juice, sprinkle half an envelope of unflavored gelatin. When it is softened, cook over low heat, stirring, until it is thoroughly dissolved. Let it cool, and then refrigerate it.

Combine the minced clams with the cooked shrimp. Refrigerate the seafood. All the other ingredients should be frigid, also.

Using a large, show-off bowl, combine all of the ingredients, except jelled juice. The clam juice will have jelled. Cut it up into small cubes and toss it into and on the mixture. Taste it. Add mayonnaise and the salt and pepper you think it needs and enjoy! Black bread, lashings of butter, some cheese like Liederkranz, and buttermilk and thou would be paradise enow. Well, if not buttermilk, maybe some beer.

SERVES FOUR.

Scene: Court of Domestic Relations.

Characters: attorney for the defendant being sued for alimony, and lady plaintiff.

Q. Do I understand you to say that you have been married to the defendant in this action for twelve years?

A. Yes.

Q. Where, and under what circumstances did this alleged marriage take place?

A. It took place in the apartment he rented and where we still live, where his mother came to visit us, and she said, "I wish you a happy, and long marriage." And that night, I said to him, "Maxwell, your mother thinks we are married." And he said, "Well, if you think so, too, then I guess you are my wife." So I said, "Well, if I am your wife, then you are my husband." And he said, "Okay, wifey, turn out the light and let's get to sleep," and I said, "Okay, honey, good night."

Q. So you claim that from that night on you have been his wife, and he has been your husband?

A. You can say that again, Mr. Lawyer, and what's more, I have nine kids to prove it.

What I would like to prove to you is that a wonderful dish is:

CHICKEN SALAD (U.S.A.)

3-pound broiler-fryer chicken, cut up, or 3 pounds parts, or 3 to
    4 cups cooked chicken meat
1 teaspoon salt
1/4 teaspoon pepper
1 teaspoon turmeric
1/4 cup rendered chicken fat, oil, butter, or margarine
1 large onion, chopped
2 cloves garlic (or more), pressed
mayonnaise or chili sauce
1/2 head lettuce, shredded
2 tablespoons each, oil and vinegar, and salt and pepper to
    taste
a lot of cherry tomatoes, or thick tomato slices
1 10-ounce package frozen tiny green peas, thawed, drained,
    but *uncooked*, hear?
4 hard-boiled eggs

Remove the skin from the chicken parts. Cut the skin into 1-inch squares. Put them in a large cold fry pan. Cook over very low heat, stirring often, until the bits of skin are almost thoroughly browned and crisp. Leave fat melted out of skin in the pan. Rub the skinned chicken parts with salt, pepper and turmeric. Cut the meat off the bones—saving wings for stew or soup—in bite-size chunks.

Add to the pan the 1/4 cup of rendered fat, and, over medium heat, in covered pan, fry the chicken chunks until they are browned and cooked through, stirring often, adding the onion and garlic. After 25 minutes of frying taste one of the chicken chunks to see if they are done. Remove everything to a large bowl, cover it, and when the stuff is cooled, refrigerate it for hours.

When you are ready to serve this, combine the chicken mixture with mayonnaise or chili sauce—about ½ cup of either —toss the shredded lettuce with oil, vinegar and salt and pepper. Arrange the lettuce on a large platter. Mound the chicken mixture on the lettuce. Garnish with tomatoes, thawed uncooked tiny green peas, and the hard boiled eggs, cut in halves the long way. Have additional mayonnaise or chili—or both—at the table. With bread and butter. If you're going to use white bread, make it French or Italian, hey?

SERVES FOUR.

It was the funeral for the unpopular president of the company, and one gentleman arose and volunteered: "In the 30 years I have worked for our company, I got to know our president as well as anyone, and I would like to correct a commonly held misapprehension about him. He was not always as rotten as he was sometimes."

What I always like in the summer is:

CUCUMBER AND TONGUE (or whatever) SALAD (My House)

2 large cucumbers
1 teaspoon salt
1 large sweet onion (preferably a purple one), sliced and rings
    separated)
1 green pepper, seeded, chopped and parboiled for 5 minutes
as much cooked tongue, ham, chicken and whatever, cut into
    strips or cubed, as you like
at least 1 cold, boiled potato, cubed
2 strips pimiento, chopped
¼ cup wine vinegar (or dry red wine) or lemon juice
1 clove garlic (at least), pressed
¼ cup oil

Peel the cucumbers and cut them into slices as thin as you can manage. Sprinkle them with salt. You have a colander? Fine. Put the sliced, salted cucumbers into the colander, put on them a heavy bowl, and let it stand in your sink for an hour or so and a lot of juice will drain out.

Put the cucumber, onion rings, green pepper, tongue or whatever, potato, and pimiento into a large mixing bowl. In another bowl, combine the vinegar or whatever, the pressed garlic, oil, parsley and pepper and beat it with a fork. Pour it over the stuff in the other bowl, toss, cover the bowl and refrigerate it for hours and hours.

This is, of course, one of those things on which you can substitute anything for anything in this list of ingredients we've given you. You can add pickled artichoke hearts; you can add black or green olives; you can add cooked shrimp, crabmeat, or lobster or lobster tails. You can add anchovies. What I want is for you to swing. How else are you going to enjoy cooking, for goodness' sake?

All the time I get letters from people who ask, like: "Instead of parsley, can I use basil?" Of course you can. You think I'm going to come to your kitchen and give you a clop on the noggin if you don't follow a recipe precisely?

SERVES WHO KNOWS?

The bum sat down next to the dignified, well-dressed elderly man sitting on the park bench and immediately began his tale of woe. The elderly gent heard him out, nodding and clucking sympathetically all through the bum's pitiful recital of how tough things were for him.

When the bum finished his pitch, the elderly fellow said, "My friend, I'd help you out, if I could, but you see, I have no money either, I'm being supported by a miserly son who makes me account for every cent he gives me. But what I can give you is some very good advice."

This time the bum snorted derisively. "Lissen, Mac," he said, "anybody's got no money ain't got no advice worth taking."

What I like to take along to a picnic on the beach or wherever in a large bucket filled with ice and beer is:

BEEF AND HERRING SALAD IN ASPIC (Finland)

1 envelope unflavored gelatine
one 10-oz. can water (or beer?)
one 10-oz. can condensed beef broth
2 tablespoons lemon juice
1 tablespoon dry mustard
2 pound cooked roast beef
small jar Bismark herring fillets, skin removed and thrown away
2 hard-boiled eggs, sliced
1 large sweet onion, chopped
1 cucumber, peeled and sliced thin

Soften the gelatine in the water (or beer?). Put it into pan with condensed soup, lemon juice, and mustard, and bring to the boil, stirring. Remove it from heat when you are sure the gelatine and mustard are thoroughly dissolved, let it cool, and then chill it. Be careful not to let it set. When it has thickened slightly pour half of it into a long shallow container, and if you're going to take it to a picnic or a non-cook-out (which I like in the summer) make sure the container has a cover that fits very tight.

The beef should be cubed or cut into thin strips (like the latter better). Distribute pieces of meat over the aspic. Tear the herring into small bits and distribute them, set slices of the hard boiled eggs helter and skelter, sprinkle with chopped onion, and arrange cucumber slices all over the place. Spoon the rest of the aspic over all, refrigerate it overnight.

All you need with this is thick pumpernickel or corn or maybe rye bread (and did I mention beer?) and butter to make everyone happy at the beach, in the woods, in a meadow, in your dining room, on the terrace, or maybe on the fire escape. You say you never heard of beef with herring? Well, now you have, haven't you?

SERVES FOUR.

I have a couple of learned friends—couple, of course, is two—and these two highly educated ginks, when I was with them recently, went on and on, each trying to outdo the other, while I, of course, sat silently wondering at their erudition.

What they were doing was to see which one could outdo the other with the Greek names for fears, which, as you know, all end in "phobia."

They paid me no attention, except that one of them sneered slightly, which they wouldn't have done had they known this chick named Dora as I knew her. (Doraphobia means: "fear of touching animals.") I learned from their cross-talk, however, that I had several phobias I wasn't aware of. Like "domatophobia" which means "fear of being in a house I lived in for many years in imminent danger of having fall on it a large mortgage, held over it with a thin, fearsomely frayed string, by the Damocles Savings Bank."

I also learned that I have "rhadophobia," which means "fear of being beaten."

Also, I have "sirerodromophobia," which is "fear of railroad travel" and if you know anything about commuter lines these days, you know that this is not an uncommon phobia. I escaped from the company of these two over-educated shlumps when one of them won the game by mentioning another fear which afflicts me, one called "pantrophobia" which means "fear of everything."

You need have no fear, for nothing in this recipe is critical, but depends entirely on your judgment, when you make:

MISHMASH SALAD (Connecticut)

½ cup salad oil
2 cloves, or more, garlic, pressed
1 teaspoon salt
¼ teaspoon cayenne pepper
¼ cup—or more—lemon, or lime juice, or wine vinegar
¼ teaspoon sugar

In a small fry pan, hot up ¼ cup salad oil, and fry the pressed garlic until it turns golden. In a small mixing bowl, combine the garlic and garlicky oil with the rest of the oil, the salt, cayenne pepper and lemon juice and sugar. This, of course, is the dressing for the:

SALAD

1 can (7 to 8 ounces) tuna fish, drained and flaked
¼ pound of 3 (or more) lean, chopped deli meats: corned beef, tongue, pastrami, salami, baloney, Polish sausage, or skinned franks
At least 3 cups shredded lettuce
3 ribs celery, chopped after strings are removed by scraping with knife or parer
1 cup cherry tomatoes, skins removed (plunging them into very hot water for one minute makes them easy to peel)
¼ cup chopped pimiento
one 10-ounce package frozen, raw green peas, thawed
6 strips roasted sweet red pepper
12 or more pickled cocktail onions

In a large salad bowl, preferably glass, combine all the salad ingredients. Pour sauce, well beaten, over all, and toss.
SERVES SIX TO EIGHT.

The young boy was in the dentist's chair for almost an hour. Finally, the dentist told the boy that he was finished working on his teeth for this session.

"How do you feel, Doc?" the boy asked. The dentist was surprised. "Why, I feel just fine, Billy, why do you ask?" he said surprisedly.

The boy nodded. "Now I know what you mean by that sign on your door that says 'Painless Dentist.' "

Whenever I see a cookbook which lists product brand names among the ingredients, it causes me to throw the book against the wall with a howl of rage. I have one which has a recipe for a barbecue sauce in which the author gives the brand names for three strong-flavored ingredients that are salty, plus 1 teaspoon of flavored salt, ½ teaspoon white pepper, plus "several generous grindings of black pepper," 1 tablespoon of horseradish and then, for some reason best known to himself, ½ teaspoon monosodium glutamate. This last-mentioned ingredient is known, of course, as "MSG" and is used to heighten the flavor of foods.

But, do the flavors of horseradish, salt, pepper, a hot pepper sauce, mustard, catsup need heightening? NO. Where MSG is helpful, if not overused, is in cooking bland vegetables, like, for instance:

MUSHROOM-GREEN BEAN-TOMATO AND OTHER VEGETABLE CASSEROLE

2 tablespoons each, butter and oil
2 sweet peppers, chopped
1 bunch scallions (green onions), chopped
1 pound fresh mushrooms, sliced through stems and caps
one 10-ounce package frozen green beans, thawed and dried
1-pound can tomatoes, or 1 pound fresh tomatoes
very little salt
very little pepper
½ cup grated Swiss or other mild cheese

In a large fry pan, get the butter and oil hot. (The oil allows you to fry for a longer time than would otherwise be possible without burning the butter.) Fry the peppers, scallions and mushrooms over low heat, stirring to coat them with the fat, and cover the pan for 10 minutes. Remove the cover, add the thawed green beans, raise the heat to high and cook stirring, for 2 or 3 minutes.

The canned tomatoes should be well mashed. If you use fresh tomatoes, peel and core them, and then mash them up well. Tomatoes are peeled easily if you drop them, one or two at a time, in boiling water for about ½ minute, cut off the stem, core the tomato, and then strip the peel with small knife. Add to the pan with the mushroom-bean mixture, stir. Taste, add salt and pepper sparingly.

Butter a casserole or baking dish, spoon the mixture in, sprinkle with the cheese, and bake in oven preheated to 350 degrees until the cheese is slightly browned.

SERVES FOUR.

The man put the watch on the jeweler's counter. "It stopped running when I made the mistake of dropping it," he said.

The jeweler opened the case and looked at the cheap watch's works. "When you dropped it," he said, "it was an accident; when you picked it up, that was the mistake."

You can't go wrong for a lovely inexpensive, easily made lunch or late week-end breakfast by cooking:

SAUERKRAUT-APPLE-AND-STUFF SALAD

1-pound can sauerkraut
2 cups raw apples, peeled, cored and sliced thin
2 cups any kind of cooked meat, poultry, or seafood
1 tablespoon caraway seeds toasted for ½ minute in teaspoon
    butter or oil
pepper

Drain the sauerkraut (of course you can use homemade) and taste it. Many people don't like it too sour. If you are one of those, put the drained sauerkraut into a kitchen towel, press out more of the liquid, then pour cold water over the sauerkraut balled-up in the towel, until it tastes the way you prefer it.

Combine everything thoroughly in a large bowl, add pepper to taste, refrigerate it for hours and serve it, with black bread, lots of butter, maybe some cheese slices, maybe with onion rings on top of the cheese which is on top of the buttered bread. Buttermilk is wonderful with this. Real cold buttermilk. Or beer.

SERVES FOUR.

Three days after his arrival at the camp to which they had exiled him for the summer, a small boy sent a postcard to his parents. His parents were overjoyed to receive this first communication.

"Dear Mom and Pop," the boy wrote, "on the first day I didn't have any friends. On the second day I made friends with two boys. Now I have two friends and nine enemies."

A refreshing, delicious hot-weather lunch or dinner dish that will make friends for you with very little work is:

VEGETABLES IN SOUR CREAM

½ stick butter
½ pound mushrooms, sliced the long way through stems and
    caps
1 cup scallions, chopped
1 clove (or more) garlic, pressed or mashed
1 large cucumber, peeled and sliced thin
3 or 4 white radishes if you can get them, sliced thin, or ½ cup
    sliced small red ones
4 large tomatoes, peeled and chopped
1 quart sour cream
salt and pepper to taste
parsley, minced
1 tablespoon capers, minced, drained, and dried
paprika

In a large fry pan, get the butter hot and in it fry the mushrooms, onion and garlic until they are soft. Remove from the pan, cool, and then refrigerate it all for at least 1 hour.

Combine with the sliced cucumber, sliced radishes, chopped tomatoes, and sour cream, and add salt and pepper, and stir.

Refrigerate once more. Just before serving, sprinkle with chives or parsley, capers and paprika. Pumpernickel, corn or rye bread, with butter and cheese—cream cheese combined with a couple of drained mashed anchovies—are good accompaniments. So is beer. Or buttermilk.

SERVES FOUR.

A thing happened to me and it wasn't one durn bit funny, on the way to get on a paddlewheel boat at Louisville to go up the Ohio River on an overnight cruise to Cincinnati. The Ohio River has always been, to me, one of the dream places of the world because it was the setting for some of the best fiction I've ever read. So when the invitation came I was ecstatic. What happened was I got into a taxicab in Manhattan to go to J. F. Kennedy Airport to get on a plane to go to Louisville and the cabbie forgot that his name was Nopar King, or thought he was Henny Youngman and he laughed so hard at his stupid jokes that he finally managed to miss the plane by precisely four minutes.

"Nopar," I kept telling Mr. King the cabbie, "if you don't stop slowing down to tell me those terrible jokes, I'll miss the plane," which, of course, made him laugh all the harder, and you should have heard him howl with joy when he found I'd been right. So right away I went back to New York and told him that if he didn't keep his big mouth shut all the way back I'd put a hex on him which wouldn't ever again let him eat:

DELTA QUEEN SALAD WITH NAUVOO BLUE CHEESE DRESSING (Ohio)

1 head lettuce, torn up
1 carrot, grated
about 6 red radishes, cut into thin slices
1 bunch endives (if you are rich—if not, forget it and use celery)
1 pound fresh tomatoes, peeled and cut into small pieces
$\frac{1}{4}$ pound blue cheese
$1\frac{1}{2}$ to 2 pounds shrimp, cooked, chopped
1 quart buttermilk
2 tablespoons lemon juice or vinegar
salt and pepper to taste

"Delta Queen" is the name of that boat I didn't get to ride on up the Ohio River, but this is the recipe for one of the delights usually served on the ship.

What you do to the ingredients is just do what you can see plainly that I told you to do with them. Peel the tomatoes (plunge them into very hot water for about one minute, unplunge, and cool them, then skin them) and cut them up. Stir up all the other stuff, but leave the cut-up tomatoes until I tell you to do with them what you should do.

In a bowl, crumble the blue cheese, add chopped shrimp and the buttermilk and the lemon juice. Add this to the bowl with the vegetables. Toss the stuff to combine it all completely, adding a little salt and pepper at a time until the seasoning seems right. Now, gently, add the cut-up pieces of tomato. Chill it for hours and hours. This will serve a lot of people. Oh, yes. About those endives. Mostly, they're imported, and I like them very much. But I eat them only when I freeload (because they cost like crazy) like I missed doing on the Delta Queen, a veritable floating gin palace that trip, I hear tell.

SERVES FOUR TO SIX.

STUFFED VEGETABLES

PART TWELVE

The New Yorker was trudging through the Florida Everglades doing his best to walk in the footsteps of the guide who was leading the way when suddenly he slipped and fell off the trail into the swamp. "Help! Help!" he cried out. "An alligator just bit off my foot!" The guide stopped and came running back to him. "Which one?" the guide yelled. "How should I know?" the New Yorker said angrily. "All these damn alligators look alike to me."

As I put that down on paper, it looked like a good day to have:

BAKED ONIONS STUFFED WITH SHRIMP AND OTHER GOOD STUFF (Brooklyn)

8 large onions
butter, oil, or marge
2 cloves minced garlic
½ pound chopped mushrooms, or two 4-ounce cans drained, dried and chopped
1 pound shrimp, shelled if "fresh," thawed if frozen, dried and chopped
1 cup cold cooked rice
1 teaspoon salt
½ teaspoon pepper
1 egg beaten
2 tablespoons flour
1 cup milk
1 cup grated cheese (any kind you like)

In a large pot, in water to cover, boil the onions for 10 minutes. Drain and cool them. Cut each one in half and scoop out the inner rings, leaving a shell of about ¼ inch.

Chop the inner rings. In a large fry pan, hot up 2 tablespoons of butter or whatever, and in it fry the chopped onion, garlic and mushrooms until the onions are browned, stirring constantly over high heat. Put this mixture into a bowl. In the same pan, get 2 more tablespoons of butter hot and in it, over medium heat, stirring constantly, fry the chopped shrimp for about 3 minutes. Add the shrimp to the bowl with the cooked onion mixture.

Add 2 more tablespoons of butter to the pan, when it is bubbling spoon in the cooked rice, sprinkle it with the salt and pepper, and while stirring constantly, pour the beaten egg slowly over the rice, stirring rapidly in order to coat the rice with the egg before the egg gets cooked. When the rice is browned, add it to the bowl with the onion-mushroom-shrimp mixture, and stir to combine all the ingredients thoroughly.

In the same large frying pan, get 2 more tablespoons of butter hot, add the 2 tablespoons of flour, and cook, stirring, for 2 minutes, until the flour is golden, and the mixture smooth. Add the milk slowly, beating with a fork or whisk until the mixture is smooth and somewhat thickened.

Pour the sauce into a large shallow baking pan. Put in the onion shells and stuff them with the fried onion-mushroom-shrimp-rice mixture, leaving some over to put into the sauce. Sprinkle the stuffed onions with the grated cheese and bake in oven preheated to 350 degrees until the cheese is melted and beginning to brown. Put the stuffed onions on a pretty, deep platter, pour the sauce over all.

SERVES FOUR.

There are many witticisms written by newspaper people that have become classics of displays of venom and cruelty. Dorothy Parker is credited with having dismissed the theatrical performance of a noted actress thus: "Miss Yifnif ran the gamut of emotions from A to B." Heywood Broun, who had been publicly berated by an actor whom he had criticized pitilessly for a bad performance, wrote, next time the actor appeared in a play: "Mr. Mitnick's performance was not up to his usual standard." You probably know Eugene Field's devastating review of a famous star's performance in *King Lear*. "He played the King," wrote Field, "as though under the premonition that someone was about to play the Ace."

What brought all this on was a story, printed the day after Spiro T. Agnew was nominated as Richard Nixon's running-mate, with the headline: "JUDY AGNEW—FROM OBSCURITY TO NATIONAL SPOTLIGHT IN 10 MINUTES." Among other things, the story said: "In their spare time the Agnews gather after dinner in a downstairs recreation room where they play pingpong and pool together. Mrs. Agnew's official biography also indicates that she reads." This, I submit, is carrying cattiness far beyond the call of duty, and is but one more illustration that man's inhumanity to man is as nothing compared to woman's inhumanity to woman, for this venomous stinger was writ by a woman.

A stinger—which I'll talk about at the end of this sermon—is what I like to have after a main course of:

LIGHTLY CURRIED CRAB-STUFFED PEPPERS

4 large green or red peppers
1 pound crabmeat, fresh, frozen or canned
2 eggs, beaten
4 tablespoons butter
1 medium-sized onion, minced
$\frac{1}{8}$ teaspoon each, salt and pepper
1 teaspoon curry powder
$\frac{1}{2}$ cup grated cheese (any kind you like)

Cut the peppers in half, horizontally, remove seeds and pulp, and parboil them in water to cover for about 3 minutes. Canned crabmeat, as is everything that comes in cans, is cooked. If you have frozen crabmeat (which comes cooked), thaw it in a colander. Whether it is fresh, frozen, or canned, you should flake the meat carefully and throw away any cartilage you come across, and dry it thoroughly on paper towels. In a mixing bowl, combine the crabmeat with the beaten eggs. In a large fry pan, hot up 2 tablespoons of the butter and in it fry the minced onion until it becomes soft and golden. Add the salt, and pepper, and curry powder, and stir and cook for 2 minutes.

If you are using fresh crabmeat, add it to the fry pan, stir, and cook over low heat, stirring occasionally, for 15 minutes. If your crabmeat is the frozen or canned kind, 2 or 3 minutes of cooking, just long enough to hot it up, will be all that is required. Taste the mixture and wait for the aftertaste, and correct the seasoning—including the curry powder—if you think it needs correcting. Crabmeat is so delicately flavored that it is shameful to kill it with overpowering seasoning. Stuff the par-boiled pepper halves with the mixture, sprinkle grated cheese over each one, and rub 1½ tablespoons of the butter on the halved peppers. Rub the remaining ½ tablespoon of butter on a baking pan, and bake the stuffed peppers in a 350 degree oven until the cheese begins to brown, about 15 minutes. Oh, yes, the stinger. Stir 2 ounces of brandy and 1 teaspoon of white creme de menthe together, and pour it into a stemmed glass holding crushed ice. Mmmmm. Good.

SERVES FOUR.

When the tide of war turned against their cause, newpaper editors all over the South bitterly criticized every general in the Confederate army. Gen. Robert E. Lee, commander-in-chief of the Confederates, was reading a Southern newspaper one day, sighed, shook his head sadly, and put the paper down. "You mustn't let the newspaper articles bother you, sir," said one of the officers on his staff. "They don't know what they're talking about." General Lee shook his head. "No, no," he answered, "You're all wrong about that. When this war broke out we made a fundamental mistake that is going to ruin us, and there's nothing we can do about it now." His staff officer paled. "What mistake was that, sir?" he asked. "Well," said General Lee, "it seems that what we did was to take all of our best generals and make newspaper editors of them and we took the editors and made them our generals."

You can take all your best leftovers and make:

STUFFED SWEET PEPPERS

8 small sweet peppers, green or red
2 tablespoons oil
1 baseball-sized onion, minced
1 tablespoon garlic, minced
$\frac{1}{4}$ cup fresh parsley, minced (1 tablespoon dried parsley flakes)
1 pound cooked meat, ground or chopped fine (leftover beef, pork, etc.)
1 cup chili sauce
$\frac{1}{2}$ cup bread stuffing (corn, preferably)

Cut the top off each pepper, not just the stem, but all around the pepper, which will leave it with more-or-less straight sides, making it easier to cut out the seeds and the pulpy white parts (both of which you can throw away). Be careful not to rub your eyes while doing this because the seeds and pulp have something in them that will irritate eyes. Wash the peppers, of course, under cold running water. Put the peppers into boiling, salted water for about 2 minutes and drain them. Get the oil hot in a large fry pan and in it fry the minced onion, garlic, and parsley until the onion is soft. Away from heat, combine the stuff in the pan with the cooked ground or chopped meat, chili sauce and the bread stuffing.

Reason I say to combine everything in the large fry pan is to save you the trouble of using a mixing bowl which will make an additional utensil to wash up. Taste the mixture. Add salt if you think it needs some; same goes for pepper. You want it real hot? Mix in some chili or curry powder, but be careful because these two ingredients are made more powerful by cooking, which you are going to do right now. Stuff all the stuff into the peppers. Make mounds over pepper tops if you have enough stuffing.

Put the peppers on a baking pan, bake in oven preheated to 350 degrees for about 15 minutes, just long enough to hot up everything without burning the peppers. If, after you have made mounds of stuffing on top of each pepper, you still have stuffing left over, put it on pan in last 5 minutes.

SERVES FOUR.

Somebody told us about a department store where the clerks in each department had to write a report telling the reason why any customer walked out without making a purchase. One saleslady in the dress department made this entry: "Lady looked at black dresses, tried on ten different ones. She didn't buy anything because her husband is in the hospital, but he hasn't died yet."

Do I hear you say: "That's a terrible story"? Well, you know what? Now that I think it over, I agree with you, that is a terrible story.

But what's wonderful is:

STUFFED BAKED POTATOES (Brooklyn)

4 large baking potatoes
1 pound canned salmon or tuna
1 or 2 anchovies, well mashed, or salt to taste
4 tablespoons butter
½ cup onion, minced
¼ teaspoon pepper
½ cup milk or light cream, heated
½ cup cheese, grated
½ pint sour cream
2 tablespoons snipped fresh chives or minced parsley

If you don't eat the skin of baked potatoes it is a ding-dong shame; not only does it taste wonderful, but it is full of vitamins and stuff that are wonderful for your health. So wash and scrub the potatoes, and dry them thoroughly. Bake them for 40 minutes to 1 hour, depending on their size, in a 350 degree oven. If you prick them with a fork in the last 10 minutes of baking it will allow steam to escape, and make the potatoes wonderfully flaky.

While the potatoes are baking, make the stuffing. If you are using salmon, remove skin and bones. Combine the salmon and anchovies—or salt—in a mixing bowl. Get 1 tablespoon of butter hot in a fry pan and in it fry the onion just until it is soft. Put the fried onion into the bowl, add pepper, and combine with mixture.

Cut the potatoes, the long way, down to but not through the bottom and with a spoon scoop out the meat, leaving a hollow shell. Add the scooped out potato to the bowl, pour in the hot milk or cream, the grated cheese and sour cream. Combine all the ingredients thoroughly.

Pack the mixture into the hollowed out shells and sprinkle with the chives. Put it back into the oven and bake for 10 minutes, just to hot it all up. You can make infinite variations on this by substituting cooked chicken, any cooked meat, or shrimps or clams.

Serve 2 potato halves to each person, putting a generous dollop of sour cream on each, and sprinkle with chives or minced parsley. Buttermilk is lovely with this. So is beer. Or wine.

SERVES FOUR.

Small boy went to the supermarket with his mother, and as they walked home, the mother, heavy laden with two big bags full of food, slipped on a patch of ice, fell with a severe crash, and, when she saw the bags burst, scattering the food all over the street, she burst into tears.

"Now, now," said her small son, "upsa-daisy, Mummy, and now we'll jump up and down, and laugh and laugh, to show how brave we are."

Let us all jump up and down and holler to show how happy we are to eat:

STUFFED CABBAGE WITH REAL GOOD STUFF (Brooklyn)

1 small head of cabbage (a red one if you can get it)
peanut oil
1 pound ground beef, chuck or shoulder
1 cup onions, chopped
$\frac{1}{4}$ teaspoon each, salt, pepper, and oregano or thyme
1 cup baked beans (no pork)
1 egg, beaten
1 can (about 10 ounces) condensed cream of mushroom soup
$\frac{1}{3}$ canful dry vermouth, or dry wine, red or white
2 tablespoons lemon juice
1 teaspoon lemon rind, grated
$\frac{1}{4}$ cup chopped seedless raisins

Throw away the tough, probably discolored, outer leaves of the cabbage, and pick out 12 fairly even-sized tender leaves. Put them into a pot with water to cover, bring to the boil, and drain instantly. Let the leaves cool.

While the cabbage leaves are cooling, hot up 4 tablespoons of oil in a large fry pan. In the hot oil, cook the beef and onions, stirring to break up the meat, add salt, pepper, and oregano, and cook until all the beef has browned and the onions are soft. Remove the pan from the heat. Combine the cold beans and the egg, then stir this mixture into the beef in the fry pan. Spread out the wilted cabbage leaves. Put equal amounts of the beef-bean mixture into the center of each leaf. Fold one side of the leaf over the mixture, roll it up, and tuck in the ends.

Put the stuffed cabbage leaves into the fry pan. In a mixing bowl, combine the soup with the vermouth, or whatever, add the lemon juice and rind, and raisins. Pour this over and around the stuffed cabbage leaves. Cover the pan, bring it to the boil, and simmer for 15 minutes.

Fried noodles are good with this. Dry cooked noodles on a kitchen towel, and fry them in oil or butter, stirring. Season the noodles lightly with salt and pepper. Try a salad made with the crisp, inner leaves and heart of the cabbage, chopped up, seasoned with salt and pepper, and a little oil and vinegar.

SERVES FOUR.

The doctor and his wife were having dinner in an expensive restaurant when a beautiful young girl accompanied by two men, both much older than she, was led past their table by the headwaiter. The girl smiled broadly, patted the doctor fondly on the head as she passed, and said, "How are you, Doc?" The doctor's wife glared at him. "How did you get to know a girl like that?" the wife asked. "Just professionally, just professionally, darling," the doctor said. His wife still glared at him. "Professionally, hey?" she asked glaringly, "Whose? Yours or hers?"

Whatever his profession—or job—few men will not be happy with:

FISH STUFFED BAKED POTATOES (Russia)

4 large baking potatoes, washed and thoroughly dried
4 fish fillets (flounder or any other fish you like)
4 anchovy strips, dried
4 tablespoons ($\frac{1}{4}$ cup) parsley, minced fine
1 teaspoon dried dill weed or thyme
$\frac{1}{2}$ teaspoon pepper
flour
2 eggs, beaten with 2 tablespoons any cheese, grated
$\frac{1}{2}$ stick (4 tablespoons) butter
1 small onion, minced fine
$\frac{1}{4}$ teaspoon each, salt and cayenne pepper
2 tablespoons milk or light cream

Preheat your oven to 350 degrees. Put a thin film of oil or butter on a baking sheet large enough to hold the 4 potatoes. Put the washed, thoroughly dried potatoes on the pan and bake for 20 minutes. While this is going on, dry the fish fillets, put one strip of dried anchovy on each fish fillet. Sprinkle each one with parsley, dill—or thyme—and pepper. Roll up the fillets and fasten them with toothpicks. Dip each rolled-up fillet into the flour and then into the egg-cheese mixture.

In a large frying pan, melt 2 tablespoons of butter. When the butter is hot fry the rolled-up, eggy fillets over low heat until they are browned all over.

When the potatoes have been baked for 20 minutes take the pan holding them out of the oven. Using a pot holder to protect your hand, cut off the top of each potato and scoop out most of the inside, leaving a shell about ¼ inch thick. Put the potato insides into a bowl.

In the same pan in which you fried the fish fillets, hot up the remaining 2 tablespoons of butter. Fry the minced onion until it is soft, add the potato insides to the pan, sprinkle with salt, cayenne pepper, add milk, and cook over medium heat for 2 minutes, mashing and mixing all the while.

Take the toothpicks out of the fried, rolled-up fish fillets, put the fish fillets into the hollowed potatoes, heap each one with the onion-potato mixture, put a piece of foil over each one, and return to oven to bake for another 40 minutes, removing foil during last 10 minutes. One to a customer.

SERVES FOUR.

The traffic cop was testifying about the events that had led him to arrest the man for trying to make a U-turn where such a maneuver was forbidden. "Why didn't you just give him a ticket?" the judge asked. The cop blushed. "Well, he called me something awful," the cop said. He apologized to the judge but refused to say what the awful thing was that the defendant had said to him.

"Judge," the defendant cried out, "I'll tell you what I said to him. He was bawling me out for being a rotten, stupid driver, and without thinking I said to him just what I say to my wife when she does that." The judge glared at the defendant. "You mean you call your wife awful things?" the judge asked glaringly.

"Well, it's not so awful when I call my wife that," the defendant said, "because what I said to the cop, without thinking was: 'Yes sweetie, yes my little pussycat.'"

That's what your husband, boy friend, or whatever, will call you if you give him:

SOUP, AND PEPPERS OR TOMATOES STUFFED WITH GOOD STUFF (Brooklyn)

2 cans (each 13¾ ounces) chicken broth
4 large green peppers or tomatoes
¼ cup oil (I prefer olive oil for this) or ½ stick butter or marge
½ pound mushrooms, sliced
1 bunch scallions (green onions) minced with some greenery
1 (or more) large clove garlic, pressed or minced very fine
1 pound chopped beef (round, preferably)
½ teaspoon each, salt and pepper
¼ teaspoon oregano, or thyme, or Italian seasoning

Bring to the boil the two cans of chicken broth. (Of course you can use homemade soup.) Cut the tops off the peppers or tomatoes. Cut out and throw away the seeds and white pith if you use peppers. If you're using large tomatoes, cut out and throw away the white core, then remove pulp—save it—to leave a shell of about ¼ of an inch. Put the peppers or tomatoes into the broth, reduce the heat so it barely simmers, and cook for 5 minutes.

In a large fry pan, hot up 2 tablespoons of the oil, or whatever, and in it, over high heat, stirring constantly, cook the sliced mushrooms, scallions, and garlic until the mushrooms are well-browned. Remove this mixture to a bowl.

Hot up the remaining 2 tablespoons of oil in the same large pan, and in it cook the meat, breaking it up with a kitchen fork or spoon, stirring until it is browned, sprinkling with salt, pepper, and oregano, or whatever. Taste the mixture and correct it to suit yourself.

Combine the cooked meat with the mushroom mixture and the tomato pulp (if you're using tomatoes). Stuff the peppers—or tomatoes—with the mixture, making high mounds. Put a very thin film of oil on a pan and bake the stuffed whatever for about 15 minutes, to hot it all up. Have the chicken soup, as a prelude.

SERVES FOUR.

EGG DISHES

PART THIRTEEN

Father and his young son got on a bus together and found seats. The father had given his son more than enough money to pay his own fare. When they had been sitting for a moment, the boy nudged his father.

"Daddy," he whispered, "I still have the money you gave me, because I forgot all about giving it to the bus driver to give me change so I could put the fare into the box, and the driver didn't say a word to me." The lad was, obviously, elated because he had got something for nothing, even though it was done somewhat innocently. This made the father angry.

"You go right back there and hand the driver the money," he said angrily, "and apologize, and put the fare into the box. Haven't I told you often enough that honesty is the best policy?"

Sulking, the lad got up, talked to the driver, gave him the money, received change, and dropped the fare into the box. When he came back to his father he was no longer sulking. Indeed, he was elated. He sat down and whispered to his father.

"Daddy, you sure are right about honesty being the best policy," he said. "When I gave the driver the dollar he gave me change for $5.00."

It'll cost you more than a dollar for this wonderful dish, but I'm sure you'll agree that it was worth it when you make:

BAKED MUSHROOM AND ARTICHOKE OMELET (California)

    4 tablespoons butter or oil
    1 cup onion, minced
    ½ pound mushrooms, sliced the long way through stems and
        caps
    small jar marinated artichoke hearts, drained and dried and cut
        in half
    1 cup chopped, cooked tongue, ham, or Canadian bacon
    salt and pepper to taste
    8 eggs, beaten
    ½ cup grated cheese

In a large fry pan, get 3 tablespoons of butter or oil hot, and in it fry the minced onion and sliced mushrooms until they are both soft. Remove from the pan to a mixing bowl.

Add to the bowl the artichoke hearts, and taste the cooked meat for saltiness.

All this won't take very long, but if you like you can prepare all this, up to this point, the night before, or hours before you are going to serve it, and refrigerate it.

Butter a baking dish and preheat your oven to 350 degrees. Add the beaten eggs to the mixture, stir to combine and spoon it all into the baking dish, sprinkle cheese over all, and drizzle with the remaining tablespoon of butter. Bake it until the cheese is bubbling and slightly browned, for about 20 to 25 minutes. If you like your eggs dry and set well, bake it until a knife stuck into it comes out without egg on its face. If you like your eggs moist, test it with a knife after about 15 minutes of baking. What to drink with this? Well, I like Bloody Marys. You have what you like. Look, if you like Bloody Marys, try it sometimes with clam juice, with no tomato juice at all. Unbloody Mary. Marvelous.

SERVES FOUR.

Our friend Joe McCarthy told us this story about a Sunday school class for pre-school children: "Can any of you tell the class," said the teacher, "who were Matthew, Mark, Luke, and John?" The classroom was quiet. The teacher sighed, and said, "Well, what about Peter? Does anyone know who Peter was?" A small boy in the first row raised his hand timidly. "I don't know about those other fellows," said the boy, "but I think Peter was a rabbit."

Quick as a bunny you can make:

EGGS AND ALL KINDS OF STUFF (Spain)

1 teaspoon oil
$\frac{1}{2}$ cup scallions, chopped with some greenery
2 cups cooked meat (or shrimp), chopped
1 can (approximately 10 ounces) condensed tomato soup
$\frac{1}{4}$ can any liquid (milk, wine, even, for goodness' sake, water)
1 package (approximately 10 ounces) frozen mixed vegetables, thawed and dried
taste for salt and pepper
8 eggs (unbroken)
$\frac{1}{4}$ cup parlsey, minced
$\frac{1}{2}$ teaspoon paprika

In a large fry pan, get the oil hot and in it fry the onion and chopped meat, stirring, until the onion is soft. Stir in the condensed soup and other liquid, and add thawed vegetables. Cook, covered, over low heat, stirring at least twice, for 5 minutes.

Taste the mixture for seasoning, add pepper—which you'll probably need—and salt, if you think it needs some.

Break the eggs on top of the mixture, sprinkle with parsley, and then with paprika. Cover the pan and cook over low heat until the whites of the eggs are set. I like to have the yolks runny, with a slight film over them, but if you like the yolks to be harder, you just go right ahead, friend, and have the eggs as you like them.

SERVES FOUR.

Young fellow was finished with school and he was going out into that fearful, menacing jungle that he'd always been told existed outside the relatively safe world of academe, and his old daddy was giving him advice. "Whatever kind of business you go into, my son," said the daddy, "you must always remember two rules." The lad nodded dutifully. "Yes, Old Daddy," he said dutifully, "tell me, if you will, pray, what is the first rule?" His daddy looked his son in the eyes sternly.

"First rule is that you must make a reputation," he said sternly, "for being an ethical businessman." The boy nodded. "Tell me please, Old Daddy, how can I establish such a reputation?" His daddy nodded. "I am glad you asked that question, my son," he said. "Everyone you deal with must know that when you give your word of honor to do something or other, you will always keep your word."

The lad nodded eagerly. "Yes, Old Daddy," he said eagerly, "and what is the second rule, please?" His daddy stood up and glared at his son angrily. "Why, you loutish dullard," he hollered, "the second rule, of course, is that you must never give your word of honor."

I have the honor now of giving a sermon on:

FRIED FISH BALLS AND SCRAMBLED EGGS

1½ pounds of fish fillets
five 8-ounce bottles of clam juice, very cold
½ teaspoon salt
1 cup onion, minced very fine
¼ cup parsley, minced fine
2 cups instant mashed potatoes made according to package
    directions
2 eggs beaten
bread crumbs
6 tablespoons butter
2 tablespoons oil
cayenne pepper (use sparingly)
8 more eggs, beaten
½ stick (4 tablespoons) butter

Cook the fish fillets tenderly in a covered pan which has in it one 8-ounce bottle of clam juice, simmering gently. About 5 minutes will do it. Dry the fillets and flake and chop and mash them, together with ½ teaspoon salt, and combine the fish, in a bowl, with the onion, parsley, and mashed potatoes, adding 2 tablespoons of the 2 beaten eggs. Refrigerate this mixture for at least 1 hour. Save clam juice in which the fillets were cooked. With wet hands, fashion the mixture into balls about the size of golf balls.

Dip the balls into the remainder of the 2 beaten eggs and roll them in a pile of bread crumbs, getting them well-coated. Refrigerate them for hours. In a large fry pan, get 2 tablespoons each of the butter and oil hot, and in it fry the fish balls, turning them gently with a spatula, until they are well browned all over. Sprinkle them cautiously with cayenne pepper. Keep them hot. You know how to scramble eggs, for goodness sake, don't you? This is for 4 people, so put those 8 beaten eggs, beaten with a little salt and pepper, into a fry pan with remaining butter (4 table-spoons) hotted up, and cook over low heat, stirring with a fork all the while until they are done as you like them.

Serve some fish balls and eggs with buttered toast. You say you don't like fried fish balls? Well, omit them. And you don't like scrambled eggs? Well you can omit them, too, of course. And you don't like buttered toast? Well, that's your problem, not mine.

SERVES FOUR.

The grade school class had been taken on a tour through Monticello, in Virginia, and had listened to the guide telling how Thomas Jefferson had designed his mansion, and had had all the bricks, the lumber, and everything else that went into its building made or grown right there on his estate, by his own people (slaves). When the tour was ended their teacher asked if anyone had any questions.

A small boy raised his hand. "I have a question," said the small boy. "Thomas Jefferson was President of the United States, right?" he asked. The teacher and the guide nodded. "He also founded the University of Virginia, and wrote the Declaration of Independence, right?" asked the small boy and the adults again nodded. "And this house is just the way it was when he lived here?" the small boy asked, and once more the adults nodded.

The small boy laughed. "Who you trying to put on?" he asked scornfully. "You mean to say the President of the United States, author of the Declaration of Independence, and founder of the University of Virginia couldn't afford to have a television set?"

Your family will howl with pleasure if you set before them a dish of:

CORNED BEEF PANCAKE (Jewish deli-style)

8 slices corned beef (or ready-to-eat tongue, or salami, maybe pastrami, or whatever)
oil (salad or peanut)
8 eggs
4 tablespoons water
$\frac{1}{8}$ teaspoon each, salt and pepper
mustard and pickled cucumbers and tomatoes
rye, corn, or pumpernickel bread

Trim the fat off the corned beef—if it doesn't have any fat it probably isn't a very good corned beef, which should be quite juicy, and the meat can't be juicy if it doesn't have fat. Hot up 1 tablespoon of oil in a large fry pan and in it fry the meat on both sides, using a spatula to prevent the meat from sticking to the pan. When the meat has been fried on both sides, remove it from the pan. Add 2 tablespoons of oil to the pan, and if any meat has stuck to it, scrape it up with your spatula because if the pan isn't altogether smooth, the pancake will stick to it.

While the meat is frying, beat the eggs until frothy, with the water, salt, and pepper. Pour the eggs into the pan, and when the bottom has begun to set, put the meat slices into the pan. Cover the pan and cook over low heat, for about 5 minutes, until the top is set. Covering the pan will make it puff up, somewhat like a souffle, and it will be moist. If you want it well-done, loosen the pancake with your spatula, slide it out on a large plate, and put it back into the hot fry pan, top-side down.

SERVES FOUR.

INDEX

Africa, 83
Anchovy-bourbon-clam sauce, 116–117
Apple and sauerkraut salad, 335–336
Artichoke and mushroom omelet, baked, 352
Asparagus sauce with breaded veal chops, 238–239
Aspic
    beef and herring salad in, 331–332
    lox in, 144–145
    pickled salmon steaks in, 107–108
Australia, 321–322
Austria, 202–203

Bacon
    Canadian, hash, 303
    tomato pie with, 297–298
Bananas, with lamb or pork chops, 311–312
Beef
    beefballs

    curried, 223
    with sweet and sour sauce, 226
    cakes, 216–217, 218
    and chicken liver pie, 259–260
    and chick peas in mushroom sauce, 205–206
    frankfurters
        with chick pea soup, 4
        eggplant and mushroom gravy casserole, 233
        lentil casserole, 235
    and herring salad in aspic, 331–332
    and liver loaf, 264–265
    London broil, marinated, 194
    meat balls, fried spaetzle and, 221–222
    meatloaf, Chinese, 219–220
    mishmash, 218
    pie, open face, 224–225
    pot roast, wine marinated, 200–201
    potted, 202–203

Chili con carne, 19
China, 26–27, 31, 39–40, 42–43, 160, 166–167, 169–170, 187–188, 189–190, 211–212, 219–220, 279
Chowder, New York fish, 11–12
Clam(s)
  gallimaufry of shrimp and, 156–157
  jellied salad a la vye, with shrimp, 326–327
  pie, 173
Clam-tomato sauce, 164–165
Connecticut, 333
Corn with shrimp, baked, 151
Corned beef
  hash, with boozy sauce, 229–230
  home-made, 231–232
  pancake, 356–357
Cornish hens. See Rock Cornish hens
Costatelle di maiale con vino (pork chops), 285–286
Crabmeat
  baked curried, 179–180
  cakes, 176–177
  with cheddar cheese sauce, 181
  soufflé, 178
  stuffing for peppers, 341–342
Crabs, soft-shelled, 175–176
Creole recipes, 89–90, 151, 161–162, 227–228
Crepes
  salmon-filled, 15–16
  smoked salmon, with black-eyed peas, 143–144
  tuna-filled, 15–16
Cucumber salad, 329–330

Duck, stuffed
  roasted, 83
  with strawberries and noodles, 82–83

Eggplant, frankfurter and mushroom gravy casserole, 233
Eggs
  baked, with chicken livers, 261–262

baked mushroom and artichoke omelet, 352
in corned beef pancake, 356–357
poached, in casserole with shrimp and celery soup, 155–156
scrambled, and fish balls, 354–355
Spanish baked, and rice, 21–22
and stuff, 353
stuffing, with sausage and mushrooms for veal roast, 251–252
England, 156–157, 224–225, 244–245, 263–264, 266–267, 273–274, 313–314

Fagioli e pasta, 17–18
Fazoola, pasta, 17–18
Fettuccine, 27–28
Finland, 331–332
Fish
  with anchovy-bourbon-clam sauce, baked, 116–117
  casserole with potato, baked, 140
  charcoal (or oven-broiled), stuffed, 91–92
  chowder, New York, 11–12
  eggy poached, 110–111
  fillets
    baked-fried stuffed, 118
    baked stuffed, 128–129
    Florentine, fried, 125–126
    marguery, 100
    poached, 98–99
    with sauce, 120–121
  flounder pie, baked fried, 130–131
  fried, for stuffing, 115
  gefilte fish, 132–135
  herring and beef salad in aspic, 331–332
  with horseradish sauce, 127
  loaf, 101–102
  marinated, baked, 95–96
  omelet, puffy baked, 122
  and rice, 119–120
  salmon
    and sardine loaf, 135–136
    steaks, cold, with sour cream, 105–106

Kasha varnitchkes, 80–81
Kentucky, 117, 229–230, 309–310
Kidney pie, steak and, 273–274
Knishes, chicken liver potato, 20–21
Korea, 216–217, 269–270
Kugel, smoked salmon-onion-potato, 29

Lamb
  fooleeyee, 320–321
  shanks, baked, 321–322
  shishkebobs, 317–318
  stew, 319–320
Lamb chops
  with bananas or pineapple, 311–312
  English grill, 313–314
  with meat sauce, 308–309
  a l'orange and sour cream, 315–316
  sauced, 309–310
Lemon sauce, poached oysters in, 174
Lentil-frank casserole, 235
Liver
  and beef loaf, 264–265
  calf's, Florentine, 267–268
  calf's or beef, with onion-mushroom sauce, 266–267
  loaf, baked, 263–264
Lobster
  or lobster tails, broiled, 182–183
  spaghetti casserole, curried, 184–185
London broil, marinated, 194
Lox in aspic, 144–145

Maine, 128–129, 130–131
Maryland, 176–177
Meat balls, fried spaetzle and, 221–222
Meatloaf, Chinese, 219–220
Meat sauce for lamb chops, 308–309
Mexico, 25–26, 261–262, 277–278, 294–295
Middle East, 317–318
  See also names of countries

Midwest (U.S.), 259–260, 264–265
  See also names of states
Mishmash
  beef, 218
  salad, 333
Mulberry Street (New York City), 17–18
Mushroom(s)
  and artichoke omelet, baked, 352
  in chicken liver gravy, 70
  with scallops, baked, 171
  stuffing, with eggs and sausage, for veal roast, 251–252
  veal with ham and, 248
Mushroom barley beef soup, 7–8
Mushroom sauces, 263–264, 323, 324
  with beef and chick peas, 205–206
  with onions, for liver, 266–267

Near East, 205–206
  See also names of countries
New England, 11–12, 171, 181, 182–183
  See also names of states
New York, 140, 169–170
  See also Mulberry Street; Bronx; Brooklyn; Spanish Harlem
Noodles and strawberries as duck stuffing, 82–83

Ohio, 338
Okra-beef-tomato bake, 227–228
Omelet
  baked mushroom and artichoke, 352
  puffy baked fish, 122
Onion(s)
  baked, stuffed with shrimp, 339–340
  kugel (pudding), with salmon and potato, 29
Onion sauce
  for fried chicken and ham, 60
  with mushrooms, for liver, 266–267
  for pork chops, 283–284